FIGURES IN THE FOREGROUND

By the same author

DEATH OF A HIGHBROW	ELIZABETH
THE GRACE DIVORCE	THE GEORGIAN HOUSE
A TIGRESS IN PROTHERO	SKETCH OF A SINNER
THE WOMAN FROM SICILY	A BROOD OF DUCKLINGS
THE SUMNER INTRIGUE	SUMMER STORM
A MONTH IN GORDON	THE ELDER SISTER
SQUARE	YOUNG FELIX
MASTER JIM PROBITY	THE THREE LOVERS
A FLOWER FOR CATHERINE	COQUETTE
THE DOCTOR'S WIFE	SEPTEMBER
COMES TO STAY	SHOPS AND HOUSES
FAITHFUL COMPANY	NOCTURNE
ENGLISH MAIDEN	THE CHASTE WIFE
A WOMAN IN SUNSHINE	ON THE STAIRCASE
THANKLESS CHILD	THE HAPPY FAMILY
THE FORTUNATE LADY	THE CASEMENT
THE TWO WIVES	THE YOUNG IDEA
HARVEST COMEDY	THE MERRY HEART

BACKGROUND WITH CHORUS
SWINNERTON: AN AUTOBIOGRAPHY
THE BOOKMAN'S LONDON
LONDONER'S POST
AUTHORS AND THE BOOK TRADE

THE GEORGIAN LITERARY SCENE
TOKEFIELD PAPERS
A LONDON BOOKMAN
GEORGE GISSING: A CRITICAL STUDY
R. L. STEVENSON: A CRITICAL STUDY
THE REVIEWING AND CRITICISM OF BOOKS
(J. M. Dent Memorial Lecture)
THE CATS AND ROSEMARY: A BOOK FOR CHILDREN

FRANK SWINNERTON

•

FIGURES IN THE FOREGROUND

LITERARY REMINISCENCES
1917–1940

DOUBLEDAY & COMPANY, INC.
GARDEN CITY, NEW YORK
1964

820.9
S978f
102568

Note

The aim of this book and its predecessor, *Background with Chorus*, is modest. It is to give one long-lived man's impressions, gathered at first hand from contact at three points, as original writer, publisher, and reviewer, of literary fashion in the first half of the twentieth century; and to do this, where possible, by accounts of the men and women who contributed, if not to fashion, at least to the general picture. *Background with Chorus* covered the years between 1900 and 1917; *Figures in the Foreground*, after an introduction for new readers, continues the story until the late 'thirties. There will be no successor.

F.S.

Old Tokefield
Cranleigh
Surrey

Acknowledgements

I thank Rupert Hart-Davis for permission to use extracts from letters written to me by Hugh Walpole, and Miss Dorothy Tomlinson for a similar permission to quote letters written by her father, and to use a passage from *Norman Douglas*.

I have also quoted from my own contributions to *The New Weekly*, *The Manchester Guardian*, *The Evening News*, *The Athenaeum*, *The Spectator*, *The Observer*, *John o' London's Weekly*, and *The American Spectator*, and from an introduction to *An Anthology of Modern Fiction*, published in 1937 by Thomas Nelson & Sons, Ltd.

I gratefully acknowledge my debt to the following authors and publishers for permission to use brief illustrative extracts from the books listed below:

CHARMES, LESLIE DE. *Elizabeth of the German Garden*. Heinemann, 1958, for quotations from Countess Russell's diary, and an account of Lady Russell by E. M. Forster.

CHEVALLEY, ABEL. *Le Roman Anglais de Notre Temps*. Humphrey Milford: The Oxford Press, 1921.

ELIOT, T. S. *After Strange Gods*, 1934; *The Cocktail Party*, *The Elder Statesman*. Faber and Faber. And a *Times* report of a speech made in Leeds in July, 1962.

GOODWIN, Geraint. *Conversations in Ebury Street*. Benn, 1929.

HARROD, R. F. *Life of John Maynard Keynes*. Macmillan, 1951.

HULME, T. E. *Speculations*. Edited by Herbert Read. Routledge, 1924.

HUXLEY, Aldous. *Do What You Will*, 1929; *Point Counter*

ACKNOWLEDGEMENTS

Point, 1928; *After Many a Summer*, 1939. All Chatto & Windus.

ISHERWOOD, Christopher. *Lions and Shadows*. Methuen & Co. Ltd, 1938.

JAMES, Henry. *The Notebooks*. Edited by F. O. Matthieson and Kenneth B. Murdock. Oxford University Press Inc., 1947.

KEYNES, J. M. *Two Memoirs*. Introduced by David Garnett, Hart-Davis, 1949.

LEA, F. A. *The Life of John Middleton Murry*. Methuen & Co. Ltd, 1959.

LEAVIS, F. R. *Mass Civilization and Minority Culture*, 1930; and *The Common Pursuit*, 1952. Chatto & Windus.

LEAVIS, Q. V. *Fiction and the Reading Public*. Chatto & Windus, 1932.

LUCAS, E. V. *Reading, Writing, and Remembering*. Methuen & Co. Ltd, 1932.

LYND, Robert. *Essays on Life and Literature*. Everyman's Library. Dent, 1957.

MAUGHAM, W. S. *Cakes and Ale*, 1930; *The Summing Up*, 1938. By permission of Mr Maugham and Wm Heinemann Ltd.

MOORE, George. *Confessions of a Young Man*. Heinemann, 1933. By permission of C. D. Medley.

MUGGERIDGE, Malcolm. *The Thirties*. Hamish Hamilton, 1940.

MUIR, Edwin ('Edward Moore'). *We Moderns*. Allen & Unwin, 1918.

PLOMER, William. *Poems*. Jonathan Cape, 1962.

SASSOON, Siegfried. *Rhymed Ruminations*, Chiswick Press, 1939.

STEPHENS, James. *Insurrections*. Maunsel, Dublin, 1909.

TOMLINSON, H. M. *A Mingled Yarn*. Duckworth, 1953.

TURGENEV, Ivan. Translated by Constance Garnett. *Rudin*. Heinemann, 1900.

TURNER, W. J. *The Duchess of Popocatapetl*. Dent, 1939.

WOOLF, Leonard. *Sowing*. Hogarth Press, 1960.

WOOLF, Virginia. *A Writer's Diary*. Edited by Leonard Woolf. Hogarth Press, 1953; and *Virginia Woolf and Lytton Strachey: Letters*, Edited by Leonard Woolf. Hogarth Press; Chatto & Windus, 1956.

F. S.

Contents

There are many invisible circumstances which, whether we read as inquirers after natural or moral knowledge, whether we intend to enlarge our science or increase our virtue, are more important than public occurrences. Thus Sallust, the great master of nature, has not forgot in his account of Cataline to remark that his walk was now quick and again slow, as an indication of a mind revolving something with violent commotion. Thus the story of Melanchthon affords a striking lecture on the value of time by informing us that when he made an appointment he expected not only the hour but the minute to be fixed, that the day might not run out in the idleness of suspense. And all the plans and enterprises of De Wit are now of less importance to the world than that part of his personal character which represents him as careful of his health and negligent of his life.

SAM JOHNSON: *The Rambler*

The General Picture

○

1 WHEN I WROTE *Background with Chorus*, which covered, roughly, the first twenty years of this century, I relied upon a strong and flexible memory, assisted in respect of my boyhood and very early manhood by letters written from the age of fifteen onward to an old friend, Garfield Howe, who had preserved them.

It was through Garfield Howe's introduction that I joined the staff of J. M. Dent and Co. at the beginning of 1901, thereby leaving Fleet Street (where I had hoped to make a living) for the trade of book publishing. While Howe moved on to other firms (he left Dent because I was given the newly-created job of confidential clerk to Hugh Dent which he had suggested for himself), at length ending in responsible employment by Peter Davies, I made only one publishing move, in 1907, from Dent to Chatto & Windus. Three years later I became what is called in England 'reader' and in the United States 'literary editor' to Chatto's, a post I held until 1926, when I went to live permanently in the country.

Having read *Background with Chorus*, Garfield Howe wrote:

This is the London literary scene as known to you and me —the personalities, the papers, the politics. . . . Needless to say, it fills in many a fact or detail previously unknown to me. But my own memory, such as it is, confirms you at every point. Your strength lies in your interest in persons—the man behind the name. . . . The trouble with this book is that there are so few contemporaries who can understand the background in the light of the accumulated facts.

I think this last comment high-lighted a fault. The book was crowded; and in some respects was as 'difficult' to unravel as the work of a modern pastiche poet. To a few young readers it seemed to be concerned with fuddy-duddies (whereas I had meant to indicate that there is nothing new under the sun); while at least one older reader was sadly depressed because it dealt almost exclusively with the dead. A suspicion also arose that I had kept a Journal, as Arnold Bennett and James Agate did. This, unfortunately, is not the case. My pencilled diaries hold nothing but notes of engagements, sometimes the titles of books read, and names of people I met or places I visited while travelling. Owing, furthermore, to the rubbing of a small calligraphy they often cannot be read at all. Memory, checked by a reading and annotation of biographies or printed correspondence, was my stand-by.

Memory grows less precise, I find, when one is over seventy-five. In writing the present book, however, I have enjoyed some luck. I have been a great preserver of letters; and a re-perusal of some of these has quickened recollection. In particular I would note that Rupert Hart-Davis, having published his superlative biography of Hugh Walpole, handed over the entire correspondence exchanged between Walpole and myself between the years 1914 to 1941. He made one stipulation, which was that I should not destroy this correspondence. 'It will be interesting,' said he, 'in fifty years' time.' My reply was: 'In fifty years' time nobody will remember Walpole or myself.' Mr Hart-Davis laconically retorted: 'Nevertheless, it will be interesting.'

Well, will it? I have my doubts. And yet when I think of the odd scraps of interest to be picked up in all sorts of books by obscure men, I refrain from pressing those doubts. Also, I find in the Walpole-Swinnerton letters, among much that is trivial, even silly, some lively candours about ourselves and our literary contemporaries which cast candlelight upon a half-forgotten period.

Having gaiety in common, he and I teased, riposted, and gossiped; and as we belonged to an undisillusioned generation the note throughout was one of cheerfulness. The future spread wide; the novel as an art form, with Turgenev and Henry James as high-priests of the art, seemed important; we wrote stories about imaginary characters because it was our bent to write stories about imaginary characters; and we light-heartedly, with an absolute minimum of jealousy, enjoyed our very different kinds and degrees of success.

Walpole needed affection, prosperity, social *réclame*, and incessant literary activity. I did not. I entirely lacked his physical energy, did not want fame or fortune, and was far less generous than he in the assessment of contemporaries. I do not think I was ever a curmudgeon; but being almost completely irreverent I did not, and cannot, take other men and women, even the geniuses, and especially those in whom I detect no genius, as seriously as they sometimes take themselves. Indeed, I remember sitting at Walpole's table with perhaps a dozen other writers, all very talented, and so ribaldly mocking our fellow-craftsmen that Sinclair Lewis, who was a guest, exclaimed in consternation: 'My God! Is there anything he *does* like?' I should add that I never resent contradiction; unlike those who disagree with me, I am for liberty in taste and opinion, which I think makes for that unpopular virtue, charity.

Walpole, equally good-humoured, but more excitable, was frequently over-generous. I think he could have been called a spontaneous fan, who fired off letters to any writer whose work he had sampled with admiration. In that way he made a tremendous number of cordial literary acquaintances; so many that at one time he proposed to entertain his fifty best friends to dinner on his fiftieth birthday. I never had fifty best friends; I should not, although we were on terms of affectionate cordiality, include Walpole among the dozen or so with whom, through the years, I have indulged almost complete unreserve. However, Walpole's delights, like his occasional cries of facile wrath at detractors, remain in these letters as endearing as ever, and even in vagary they are valuable pointers to contemporary preferences and reputation.

They often correct mistakes made by present-day critics, who, having never met their subjects, accept false reports, and repeat old slanders as truth. I do not know why the false reports should have gained currency; but there are many about Walpole himself. I therefore hope that my quotations or paraphrases will do good. If they seem antediluvian, I shall be sorry, but not contrite. I think they may have a moral for the latest generation, which will fade as quickly from memory as its predecessor.

While in old age tending my garden, literally as well as figuratively, as Voltaire said one should do, I ruminate. As I saw a log, pull out a weed, or prune a rose, I hear myself ejaculate, and find that I have been unconsciously reviewing the impressions of more than three-quarters of a century. It is sometimes, though not always, a delightful discovery. Arnold Bennett used facetiously to say 'a dirty mind is a continual feast'; so is an amused mind, such as mine. Being a natural ruminant, and not a slave to culture, I do not coerce impressions into material for a thesis; I enjoy them for their own sake. I see my favourite cricketer, George Cox, make a glorious one-handed running catch on the boundary at Horsham, recall the splendour of an entry to Dover Harbour on Bennett's yacht, the *Marie Marguerite*, with all sails spread and the brilliantly blue water flying across the deck, laugh again at one or other of our cats, or at preposterous speeches made by men in anger, repeat sentences from *Pride and Prejudice*, Boswell, *Kim*, or *The Prisoner of Zenda*, return to rooms I have known, and recall with kindness dead friends. Sometimes, but more rarely, I think of slanders directed against myself, and realize that I implacably resent them. In a sense, of course, I have been cultivating my garden for seventy-nine years; as I shall do until I die. When I die I expect to forget everything, and be forgotten. I am content that this should be so.

My impressions have been gained in several parts of England, Europe, and the United States, but chiefly in London, where I was born and where I lived until my happy marriage in 1924;

and except when I feel that some little personal anecdote will cast a beam I record here only those relating to books, publishing, and literary fashion.

On the subject of literary fashion I remark, for readers who do not know a former book, *Background with Chorus*, that in boyhood I saw and even helped at the birth of Everyman's Library, which gathered together, for a shilling a volume, the literature of three thousand years. I saw the passing of Victorian giantism and the eclipse of Kipling as spokesman for the British Empire. In the novel I saw the 'naturalism' of the 'eighties and 'nineties, the romanticism of Stevenson, Maurice Hewlett, Anthony Hope, and Henry Seton Merriman, and the monster performances, so different, yet so comparably popular, of Mrs Humphry Ward, Marie Corelli, and Hall Caine, which yielded to the humane realism of a new century. I still rely on that humane realism.

I saw George Moore turning from grubby records of stables and provincial back streets and gas-lit theatres in London to exquisitely malicious autobiography, but not until later his retelling of ancient fables with simple cynicism. I found and adored Henry James at a time when he thought nobody wanted him; and watched with approval his exaltation to the rank of a Grand Panjandrum. Through some forgotten agency I was able to attend the memorial service to George Meredith in Westminster Abbey, and I saw his reputation—in spite of *Modern Love* and the thrilling *Woods of Westermain*—drop lower and lower, year by year, until a charge of resemblance to him, levelled abusively some years ago at myself, showed that in the minds of English reviewers he had become mud.

The fashion moved, while these things were happening, from admiration for William Watson's dignified poetry to respect for the grim *Testaments* of John Davidson and ecstasy over Francis Thompson, and from the inexplicable acclamation of Stephen Phillips's poetic dramas to joy in the melodies of such Irish Poets as Yeats and A. E., and excitement at the vehement colloquialisms of *The Everlasting Mercy*.

In polemics and general literature, Shaw, Belloc, and Chesterton captured our young fancies and gave us finger-posts to endless argument during summer walks about the suburban countryside. In the theatre, besides Shaw, Galsworthy, and Masefield, the Irish Players from Dublin triumphed at the Court with Synge, Yeats, and Lady Gregory. When Ibsen's plays were at last performed in the West End, *Rosmersholm*, at a curious old-fashioned theatre in the Strand called Terry's, seemed to me the most fascinating play I had ever seen. Sudermann was actually performed in a fashionable theatre in St Martin's Lane, where he proved unaccountably sentimental. By 1912 I had seen at least two of Chekhov's plays, *The Cherry Orchard* and *The Seagull*, the former of which I still rank with *Rosmersholm*.

We heard nothing then of 'great acting'. Irving in old age revived Tennyson's *Becket* and declared, with an aged elaborateness which made the word sound multisyllabic, 'I will anathematize him!' Charles Wyndham, as Garrick, spoke in a whisper that without amplification could be heard in the gallery. Forbes Robertson was equally audible when he delivered the speech 'most potent, grave, and reverend seigneurs' with his back to the audience. John Hare was quietly perfect in drawing-room comedy; Beerbohm Tree was a highly-coloured Dr Stockmann; George Alexander turned without effort from Pinero to the part of a student prince in *Old Heidelberg*. But the famous actor-managers, whom everybody went to see, whatever their parts, were dying. H. B. Irving, indeed, unaware of the fact, expressed amusement at a clergyman who, after buying tickets for his production of *Hamlet*, turned back at the box-office to ask: 'By the way, who is playing Hamlet?'

We had in place of the actor-manager a new and overwhelmingly important boss who was named The Producer. Even Ellen Terry appeared in old age under Granville Barker's direction, though her performance in *Captain Brassbound's Conversion* was that of the old Ellen Terry, a creature of intoxicating charm.

In other productions, Granville Barker imposed the subordination of all individual actors to the play's design. One well-known author-actress, Cicely Hamilton, after giving what I thought a splendid performance in *Fanny's First Play*, bitterly condemned him to me in conversation as a ruthless martinet who had ruined the theatre by (as we should now say) 'brain-washing' his cast until they went through their parts as automatons.

They were not automatons; they were actors magically enthralled. Barker was a very tall man, with great charm and grace and courtesy of manner; but his jaw was abnormally wide, and his determination to go his own way, though at last it meant wholly abandoning friends and theatre for the sake of a possessive wife, was imperious. It caused even a deliberate break with Shaw, whose plays he had carried to triumph, and whose loyalty to him was never in doubt. My recollection (which as we had the slightest possible acquaintance may be faulty) is that his eyes, of a singular reddish brown, held more than human fire. He probably did, with those eyes, mesmerize his cast. He would sit through entire performances, long after the first nights, considering whether some minute change in movement or diction would heighten the play's meaning; and rehearsals for the principals continued until he was satisfied.

Thus, in brief, and with a jumble of names which may confuse modern readers, literary fashion moved before the outbreak of war in 1914. My own enthusiasms had carried me in fiction from R. M. Ballantyne and Louisa Alcott at the age of six to the romantics in boyhood and, as I developed normally, to Balzac, Henry James, Turgenev, Dostoevsky, Stendhal, Jane Austen, and Chekhov, in that order. To *Rosmersholm* and *The Cherry Orchard* I added Barker's *The Madras House* (excepting a futile last act) as the third most absorbing play I had ever seen. Keats, Browning, and the Meredith of *Modern Love* were my poets; Hazlitt my essayist; Gibbon, Buckle, Macaulay my absorbing historians. But for specific reasons I had read the entire works of Sam Johnson and Charles Lamb; and before the War began I had, in order to write about them, read every published word of George Gissing and Robert Louis Stevenson.

It never occurred to me that one day men would consider it disgraceful for a writer to earn money by the popularity of his writings. The authors I admired, whether dead or living, from Shakespeare to Shaw, had all done this; we who followed them hoped to share our interest and pleasure in life with innumerable fellow-creatures, and not only the esoteric few. We aimed at being professionals. Such rivalry as we felt was friendly without rancour. The country was Liberal in politics and government, and Liberal in outlook. We still believed that England was good and beautiful, that cheats did not prosper, that in the end right would always triumph; that the word 'progress', meaningless as it might be, could be spoken and heard without a sneer.

The War changed all this.

Poetry and Fiction

•

2 AS IT ended, Thomas Hardy was still called, in succession to George Meredith, who died in 1909, the Grand Old Man of English Letters. Poetry was in the air; *The Dynasts* was greatly admired; the long series of late poems resulting from sudden vivid memory of his first wife held gloomy rapture; and a figure-head is necessary to any aesthetic enthusiasm.

Hardy was a curious choice for grandeur. He was not temperamentally a leader. He had never indulged in bravura, as Meredith and Swinburne had done. He had no school. While Eden Phillpotts, who settled in Devon and used Devon types and backgrounds for his conscientiously regional novels, was often likened to him, there was no real resemblance. Phillpotts was not a West-countryman; he was born in India. His inspiration was not Classic, but Biblical. In all his serious novels he elaborated simple themes which he had found in the Old Testament. The only likeness between the two men was that both lived 'far from the madding crowd's ignoble strife', content to work and potter in garden or countryside, and indifferent to Metropolitan sophistication. Phillpotts, who in 1912 was regarded as a great novelist, paid the penalty of rusticity by sinking from notice; Hardy has only done that since the rise of other gods.

Hardy was so much the West-countryman that it came as a surprise to many, when his mysteriously-composed 'life' was published, to learn that formerly he had dwelt in London. And although in old age he was sometimes persuaded to hob-nob in Barrie's flat with Shaw, Wells, and Bennett, he was more at ease in Dorset. There, at Max Gate, he entertained most of the Georgian Poets, and such neighbours from the Chesil Beach as H. M. Tomlinson and Middleton Murry. They listened attentively to his quiet, undistinguished table-talk, and approached him with affectionate awe. He did not object; he was quite without pose; whether he enjoyed being called the Grand Old Man of English Letters I do not know. Although George Moore afterwards maliciously nominated Virginia Woolf for the succession, he was the last of the species.

The Georgian Poets. I have already, in *Background with Chorus*, told how the term came into use before the War, and I consciously repeat myself in the present book only for the sake of narrative; but will say here that it was neither invented nor adopted by the men themselves. Certain small widely-read anthologies of current verse began to be produced in 1912 under the editorship of Edward Marsh, who called them *Georgian Poetry*. This name, for purposes of publicity, until it was turned by adversaries into a reproach, was valuable. It drew attention to writers who might otherwise have been overlooked. It also gave modern poetry a standing and popularity with ordinary readers which had previously been in doubt. That was its modest intention.

Marsh, the son of a Master of Downing College, Cambridge, and great-grandson of Spencer Perceval, the only English Prime Minister ever to be murdered, held a series of positions in the Civil Service which proved his tact and capacity. Without genius himself, he was quick to see it in others; and aided by what he called the 'murder money' (inheritance of a grant made to the Perceval family by House of Commons vote in 1812), and his own contacts with the social *élite*, he became a fairy godfather to young writers. Patronage, according to Dr Johnson, ceased to exist in England before the middle of the eighteenth century; the help given to the Lake Poets by such rich men as Sir George Beaumont and the Wedgwoods had become unnecessary to prosperous Victorian authors; a small allocation of funds for what are known as Civil List Pensions went only to those who, in middle age, could no longer support themselves (Conrad and W. H. Hudson both benefited in bad days); modern young poets, unless they had wealthy parents, needed some equivalent to patronage. Marsh supplied this. He continued to supply it until the end of his days.

In person he was large, gentle, monocled. He had a round un-ruddy face, and a tiny, rather insipid voice. His manner was extremely modest, sweet-tempered, and agreeable. He constantly recalled with pleasure Edmund Gosse's prophecy that his anthologies would enjoy a small immortality akin to that of Dodsley's *Collections*; and whenever I casually met him (for we were not intimate) he confided this prophecy to me with the most charming diffidence, seeming gratified, so admirable were his manners, when I endorsed it. I still, with my eyes lifted for a moment towards the twenty-first century, endorse it.

At the outbreak of war most of Marsh's young friends, undergraduates as idealistic as Byron, without Byron's rebelliousness and passion to escape from the over-heated London Society which he had outraged, volunteered to fight for Liberty and the Glory of Man. If, as many expected, the War had been a spirited cavalry dash across Europe, all over in six months, Marsh's choices would have been vindicated. A new burst of song and romance might indeed have followed; a few more Darleys, Tennysons, William Morrises, Stevensons, and Hewletts might have spread melodious words and inventions over many pages and lightened many hearts. A contrary movement was already active, and I do not seriously think there was any chance of revived Victorianism; but the illusion gave pleasure to many senior minds.

Instead of open warfare and an atmosphere of tournament, however, there followed a long, nauseating slaughter, in which men condemned to the misery of darkness and everlasting mud, frozen feet and trench fever, felt their idealism betrayed. What C. E. Montague, who falsified his age in order to join the crusade, recorded in his book *Disenchantment* was the lot of such poets as survived. Those who were quickly killed, or those who were brought home unfit for longer active service, could, like Sorley, Rupert Brooke, and Robert Nichols, sing to the last; the rest had time for bitter thought.

As early as 1917 one of them, Siegfried Sassoon, wrote from the battlefront to the British press, saying that what had begun as a war in defence of freedom was now a war of conquest, without justification. He spoke for millions of those, the world over, who could not speak for themselves; and he called for immediate peace negotiations. He was not shot, as Tom, Dick, or Harry might have been. He was treated as a sick man, and under the escort of his friend Robert Graves was taken to a sanatorium, where he met another sick young poet, Wilfred Owen, whose memory and verses are still acclaimed. The War, to which international politicians were committed without means of escape, continued.

I return to Edward Marsh, the poets' benefactor. As is shown by his happy translations of La Fontaine, he loved melody, irony, and polish. His range of sympathy was elegant but not wide; and the work of some new cynical rebels—for example, the Sitwells, who aimed at pruning the tree of language of its dead fruit, and called for a substitution of wit for 'this eternal humour'—pleased neither his ear nor his perhaps slightly emasculate taste. He agreed with Horace Walpole, who spoke of 'that faithful attendant of wit, ill-nature'; and he had no ill-nature. Smiling at cheeky but uninspired children, he drew nearer to his heart the beauties of Marvell, Keats, Tennyson, and the Georgians—especially his charming and heroic *protégé*, Rupert Brooke. He did not print the rebels. He thereby gave later volumes of *Georgian Poetry* some resemblance to Victorian *Keepsakes*. The rebels launched their own anthology, *Wheels*.

In doing this, they expressed resentment and independence. They did not want to be mellifluous; they wanted to be astringent, to tear apart and destroy the mentality from which the long years of war had arisen. That very discreetness which had made Marsh a perfect Civil Servant was considered disastrous to poetry. The rebels mocked his discreetness, his preference for the mellifluous commonplace, his obscurantism. They mocked, no less, his Georgians, some of whom were their friends. So far, so legitimate.

The mockers, however, were not alone. Horace Walpole might have added to his *mot* a supplement referring to 'those faithful attendants of ill-nature, the parasites'. To the mockery of the wits was added the tittering of the heartless smart. And the tittering was presently drowned by more powerful covert detraction in circles newly liberated from wartime civil occupations, where sharp minds and tongues aimed less at pruning the tree of language than at establishing a new hierarchy of culture.

Novelists also began to be made *vieux jeux* by general impatience with the Victorians and Edwardians. Edwin Muir, using the pseudonym 'Edward Moore', published in 1918 a book called *We Moderns*, in which he said:

> The fault of most modern writers—and especially of the novelists—is not that they are too modern, but that they are too traditional. It is true that they are not traditional in the historical manner; . . . but they follow a tradition also, though a much narrower one; they, too, believe in the past, but only, alas, in the immediate past; they are slaves to the generation which preceded theirs. In short, that which is disgusting in them is their inability to rise high enough to *see* their little decade or two, and to challenge it, if they cannot from the standpoint of a nobler future, then, at the least, from that of the noblest past. But how weak must a generation be which is not strong enough to challenge and supersede Mr Arnold Bennett, for example.

Denunciation by a gifted poet, then I believe very young, and a dozen years later, in collaboration with his wife, the translator and introducer to English readers of Franz Kafka's best book, *The Castle*, had absolutely no effect upon the writers so arraigned. How could it have done so? Most of them were unaware of the denunciation; and the fault he charged them with, imitation of their living seniors, took no account of the true disease.

As I look back for a point of demonstration, I naturally recall the literary world as I first played an inconspicuous part in it, and observe that of the novelists most admired when the War began Conrad had written *Youth*, *Lord Jim*, *Typhoon*, and *Nostromo* by 1904; Galsworthy's *The Man of Property* (in which he said really all he had to say in the novel) was published in 1906; Arnold Bennett's *The Old Wives' Tale* in 1908; H. G. Wells's *Tono-Bungay* in 1909. The juniors, with Rose Macaulay's *Abbot's Verney* leading the way in 1906, flocked about 1910, when these several books still strongly affected the public mind as something fresh.

It is important to remember that Conrad, Bennett, Wells, and Galsworthy represented, in their important books, a break with fashion. The three best-selling novelists of the nineteen hundreds were still Hall Caine, Marie Corelli, and Mrs Humphry Ward. All were 'teachers', whether religious, emotional, or philosophical (Mrs Ward was a niece of Matthew Arnold, and in her early novels took pains to attack problems of faith and ethics with what was then thought great intellectual power; Hall Caine specialized, as some do in our own day, in sex and religion; Marie Corelli was a critic of Society and social hypocrisy). The first two had enjoyed high praise from leading reviewers; only the general *furore*, and, in the case of Hall Caine and Marie Corelli, some ridiculous rivalry and self-advertisement, lessened their supremacy. All three were completely superseded in critical esteem by Wells, Bennett, and Galsworthy.

Where these last failed under the stress of war was that with the exception of Wells, who to journalistic genius and a unique gift for material prophecy added the illusion that he could indoctrinate the rising Labour Party, they were beyond adaptation to the most appalling experience Englishmen had ever known. As men of courage, they could endure that experience; but as artists they could not draw from within themselves the new vision needed to transcend it.

Wells the educationalist wrote *The Outline of History* and the immediately topical and very successful fiction, *Mr Britling Sees it Through*. The others, in spite of Bennett's heroic completion

of the *Clayhanger* trilogy with *These Twain*, which contains
some of his best work, had lost belief in the importance of the
novel as a philosophical representation of life. If it was not a
philosophic representation of life—and life had become a nightmare to the middle-aged liberal mind, committed to belief in
brotherly love—it was nothing.

Time is showing that their pessimism about the novel was
wrong; but in my opinion they had much earlier forsaken the
imaginative for the factual, or greatness for verisimilitude.
Henry James, whose passion was for art and form, had condemned the verisimilitude they employed, which he called
'squeezing the orange', or 'saturation'; and this was a good
point for an artist to make. James's view, however, was too
narrowly that of the technician. He himself handled ever more
intensively and elaborately themes which, when stripped of
magic verbiage, were trivial.

With surpassing skills and delicacies of understanding, James
subtilized the mean. Even when he glimpsed delicious comedy,
as he did in *The Spoils of Paynton*, he preferred to work through
the twitter of what he called 'a flurried bundle of petticoats'
rather than through the Shakespearean or Meredithian wide-
ranging mock-heroic; and, beautiful as it is to a craftsman's eye,
The Ambassadors, the perfect performance, is equally without
nobility. James's complaint against his juniors was that of one
who saw art as exquisitely measured portrayal of the small and
static, and not as poetic creation.

We are so used, nowadays, to talk of research and the
documentary, as if accumulation of the negligible, if persistent
enough, becomes important, and so used to successive essays
in sometimes highly complex and usually satirical reproduction
of contemporary manners, that we tend to despise poetic
creation. It does not lend itself to class-room analysis. Perhaps
we are right: I do not know. It seems to me, however, that in
England the tragic novel, as written on the grand scale by
George Eliot, Meredith, and Hardy (with Scott, in such a book
as *The Heart of Midlothian*, leading the way), was killed, not by
the squeezing of oranges, nor by a world war, but in the first
place by general acceptance of the Darwinian theory. You

cannot show men fighting against the Gods if you are convinced that they represent no more than the survival of the fittest.

It is possible that the post-Stevensonian romantic school, which saw out the reign of Queen Victoria, was in spite of its scamper from the commonplace the last flicker of refusal to accept a mechanic explanation of conduct. By 1910 Conrad was the only admired and practising novelist to whom men were still tragic persons at odds with Fate.

With Wells, Galsworthy, and Bennett—different as they were—pigmies struggled, or didn't struggle very much, amid a jostle of fellow-opportunists. Bennett calmly observed the individual growing older, moulded by time, family surroundings, and the day's chances. His power lay in extreme compassion and all-pervasive humour which has provoked unfavourable comparison with that statistical recorder of human animal life, Zola. Galsworthy, a man of sensitive conscience, as well as property, made the individual a centre of class conflict and family or social acquisitiveness; but did not allow him to grow or change. Wells snatched him from behind a counter for scientific training, set him amid the commercial and political scramble, and allowed him the amours incidental to a life of public advancement.

All three used as their material the surfaces of urban society: Wells with quick mimicry, Bennett as an impartial historian, Galsworthy with a humanitarian sigh. Their concern was specifically with the human *comedy*; the comedy of man escaping from or accepting his environment. At its best, the comedy was magnificent. Disparaged as they have been for the last forty years, these men had native qualities which their detractors cannot equal.

The junior novelists, also born in the Victorian age, dealt with similar aspects of existence. When they began to write there was no threat of world war. Freud and Bergson were unknown in England. The subsequently over-developed complexities of science, economics, and psychology were as remote as the moon. The difference between them and their predecessors was that whereas, with the exception of Galsworthy, the older men had been to neither Oxford nor Cambridge, most of the younger ones, whatever their family backgrounds, were public schoolboys who had subsequently taken their degrees. That is to say, they had been segregated from the bulk of their fellows until the age of twenty-four, and were having to discover innumerable unfamiliar idioms in young manhood or womanhood.

I do not know which of the newcomers were in Edwin Muir's mind when he wrote what I have quoted; but he may have seen an article published in the American *Bookman* during 1912 by W. L. George, who was one of them. In this article, apparently reprinted in book form in 1918, George named nine as possible successors to Wells, Bennett, and Galsworthy, his list of recommendations including Rose Macaulay, Sheila Kaye-Smith, E. M. Forster, J. D. Beresford, Compton Mackenzie, Hugh Walpole, Gilbert Cannan, D. H. Lawrence, and myself.

Four years later, in a small book on Conrad, Walpole tried his hand at a comparable list. It contained the names of E. M. Forster, D. H. Lawrence, J. D. Beresford, W. L. George, Gilbert Cannan, Viola Meynell, Francis Brett Young, and myself. He explained:

> Even with such avowed realists as Mr Beresford, Mr George, and Mr Swinnerton the realism is of a nature very different from the realism of even ten years ago, as can be seen at once by comparing so recent a novel as Mr Swinnerton's *On the Staircase* with Mr Arnold Bennett's *Sacred and Profane Love* or Mr Galsworthy's *Man of Property*—and Mr E. M. Forster is a romantic-realist of most curious originality, whose *Longest Journey* and *Howard's End* may possibly provide the historian of English literature with dates as important as the publication of *Almayer's Folly* in 1895.

I gather that I thought poorly of Walpole's list, and told him so in a letter which has been lost. He vigorously retorted:

That 'skinny' list was the most deliberate and considered thing in the world and I would support it till all's blue. If I'd offered it as a list of 'arrived' novelists, novelists sure of any permanence, that of course would have been ridiculous. But that is exactly what I did not do. What I did mean was that I believed these names of men all at the beginning of their careers, and all about thirty years of age, a real sign that the English novel was alive and active in the truest sense. . . . I have recently tried to read two perfectly ghastly novels of Hardy's, *Desperate Remedies* and *A Laodicean*. They are unspeakably bad. And I'm not at all sure that you'll find worse novels anywhere than Henry James's *Princess Casamassima*, Kipling's *Light that Failed*, Thackeray's *Lovel the Widower*, etc. etc. I am sure that *Sons and Lovers*, and *The Hampdenshire Wonder* and *On the Staircase* are finer than any of those. What I mean by all this is that historical perspective increases values to an incredible extent and that we are inclined to expect books to fulfil the standards of older fiction: 'Ah! but think of *Vanity Fair*,' you hear people murmuring. Now I believe that *The Old Wives' Tale* is in many ways a greater thing than *V.F.* and in many other ways not so great, but *that it stands to represent its own age through the spirit of a man of its own age*. That is I firmly believe what a novel has to do. . . .

Brave words, which assumed that peace could bring a return to normality. It did not. The War killed a generation which considered love, duty, and physical heroism the supreme virtues. It drained significance from the novel we had known, which could not be seen (as it may be in A.D. 2000) as either symptomatic or historically interesting. Easy chronicles of pre-war middle or lower-middle class family life were finished; the life itself had been disrupted. Less inevitably young novelists abandoned the simple ethical themes upon which the English novel, from Richardson to Moore, had been based for two centuries.

What could be offered instead? Rose Macaulay, who in 1912 won a novel-prize with the tale of an unlucky man forced by the loss of wife, worldly goods, and reputation to become a tramp hawking his own embroidery, gave the first of several answers. She deserted sentiment for caustic satire of those who had muddled the League of Nations; of newspaper publicity; of extremely futile class-hostilities in Spain. Wyndham Lewis, who described his novel *Tarr* as 'a very logical and deliberate grimace', attacked British 'Humour', by which he meant a special kind of self-consciousness or pride, and not the heartfelt merriment of Fielding or Dickens or the delicious mockery of Jane Austen. Aldous Huxley, who had contributed to *Wheels*, first satirized intellectual sillies and editorial hypocrites, and then satirized the sterile Utopias of Wells and others. He went on to scourge human nature as it had not been scourged since the days of Swift. Two of these writers, addressing us from heights too great for compassion, charged their work with astringent but still recognizably humane laughter; the third (Wyndham Lewis) savagely bombinated.

In other hands, also, the novel became stupendously ingenious, not with the difficult subtlety of Henry James and Joseph Conrad, who were seen by the new pathologists to have been naïve believers in personality, but with calculated cleverness which turned the form inside out and upside down in an effort to escape the obvious. Such new novelists quite eclipsed the humdrum dozen who had figured in George's and Walpole's lists. They brought to their work mental nimbleness and astonishing verbal fluency and mimetic power. This work, so far from being creative, became a literary gymnastic of the first order.

While smaller fry pottered with experiments in condensed time and fortuitous assembly, the ablest of the gymnasts—James Joyce—jollied fiction into the esoteric. He filled it with theological back-chat, wild fancies, devastating perceptions of human fallacy and folly, and ferocious researches into the subconscious; and he did this in a language which passed from the rich to the incomprehensible. Lawrence described *Ulysses* as made up of 'old fags and cabbage-stumps of quotations from the Bible and the rest, stewed in a juice of deliberate, journalistic dirty-mindedness'. Norman Douglas said 'he is too excremental for my taste'; and Virginia Woolf found it 'an illiterate, underbred book', the work of a writer who is 'tricky, doing stunts'. But the brilliant display, which was that of a cold-minded egotist, tickled those who began at this time to be called highbrows (an American word to replace the recently-imported Russian word *intelligentsia*, which Wells had applied to 'an irresponsible middle class with ideas') and people of fashion. The highbrows were enraptured by this new kind of fiction. They had read Bergson, Freud, and Jung.

Freud, in my opinion, superseded Darwin as the prime destroyer of the tragic novel of character. He and the mathematicians paralysed what had been known as the mytho-poetic faculty. Homer himself, under their influence, would have begun to doubt whether the *Iliad* would quite do. In fact, the novelists had received a knock-out. If they wanted to retain the respect of educated men and women, they had either to cease writing novels altogether or to demonstrate that they descended to such bagatelles only as vehicles for the exposure of the *libido* or a display of recondite learning.

If, still obsessed by an imaginative concept of life, they ignored the new psycho-analysis or the new severities of criticism, they were labelled—a word newly adopted from Freud's own vocabulary—'escapist', with the implied reproach of sentimentality. We saw a divorce between literature written and approved by persons of culture and an adulterate compound fit only for the entertainment of nursery-governesses. We heard inventive writers described with an unconscious adoption of Daisy Ashford's Victorian word as '*mere* storytellers'.

Sophisticated Caveman

•

3 ONE of the 'mere story-tellers' of the time, surviving, of course, from Victorian days, was William Somerset Maugham, who to his early loss and ultimate gain fell between recognized generations. He was nearly ten years younger than H. G. Wells, and fully ten years older than Hugh Walpole. Fitting in with neither the seniors nor the juniors, he stood alone among novelists, a sort of male literary Cinderella. If there had been room for pity in the minds of the new generation, he would have earned it as an orphan; but there was no room for pity in those caustic intelligences.

Maugham was alone in another respect, also; because although he attended an English public school, the land of his love was France. He went, not to an English university, but to Heidelberg; and as a young man, after studying medicine, and writing his first novel in London, he dwelt much in Paris. Even that first novel, *Liza of Lambeth*, now so familiar to his admirers, seemed then to be but one of the 'tales of mean streets' for which when he wrote it the fashion was already passing; and while I can remember seeing as a boy one or two big green posters advertising his play, *A Man of Honour*, we have Maugham's assurance that in face of such topical giants as Pinero, Henry Arthur Jones, and R. C. Carton, and a managerial reliance otherwise upon translations from the French or German, *A Man of Honour*, produced in 1903, had no friends.

It was a Stage Society venture, of which Maugham says 'the critics judged it according to their preconceptions. The more conventional abused it heartily; the earnest students of the drama praised it.' As the author was neither conventional nor earnest, and was displeased with his experience as a mean-streeter, he reconsidered his position. 'I wanted money,' said he; 'and I wanted fame.'

He was in a hurry. He could not wait for money and fame to amble after virtue. He therefore began deliberately to write brisk sentimental-cynical comedies for the theatre; and when, in 1907, *Lady Frederick* provided a triumph for an emotional actress, Ethel Irving, all the West End managers remembered that they had in their larders other plays by the same author. The larders were ransacked. In 1908, accordingly, Maugham comedies popped up everywhere, and took the town as complete novelties. Their author became suddenly, not only a social star, but a tit-bit for every theatrical gossip-writer in England.

By deserting the cause of grave unpopularity he revealed himself to earnest students of the drama as the arch example of prostituted talent. Hell hath no fury like an outraged doctrinaire. Maugham was critically ostracized thereafter for more than a quarter of a century.

This cold shouldering was never social. He was more at home in cosmopolitan society than most of his contemporaries. He was not, like Wells, emergent from the small shop and the housekeeper's parlour, nor, like Bennett, a northern provincial. He had not come, poor, from Ireland or Poland, like Shaw and Conrad. He was from Paris, the home of culture, and he could walk into any drawing-room without *gaucherie*. His plays were mordant, excellent 'theatre'; smart men and women, whether from Belgravia or St John's Wood, laughed cordially at scenes depicting their own incurable folly. Only the earnest, who also laughed in the theatre, missed in Maugham's plays the flattery to their intellects of such deep stuff as *Ghosts* or *The Master Builder*. Coming away from *Jack Straw*, they adjusted their smiles and said they had not been at all amused. 'Very light stuff,' they grumbled; 'Maugham has no philosophy.'

'No philosophy': it has been a hiss for many years now. As if

Maugham, who says he quickly forgets adverse criticism, had more decidedly noticed the charge, he once claimed to have studied the famous modern philosophers rather carefully, finding Schopenhauer, Nietzsche, and Bergson 'not too difficult'. Thus he scoffed at Bloomsbury, where between the wars Bergson enjoyed a vogue, and where popular dramatists—and indeed popular novelists and essayists—were dismissed as triflers. He added that as a dramatist he was neither prophet nor innovator, and did not feel it a duty to grapple single-handed with civilization, while 'as a writer of fiction I go back, through innumerable generations, to the tellers of tales round the fire in the caverns that sheltered neolithic man'.

Could anything have been more mere? Because obviously no sophisticate could be expected to share the crude pleasures of primitive man. We had come far from cave-dwellings; we needed Continental forms and thought as we needed Continental food and wines; the great novelists and playwrights had all come from abroad, especially from France, where they ordered such matters better than the go-as-you-please English. It cannot be denied that in spite of his defiance Maugham was found entirely insignificant in the stream of modern literature.

Still telling tales, however, he noticed, round about 1910 (which was before the days of Bloomsbury), that while his tales enjoyed some popularity they gave him no more serious a reputation as novelist than as dramatist. This also was a matter for reconsideration. Other men obtained *réclame* by writing long novels in which the backgrounds, whether in the Potteries or in Kensington, were those of their youth, and the heroes were adapted self-portraits. Why should he not do the same? The result was *Of Human Bondage*, which to a great extent reproduced, with appropriate disguises and diversions, the stages of a life intimately known to him.

Had *Of Human Bondage* been published before the first War it must have taken high place between *Clayhanger* and *Sinister Street*; but it did not appear until 1915. By then, the British were desperately engaged in fighting for their lives, and only in the still-uncommitted United States did this book receive immediate and enthusiastic attention. An insular student of the novel might have assumed that Maugham had missed the bus.

He had not done so; or at least it may be said that there was another bus, and that it was unpassengered. He had always been a devotee of Maupassant; and he knew that distant parts of the world offered endless material to story-tellers reared among neolithic man. Life in Paris had familiarized him with the ways of artists; he found himself especially attracted to the personality of Gauguin, who had abandoned respectability and 'gone native' in the South Seas. Wasn't that, in itself, quite a story?

The abandonment of conventionality, and the possibility of becoming what, quoting Hazlitt, he called 'the gentleman in the parlour', an anonymous loser of 'importunate, tormenting, everlasting personal identity', was a fascinating prospect. Interest in Gauguin's escape, and the wish to 'become the creature of the moment, clear of all ties', resulted in a new birth for Maugham. He left the world behind. He saw Tahiti. He wrote *The Moon and Sixpence*.

The Moon and Sixpence, published in 1919, was a great success with the public that reads for curiosity. It also attracted critical attention. Though still branded as 'popular', Maugham was seen to have an individual approach to life; and as the Post-Impressionists had hitherto been considered peculiarly the property of advanced culture this novel about Gauguin suggested that if only Maugham had understood the Art of the Novel he might have done something excellent in that form.

This was not my own view. I see that in a notice I wrote of *The Moon and Sixpence* for *The Manchester Guardian* I commented on the reader's dismay at 'a sense of calculated and heightened effect', and on the failure of technical accomplishment lacking 'true creative inspiration'. Such an opinion did not matter; it was a voice from the sideline. What mattered was that Maugham had really caught the bus at last.

At this time, according to my interpretation of *The Summing Up*, he told one of the arch-prophets of the Post-Impressionists,

Desmond MacCarthy, what he thought his possible, but over-looked, claims to aesthetic esteem. MacCarthy stated those claims as his own opinion in a magazine article (I think the magazine was *The Cosmopolitan*) for which Maugham expressed little gratitude in *The Summing Up*. Maugham should have been more appreciative. The article represented a thaw in the aesthetic winter, and gave the first hint of coming glory.

The glory was not yet to arrive. In 1921 Abel Chevalley's *Le Roman Anglais de Notre Temps* barely named *Liza of Lambeth* while giving extended attention to several writers younger than Maugham (including myself); in 1925 Virginia Woolf, attacking her seniors, Bennett, Wells, and Galsworthy, whose work she described as 'already a little chill', listed as the only significant novelists of the time James Joyce, E. M. Forster, Lytton Strachey, D. H. Lawrence, and T. S. Eliot. She did not mention Maugham. Even in its revised edition of 1930 the *History of English Literature* by Legouis and Cazamian brushed him off with dozens of lesser men; while A. C. Ward's *Twentieth Century Literature* (3rd edition, 1930) confined itself to unenthusiastic references to the plays, and the same author's *The Nineteen Twenties* (also 1930) did not mention Maugham at all.

Nevertheless *The Moon and Sixpence* had been observed. So, in the theatre, had *The Circle*, which was produced in 1921. Neither could wholly please those who thought success incompatible with quality (I see that as dramatic critic for *The Nation* I spoke harshly of *The Circle* on more legitimate grounds); but Granville Barker and William Archer were both enthusiastic about the play, and outside the narrow world of what Arnold Bennett used ironically to call 'the *Élite*' a stir of admiration was perceptible. It was to deepen and spread.

It deepened particularly because, having written a few short stories in young manhood, and having noticed (he has always been a great noticer of men and women and their reading) that some fuss was being made of a Russian writer named Chekhov, whom he thought inferior to his old idol Maupassant, Maugham had caught a sudden glimpse of the field in which his greatest printed triumphs have been gained. The United States at that time was eager for the pungent dramatic short story. Maugham wrote it. When in 1928 he produced *Ashenden* nobody could doubt his mastery of the form.

Ashenden was followed in 1930 by *Cakes and Ale*, an astringent novel in which the two chief characters were identified as actual people, drawn with exquisite malice. Maugham became for the first time a writer important to his age. Within a year or so of its publication Galsworthy and Bennett were dead; Shaw had removed to the country; Wells had lost his force. By 1935, when I wrote a book called *The Georgian Literary Scene*, it was natural to include Maugham, however partially and inadequately, as a serious writer.

Hugh Walpole

•

4 I **WANT** now to step back a few years, to days long before *Cakes and Ale*, in order to speak of Hugh Walpole, who was immediately recognized as the Alroy Kear of that book. My view of him differed from Maugham's; and although as a later chapter will explain I liked him very much but did not whole-heartedly respect his character, I am sure that the satirical portrait in *Cakes and Ale* was unjust.

Walpole's first letter to me was dated 'Good Friday'; and since the book it refers to was published in March, 1914, he must have written on April 10th in that year. I have already spoken of his habit of dashing off letters of praise to his contemporaries. Here is an example:

> Dear Mr Swinnerton, I've hesitated considerably but after all, a grateful letter can't do any harm. I am forced to write and tell you how fine a piece of work I consider *On the Staircase*, not that it matters a damn what I think, except that one novelist always sees more into another novelist's work than . . . well, than someone who's never tried to do the thing. Your book has given me the most extraordinary sense of charm and beauty—a charm which is utterly your own secret.

More followed, in the same vein. I imagine that this letter was not unlike those sent to other men and women; and as the writer of it had already published *Mr Perrin and Mr Traill* and *Fortitude*, both of which had received splendid praise, I have no doubt that as one who hardly regarded himself as a writer at all I felt and expressed gratitude for such generous notice. We were both twenty-nine. Although I was reviewing novels, over initials, for *The Manchester Guardian*, I still think it was generous notice, and not the interested approach of Alroy Kear to a potential log-roller.

The protest may suggest that I feel a doubt. The truth is that Walpole was a very complex character, impulsive, loyal, affectionate, laughing, but at the same time aware of the advantages of publicity and tormented by conscience, bad dreams, ambition, schoolgirlish spitefulness, and an incurable habit of self-protective secrecy, or dissimulation. When Maugham referred, in *Cakes and Ale*, to his meeting with Alroy Kear, some talk of a lunch, and Kear's innocent promise to 'look at my book when I get home and ring you up', he caustically added:

> I had not known Roy for twenty years without learning that he always kept in the upper left hand pocket of his waistcoat the little book in which he put down his engagements; I was therefore not surprised when I heard from him no further.

This exchange might have been set down as it occurred. Besides being characteristic Maugham, it touched that trait of secrecy in Walpole which I mentioned, and which all knew. I am sure that the evasiveness about making an appointment was not a smooth lie, and that it revealed, rather, a sudden impulse of distrust. Kear would certainly dread Willie Ashenden's penetration. At the heart of that dread would lurk memory of having in one of his bursts of effusiveness confessed to Willie, long before, his dream of becoming, late in life, a G.O.M. Pleasure in the thought of a longer meeting would be followed in a flash by the doubt: 'Careful! Careful! He's dangerous. I mustn't commit myself.' Indeed, I imagine that knowing Willie's cool eyes to be upon the waistcoat pocket, he would remember other pending engagements, less nerve-racking and of course socially more valuable. Slight distaste for Willie, sweeping across that sensitive mind, would be decisive.

Willie Ashenden, so placed, might have refused point-blank. His judgment was calm; Walpole's was not. And owing to his unmistakable relish for social popularity Walpole was besieged by hostesses everywhere. He was a bachelor; he looked radiant and talked radiantly. His father was a bishop; his manners were acceptably modest. He was therefore in great demand. In one early letter to me he spoke of being 'so hemmed about with masses of people that I can't be my natural self at all', while in another he said such people 'held pistols to his head'. The device of the little book was a necessary shield. In addition, he liked to remain uncommitted and mysterious. I have met him in Piccadilly when he was supposed to be abroad; and on one occasion, when we lunched, he so greatly enjoyed our talk that he asked if we could lunch again on the following Friday.

'I'm going up to Edinburgh,' said he. 'I'm telling everybody I shan't be back until Saturday; but I'm really coming back on Thursday.'

I agreed to lunch on Friday. As we left the restaurant together in high spirits he caught sight of a strange-looking man sitting alone at a side table, and stopped. I continued for a few steps, turned, glanced, and heard Walpole whisper: 'I shall be back on Wednesday.'

Well, now, that was a very extraordinary thing, wasn't it? Extraordinary and inexplicable? Was he going away at all? Willie Ashenden, saying 'No', would have drawn a devastating conclusion; but I think Willie would have been wrong. I think Walpole was going to Edinburgh, because he was much attached to his father and mother, who lived there. I think he may have been coming back on Thursday, and in the instant of seeing this unknown friend may have decided to cut yet another twenty-four hours off his stay. His reactions to individuals were always emotional. If those individuals, like Arnold Bennett and myself, impressed him with a sense of ironic stability, he responded with eager affection. For a time he trusted. Having trusted, he was seized by panic. Had he betrayed himself? How far could any man really trust another, especially another of cooler emotion than his own? It was a terrible problem. He once admitted that while extraordinarily happy in my company he always, five minutes after our parting, was pierced by the thought: 'I wonder if he was laughing at me all the time.'

That was a criticism of my levity. It did not arise during our first correspondence, in which I detect, on his part, a slightly uneasy approach by flattery and the sort of manly colloquialism which self-conscious writers sometimes use in correspondence with each other. The sense that the recipient is another writer restricts topics; the wish to boast a little without seeming to patronize restricts candour; the fear that if he says 'I think your book is no dam' good' he will receive in reply some shocking home-truths, leading to the breakage of a none-too-secure friendship, hangs heavy. Only when non-literary affection is established can there be free exchange.

At first, therefore, in Walpole's letters to me (not mine to him) there was hesitation, as well as friendliness. As I shall illustrate hereafter, he had been cruelly teased by another of his enthusiasms; but to me, as a contemporary much less prosperous than himself, he was earnest and expository. As he grew used to me he said—knowing there was no alternative—that he did not mind my laughing at him if I would always make it clear that however much I laughed I was his friend. Only in his diary did he leave a final sign of resentment by saying that I was 'untrustworthy'.

Maugham did not touch, in *Cakes and Ale*, the deep vein of hysteria which led to nightmare and the macabre hatreds of *Mr Perrin and Mr Traill* and *Portrait of a Man with Red Hair*. When I said to Walpole of the latter (I had had an operation for hernia, and he very kindly visited me with the book in his hand) 'I suppose this is your *Jekyll and Hyde*?' he was enraptured, exclaiming: 'That's an awfully nice thing to say!'

It was the more acceptable, because I had often objected to his experiments with the uncanny. I responded to this when presented by Turgenev in *Clara Militch* or Henry James in *The Figure in the Carpet*: I could not do so in Walpole's fictions. I thought it then palpably bogus, and said so. The first time I did this his reply was so characteristic that I shall quote from it here:

What a delightful letter! I liked its honesty, its clarity, everything about it. Where you mainly differ from me you will I'm afraid always differ from me. To tell you the truth what I miss in your books is exactly what you hate in mine—the fantasy—the 'spooks'—call it what you will. It's no use —it's an intrinsic part of me and it will always be there. I think the only thing that *really* absorbs me is the 'spiritual' history of the human soul—the moment and the place where and when the soul and body join and the country in *between* this world and the others. Don't think this priggish or false— it isn't. It's derived I think directly from my Puritan fore- fathers and I hail in my literary descent straight through Hawthorne, Shorthouse and Henry James who after all mainly dealt with these things. I don't mean that I do this 'spooky' business well—I don't—but I deeply deeply believe in it and I believe one day I'll do it better. Meanwhile there are of course people who like that side of my work and *feel* it and a number who don't. The only point is that I shall never get away from it and I *do* believe it.

This declaration was made some time after our first meeting, which took place in December, 1916. At that meeting he was slimmer than he afterwards became, and was not yet the 'apple-cheeked Hugh' of Ellen Glasgow's amused nickname. He was physically larger-boned than myself, and at least a couple of inches taller, with a jutting chin, thick-rimmed *pince- nez* which diminished the size of the eyes behind them (he had much trouble with short-sightedness, and suffered a good deal of pain with his eyes), a plunging energy of gait, and an im- petuous joviality of utterance which brought minute bubbles to the corners of his lips. He had no affectations of speech; his voice, neither deep nor high-pitched, seemed to come from the throat, and could be described, I think, as a resonant tenor. It served him well on the platform, as did his open, boyish manner.

Although we met at the Garrick Club, we went to a Soho restaurant for lunch, as 'we can't talk here'. He led the way; he walked fast. At table we exchanged free opinions about current books and living authors, his comments showing enthusiasm for all literature and all mankind. And as he was then attached to the Russian Red Cross and was in Russia throughout the Revolution, we met seldom. Our correspondence therefore expanded. I kept him abreast of literary affairs in London, especially of the new books published in his absence. This was what I said in 1917:

I had a go at *House-mates* [by J. D. Beresford], but did not greatly care for it. I have also reviewed Tennyson Jesse—a long huge formless feather-bed of a book, very Cornish, with 'you'ms' and 'lils' galore, and a vague figure of a gelding far away among the mists as its central male character, with skipping types of 'strong' men and artists and forlorn women like the ghosts of fleas appearing and disappearing as clouds upon a mountain top. Some of the writing not bad. Joyce [presumably *A Portrait of the Artist*] I thought extraordinary a page at a time, but tiring. I am very depressed with current fiction. I trust you to redress the balance. Lawrence is not yet announced; I rather gather his work is perambulating [the story was that Philip Morrell, resenting the portrayal of Lady Ottoline in *Women in Love*, had threatened legal action]. This is a pity. Mackenzie is reservedly aloof, charging the Gk. govt. for lost works. Cannan has completed a new work which Unwin is to do. He has also writ a little play. . . . Everything rather stagnant. [Here followed extremely adverse criticism of a still living author.] In fact, as I've said, I am displeased with current fiction. What we've got to do is to get that new criticism on its legs, to react upon the fiction of our day—or, rather of tomorrow. I picked up *Still Life* [Middleton Murry's only novel] at Mudies. It lay very still—very still and quiet. I could not hear

42

its pulse nor feel its soft breath. So I laid it down again among its fellow corpses, all rather soiled and unattractive.

We also quoted newspaper comments upon ourselves as writers. One of these, which he very much enjoyed, was made by C. K. Scott-Moncrieff, the translator of Proust, who called him 'Charlotte Yonge trying to write like Charlotte Brontë'; others were that I was 'a flower among the weeds' (a Dutch reviewer), had 'an honest humour' (this was the *T.L.S.*), and (according to *The Spectator*) was 'very clever'. An American writer, lumping us together with Lawrence and Cannan, headed his piece: 'If this is Literature, give me Death'. Whether praised or blamed, however, we were pleased at being noticed at all.

Walpole, visiting London, lunched Wells, whom he found 'very urbane albeit looking, I thought, dirty and old and hideously ugly. I like him more than I used to, but he doesn't impress me so much. Something has gone out of him. But he was nice.' This was in May, 1918. I, in return, wrote:

Do you know who's here? Confusing greatness with sales, and sales with virtues, and virtues with vices, and vices with greatness, and greatness with sentimentality, and sentimentality with sales, and sales with God? Why, your old pal Gilbert Frankau. He tells me that he and I are Artists.

On May 14th, 1919, I wrote:

Since I saw you, what have I done? I mean of interest. I've seen Arnold, who was greatly bucked one day because T. Hardy was enthusiastic about *Judith*. . . . Oh, and I've been to the Wells's for the week-end. Myself the only visitor, but all very gay and tranquil. H.G. happy and confiding. Myself extraordinarily witty—must have been the drink, I believe. Just fancy Jane and H.G. listening in silence for half an hour late at night to my conversation!

In response to my demand for the rise of a new criticism, Walpole wrote:

I've ceased to believe any more in contemporary criticism. I don't see an infallible critic anywhere and I find that I myself am all over the shop. I *know* that [Gilbert Cannan's] *Pink Roses* is shocking bad (really Cannan's worst) and I know that *The Arrow of Gold* [by Conrad] is magnificent, but in between there are things like *Judith*, *The Return of the Soldier* [Rebecca West's first novel], Robert Nichols, etc. etc: these are the difficult things. . . . Something called the Hogarth Press have been sending me strangely-coloured works including an amusing K. Mansfield and a horribly bad poem by Murry.

My reply stated that I had read Wells's *The Undying Fire*, which I admired, and *Pink Roses*, which I did not. I continued:

Cannan's reputation should be buried with the notification 'No Flowers'. . . . dry at bottom, superficial and shoved out, and I don't think it has got any imagination or brain-stuff behind it. . . . I have written one of my famous adverse reviews for *The Manchester Guardian*, which should estrange Gilbert for ever. But most likely he is made of sterner stuff. After all, we must all recognize the right of others to their estimates of our own work. I don't mind people not thinking my works good.

Marguerite [Bennett] has been to see me this afternoon—looking really beautiful in a jolly new dress with lots of yellow in it. She is full of vigour. I missed her recital a fortnight ago—through forgetfulness—and must absolutely not fail this week. I've just collected the card from my drawer and stuck it before me as a reminder. Of course I shan't be able to understand a word, as French poetry always remains incomprehensible to me, even in print.

Walpole wrote complaining that he had received no letter from me (it was a favourite gambit of his to pretend that one was long in arrears); and as he was writing *The Cathedral* with enjoyment down in the Cornish fishing village of Polperro he reported that his enjoyment would have been even greater if he had not been 'keeping my Hobgoblin tendency strongly in check for your sake'.

Although in fact I had recently written, I replied with soothing words to this complaint:

I am sorry to feel myself a skeleton at the feast of goblins. I suppose it is that being rather self-sufficing I don't ever think of people or things looking over my shoulder and leading me. I think of things within. Not the Soul, my lad; but the—what Miss Hilda Glyder [a music-hall singer of the time] would call 'the little lump of cuddle inside'. But I don't mind people doing goblins if they want to, so long as they make my flesh creep. . . .

I am sorry you have ceased to believe in contemporary criticism. In point of fact I don't worry myself about it very much. But very few things worry me now, since I began to have enough to eat. I will explain to you where you and I both go wrong in criticism. As long as we *know* anything about a subject, and we are content with our knowledge, all's well. There is harmony, and the judgment is O.K. But there are things outside. You worry about them. I don't. Having decided that I like *Judith* and hate its production, I am like a feather cushion—finally immovable. Having decided that I like *The Undying Fire* I am perfectly willing to give my reasons and die—knowing that in theme, and fabric, and aim it is quite outside the things I intricately absorb myself in. In the case of neither *Judith* nor H.G. should I claim definitely to be right. On the subject of *Pink Roses* or *The Return of the Soldier* I simply KNOW I'm right. I don't feel the same about books outside my own technical range of composition or insight or imagination.

Still upon this subject, Walpole wrote:

This is only a five minutes chat because I feel friendly, and doesn't demand an answer although of course I shall be delighted to have one. What you say about contemporary criticism is excellent and I think quite true although you're wrong to think I worry. I don't. My final conviction remains as I one day stated it to you—namely that the novel is a pudding and that many critics go wrong in looking for only one ingredient and praising and blaming accordingly. There are (1) Personality (2) Style (3) Narrative gift (4) Humour (5) Creation of character (6) Philosophy (7) Poetry (8) Observation etc. etc.

Now I think *you* have 1, 2, 3, 4, and 5 without question, that I have 1, 3, 4, (you'll see it later), 5—and would like to have 6 and 7 but haven't naturally. Mackenzie has 1, 3, 4, and none of the others, Lawrence 1 (very strong), 2, 6, and 7, and not a shadow of 3 and 4—and so on.

Now I think what the Clever Ones like [Dorothy] Richardson, K. Mansfield, W. Lewis etc, have above us is 2 and 8, but their characters are like people seen for a moment in a Tube [underground train] and no more, and their philosophy is merely transient emotion.

Now I can observe no modern critic save Arnold, yourself, Lynd, and possibly Squire who is broadly tolerant and is not angry if *such* an ingredient is not there and not ecstatic if *such* an ingredient is. Is not this what is wanted in criticism?

Tolerance? Breadth? What innocent talk was here! Such qualities were *démodé*. Well had Walpole written from Moscow in 1916:

I'm pulled immensely two ways. On one side nothing seems to matter in comparison with Art—on the other nothing in comparison with the War. . . . It all means an absolute crisis in me who before the War had believed that Henry James and the Georgian Poets were the streets to walk in, and that to be in a London literary set was the best thing on God's earth. That's all gone utterly. . . . I believe that any shoe-black is more important than May Sinclair and any minesweeper more interesting than Wells. . . . Henry James is dying, Bernard Shaw is dead, Bennett has completed his Trilogy, Galsworthy is shrivelled up like a pea—no my dear Swinnerton, the gate is slammed upon a period—they are all dead and gone.

Elizabeth and Katherine

5   MY SHORT novel *Nocturne*, published in England in 1917 and in America one year later, dealt with the events of a single evening in the lives of five people. It had a poor English press, and I was told not to play tricks again; but the warm praise of H. G. Wells, who, unknown to myself, contributed a preface to the American edition, prompted reviewers in the United States to greater cordiality. Bennett—also secretly —weighed in with a personal sketch for a small advertising brochure; and *Nocturne*'s fortune in America was considerable.

Ricochet led to a quiver of interest in England among what William Heinemann used to call 'the little West End clique'. Fifteen hundred copies of the book had been printed by Secker, whose circumstances prevented him from reprinting for twelve months. He then, by permission, used the Wells preface, and sold the whole edition of a thousand copies at once. A third followed in 1922, of I forget how many, and a fourth in 1926. In 1937 the book was included in the *World's Classics;* it was translated into almost all the European languages; and just before, or during, the second War was published at sixpence in paper covers, when about one hundred thousand were sold. This last event destroyed its reputation. A few innocents continued enthusiastic, and Maugham included the book entire in a massive anthology which he called *Travellers' Library;* but that was practically the end.

You can no longer buy *Nocturne* in the *World's Classics;* I am told that a reference to it in at least one standard work has disappeared, and that no academic literary historian of today

47

dreams of naming such an unimportant work. I make no complaint. I never exaggerated the book's merit, and I do not object to its present eclipse. R.I.P.

While critical esteem was high, I wrote in 1919 another novel about a small group of characters, but with a less arbitrary time-table. It was called *September*, and, being published by Methuen (to whom it belonged on a contract made before the War) as something very distinguished, received reviews which I des-cribed to Walpole as 'extended and respectful, but not eulogistic'. *September* sold over five thousand copies in England, about twenty thousand in America, and nearly brought me an honour which young novelists in those days coveted.

The honour was this: *The Times Literary Supplement* used to print most of its fiction reviews at the back of the paper; but one particularly noteworthy novel was given the whole right-hand column in the centre opening. Compton Mackenzie, whose book *Poor Relations* was published simultaneously with *September*, and who had good reason to expect the column for himself, sportively invited me to bet on which of us would receive it. I told him I never betted on certainties.

We waited for the Day. To our surprise and common pleasure the *T.L.S.* found its own solution to the problem. It printed the review of Mackenzie, sure enough, in the coveted column, but, breaking all custom, set a review of *September*, of the same length, immediately alongside.

This was one compliment. Another was an astonishing letter from James Stephens, the Irish poet, then a stranger, saying gravely (I have the letter still) 'there is no doubt that you are the master of English fiction'. A third, equally astonish-ing, was a public declaration by Frank Harris in the American periodical *Pearson's Magazine* that I was so great a novelist as to suggest limitless powers.

Nowadays the name of Harris is hardly remembered; but however hard it may be to distinguish true from false in the

Casanovian brag of *My Life and Loves* it is certain that fero-
ciously brilliant talk, a wealthy marriage, and bold conduct of
the *Fortnightly* and *Saturday* reviews once gave him tremendous
prestige. On the *Saturday*, for example, he employed Shaw,
Max Beerbohm, Wells, and many another bright star; so that
the paper could be read from beginning to end with a sense of
tremendous vitality. In spite of the fact that he then rid himself
of the *Saturday* and passed to other journalistic ventures which
grew shadier and shadier until he left England in disgrace,
literary praise from Harris was never easily won. I could not
help being excited, as well as amused. Moreover when I
laughingly repeated to Arnold Bennett what Harris had said,
Bennett, who never lost his admiration for Harris, said with
serious brevity: 'That . . . is my own opinion.'

In later years, for the purpose of summarizing Harris's
life-story for the D.N.B., I re-read his books. The lustre was
gone. Those once-famous short-stories, *Montes the Matador* and
Elder Conklin, proved long-winded and derivative; *The Man
Shakespeare* (1909), which for English readers represented the
first attempt to construct from allusions in the sonnets and plays
a coherent self-portrait on Freudian lines, was forced, rather
noisy; the shorter studies of famous persons, which when first
published attracted attention by their outrageous effrontery,
were dead.

The case was different in 1919. Harris said I was a great
novelist; and even a ribald smiles upon praise as something to
retort upon too-candid friends. But indeed I had nothing to rue.
I was already, at Allan Monkhouse's invitation, reviewing for
The Manchester Guardian. In succession to G. H. Mair I acted,
again by invitation, as anonymous dramatic critic for *Truth*;
and because Charles Masterman, who read my *Truth* contributions, told him I was the best dramatic critic in London H. W.
Massingham asked me to write on the theatre for *The Nation*.
Middleton Murry had returned to journalism as editor of *The
Athenaeum* and begged me to contribute to that paper. As I
was reading manuscripts all day for Chatto & Windus, and
enjoying fame in the book trade as sponsor of, among other
publications, *The Young Visiters*, it will be seen that for a lazy

young man without ambition I was in a wordly sense doing pretty well. These things had all come unsought, by luck. I had no conceit. I was just thirty-five.

For some years my freedom of movement had been curtailed by responsibility for my mother's life and happiness. She, by the age of sixty-four, was so much crippled by arthritis as to have lost almost all locomotive power. When the War ended, and my brother, who had married while in the Army, was demobilized, she suggested making her home with him, so that I could enjoy what she considered well-earned liberty. It was a truly imaginative suggestion. Scottish pride in both her sons yielded to love (we pretended that she referred to us as 'my clever boys'; but she never did that). She was an exceptional woman; full of merriment; scorn of sin, cruelty and emulation; and full also of the most simple interest in everything from cats to Henry James, who next to myself was her favourite novelist.

The next step was to find a living-place in London, and here I received unexpected help. Mrs Desmond MacCarthy's novel, *A Pier and a Band*, had been published by Chatto & Windus on my recommendation; and although I forget the circumstances I think Mrs MacCarthy must have felt resulting kindness. She lent me, for a few days, a cottage in Wiltshire, where, with Martin Secker as my guest, I received a friendly visit at her instigation from Sydney Waterlow and E. M. Forster. She also asked me home to Chelsea, where I met her mother, the famous and highly formidable Mrs Warre-Cornish, of whom a delightful sketch is given by Aldous Huxley in one of his early stories. Mrs Warre-Cornish, whose first remark was: 'And what, Mr Swinnerton, is your opinion of flogging in the Navy?' closed the proceedings with the majestic announcement: 'I go *straight* to read *all* your books— beginning with *Nocturne*!' The farewell disconcerted me almost more than the greeting.

Mrs MacCarthy, heroic sufferer from incurable deafness, was a generous and impatient woman of quiet but arrogant determination. She was married to a man who talked so enchantingly that if he visited friends for lunch he was often prevailed upon to stay the night or longer. He was Irish, Eton, Cambridge, and, in the Irish conversational manner, a celebrated raconteur. But he depended for triumphant success upon minds responsive to the elaborations of anecdote and the ingenuities of fancy; among less consciously witty, erudite consorts, such as Arnold Bennett and myself, his gift, calling for space, was not as effective.

Owing to MacCarthy's indulgence in the art of conversation, which friends encouraged (James Stephens, an even better talker, needed applause and at least two bottles of wine to become not so much an inhabitant of Fairyland, although he was that, too, as a companion for the Gods), he never wrote the book he was qualified to write by wide-ranging familiarity with eighteenth-century *belles lettres*. It was Mrs MacCarthy's wish that I should give him (on behalf of Chatto & Windus) a contract to write this book. She supposed that such a contract need be only a sort of dummy—something she could use as a persuasive to labour—but this I thought impossible. I hesitated, partly because I doubted if such a book would appeal to the firm's senior partner, who was not a literary man, partly because I did not greatly admire MacCarthy's writing. The contract was not offered. I am sorry if my stupidity robbed the world of a masterpiece.

However, Mrs MacCarthy resolved to find me suitable accommodation in London; and, meeting with Bertrand Russell in the street, she explained her errand. He at once said: 'He can have my studio.'

So briefly, among friends, are such matters decided; and I am glad to say that as landlord and tenant Bertrand Russell and I were mutually satisfied for several years. For one thing, having been poor and scrupulous, I paid my rent punctually, which he found an admirable habit; for another, having read one or two of my books, he was always friendly and courteous, which I liked. The studio I rented was on the ground floor at the back of No 5 Fitzroy Street, a grimy building with a repulsive communal water-closet and, to my intense pleasure, quietness, a gas fire, a comfortable bed, and a magnificent club-like leather-covered armchair, all of which I used until the house was sold, when Russell generously offered me other accommodation in a Bloomsbury flat.

Fitzroy Street lies at the heart of a district bounded by Tottenham Court Road on the east, Oxford Street on the south, Marylebone Road on the north, and Portland Place on the west. It was territory familiar to me because George Gissing had lived in the neighbourhood with his first wife and I had examined it while writing my little book about Gissing. I could reach any part of social London in a few minutes; I could entertain without ceremony; I could and did work very hard at night when my day's work of reading manuscripts was ended. And the blessing of freedom to go and come as I liked, never previously enjoyed, was delicious.

In order to see Bertrand Russell I had, by Mrs MacCarthy's advice, to telephone to his brother's house in Gordon Square. When I did telephone I was at first answered by a foreign voice, the owner of which was unable to grasp my name. This was interrupted by another voice, a little drawling voice; and now there was no difficulty. The voice, still drawling, but subtly animated, exclaimed: 'Oh, but you wrote *Nocturne*: do come to tea!'

The speaker was Countess Russell, who, as the Countess von Arnim, had produced many years earlier, and still continued to produce, those arch, acid, charming self-portraits, *Elizabeth and her German Garden* and its successors. By inadvertence I thus entered yet another world, a world in which lavender and furs were curiously associated with sophistication, pre-war Germany, ancient and modern love-affairs, sentiment, shrewdness, cruelty, and unflinching candours about husbands.

Very old men and women were slaves to the heroine of this world. So, through the years, were numerous young men, some of them ardent about work in other spheres, but the most interesting to me distinguished by prosperity or quality in literature. Lady Russell, when thirty-one, had been commended in her father's journal for 'surprising brightness and seventeen-year-old appearance and simplicity—rare and fascinating combination of dove and serpent'. She was now fifty-four; tragic and ludicrous happenings had impaired the outward youthfulness; the rest of the description was true as before.

Small, fair, lazy-voiced, she seemed at a first male glance to be no more than a child. Then one observed that the child was precocious. And then that she was terrifying. She was so terrifying to some men that they trembled under the gaze of her rather prominent merciless pale blue eyes, and collapsed altogether before the demurely drawling boldness of her tongue. If, personally, I never trembled it was because at our first meeting some recognition of her quality made me interrupt what was not so much brag or self-explanation as indiscreet commentary with the words: 'I trust you.' I meant: 'I can trust you not to misinterpret what I say'; but Lady Russell, alarmed by what she thought a *naïveté*, cried: 'Oh, but you mustn't do that!' An instant later she understood my meaning, and concluded that a young man who had trapped her into protest must be less simple than he seemed; less simple and not easily demoralized. She was thereafter a true and candid friend.

She was extremely kind. Her judgments of men and women, however, being unsentimental, were often destructive. What she seemed to be in *Elizabeth and her German Garden* (especially if one recognized her voice in that far from innocuous classic) she was in reality. The pleasure we take, in *The Caravanners*, in the discomfiture of pompous and overbearing persons was her pleasure. When we relish the defects of the hero of *Vera*, we are as it were hand in glove with the author, who, perceiving our enjoyment, will playfully decorate her accurate observation with newly invented absurdities of the most scathing—and, to the victim, infuriating—order. Thus the lucid ridicule of dullness and brutality which quickens nearly all her books was what produced for every hearer an awful delight in her more intimate conversation. I have never known any woman with the same *comic* detachment of mind.

Perhaps because of this characteristic, she had loyal admirers and a wide public rather than great literary reputation. It was as long ago as the eighteen-nineties that she first set a fashion for 'garden' books and drew to her side, whenever she was in England, so many of the cultivated people of her day. The survivors of that body were still loyal when I entered their circle; indeed at that first meeting we had with us for a time a considerable classical scholar named John Sargeaunt, and when I visited the Châlet Soleil at Randogne, above the Rhône Valley, I found myself in company with, besides two attractive young men, the aged Cobden-Sandersons and Henry Festing-Jones, friend and biographer of Butler. Augustine Birrell was due in the following week.

I may here remark, as I cannot regard him as part of the post-war literary scene, and therefore may have no occasion to speak in more detail, that Festing-Jones (she called him 'Senoj') was a darling. Immediately communicative about his idol and about Sicily, which he had explored with devotion, he slowly revealed with the progress of intimacy an astringent mind that explained Butler's friendship. To speak of him as a mere satellite to a great man would be an arrogant mistake.

Now a literary life of nearly fifty years is long enough to allow any reputation to wax and wane. Whether there is any other example of a writer who scored such tremendous successes of delight with her first and last books as Lady Russell did with *Elizabeth and her German Garden* and *Mr Skeffington* I cannot say. In her case the progress was from demure comedy to rueful hilarity. It was from the young wife pitilessly regardful of the idiosyncrasies of a Man of Wrath to the ageing flirt who discovers that, one by one, she has lost her adorers, and that while charm may be perpetual allure inevitably dies.

Lady Russell was only twenty-one when, a Beaumont, born in Australia, she was taken abroad by her father. She then fell straight into the arms of a noble German widower, the Graf Henning Auguste von Arnim-Schlagenthin. The Graf pursued;

Elizabeth, or 'May' as she was called by her family, however wayward could not resist; and as soon as they were married the business of producing an heir for the noble family's title was undertaken. Daughter after daughter appeared. Elizabeth, bored with the vain pursuit, refused for a time to bear further children; and it was not until 1902 that she had a son. Then indeed joyful excitement filled the hearts of Arnim and the Beaumonts. Only Elizabeth, observed her father, remained 'imperturbable, calm and childish as ever'.

Imperturbability was needed. Her husband, who among other occupations was director of a bank, survived a false charge of financial misdemeanour; other difficulties followed hard and cruelly until his death in 1910; and Elizabeth used her sportive literary gift to maintain the family income.

Her style did not change. She unobtrusively depicted herself as she was or had been, surrounded by husbands or friends seen with what Jane Austen called 'open pleasantry'. Her talent lay in fun, satirical portraiture, and farcical comedy, qualities which are scorned by those obsessed by what a correspondent describes to me as 'the modern dilemma'. Her fame has therefore sunk. If it ever recovers, as I hope it will do, she may find a place below the highest but in a discreet jostle with Fanny Burney, Emily Eden, and Rhoda Broughton.

Meanwhile a succession of young Englishmen came to Nassenheide, in Pomerania, as pedagogues for the Arnim children. One of these was E. M. Forster; another—Elizabeth selected tutors on principles known only to herself—Hugh Walpole. Because Forster was the friend and recommendation of her nephew, Sydney Waterlow, she over-rode all his characteristic scruples about taking the job; yet when he reached Nassenheide she said she almost dismissed him at sight because he wore a repulsive tie. Forster was then about twenty-four. She began at once to mock what, presumably, she thought his priggish inexperience; but superficial mockery was only one of her arts, and after reading an essay he had written upon a sixteenth-century scientist she moved to ironic and highly suspect praise, which implied that he was an extremely dark horse of genius. Forster afterwards wrote: 'Not only was she clever, but she had the power of making one accept her categories, and I wasted much time in wondering how dark I was.'

Such detachment left all power of manœuvre with herself. It kept her children unhappy but adoring; in the case of Hugh Walpole it was so lacking in tolerance as to become cruelty. Walpole's engagement followed one of his 'fan' letters and a meeting in London. This was in 1907. He reached Nassenheide jovial, ingenuous, sensitive, painfully vulnerable; and he was immediately subjected to variegated tortures.

> The Countess [he wrote to Charles Marriott] is a complex enigma. I don't see much of her but, when I do, she has three moods. (1) Charming, like her books only more so (this does not appear often). (2) Ragging. Now she is unmerciful—attacks you on every side, goes at you until you are reduced to idiocy; and then drops you, limp. (3) Silence. This is most terrible of all. She sits absolutely mute and if one tries to speak one gets snubbed.

It is appalling to learn that—possibly in the hope of placating his tormentor—Walpole had the folly to lend Elizabeth his diary, crowded with simplicities. It was returned ribaldly annotated. Two months later, as Elizabeth wrote to her daughters, he was 'requested, *höflich aber kühl*, to remove himself the end of July'. She added: 'He grows weirder visibly and is the most weird we have struck.'

With the childlike *naïveté* which caused him throughout life to cherish friendships even when he greatly suspected their genuineness, Walpole continued to send Elizabeth his books as they were published; and I think this persistency must have had its reward, for he and she seem to have felt mutual affection to the end of their days. Affection, in her case, was compatible with disdain for his work. Having read the result of a newspaper commission, *Roman Fountain*, she commented in her diary:

The archness and gush and female skittishness of it! Mixed with the most uncomfortable-making elementary philosophising. Poor Hugh. He so longs to be a great writer. I blushed for him, reading the stuff.

Elizabeth remained in her châlet at Randognę, overlooking the Rhône Valley, until the anomaly of being, by marriage, a German citizen of British birth in a neutral country drove her back to England with a mysteriously acquired British passport. She told me she had presented herself at the Foreign Office with the words: 'Here I am; German. What are you going to do about me?' They 'did' something entirely to her advantage.

In the first Randogne period she had had a love-affair with Wells, whom she described to me in retrospect as 'that coarse little man'; (his own comment was 'when you've had her for a week you want to bash her head through the wall') and one solution of the problem of nationality was re-marriage to an Englishman. It was quickly found. She was delighted with the new husband, Francis, Earl Russell, a fact which she was inclined afterwards to deny; but experience of his domineering behaviour and intolerable sexual infidelities had by that time produced disgust. She left him, and with her two countries again at peace returned to Switzerland, the Châlet Soleil, and apparent tranquillity.

The Châlet had a garden, a lawn the greenness of which was maintained by daily spraying, a wonderful view of mountains. She worked in a small separate châlet or studio. And she wrote there the narrative, with reflections, entitled *In the Mountains*, which was much discussed on its anonymous publication, and immediately recognized as hers by Earl Russell. He, having read the Bible very thoroughly while in prison charged with bigamy in marrying his second wife (he always jocosely referred to Elizabeth as 'my third'), copied from that Book every familiar reference to faithless wives, and posted the resulting dossier to her. I do not know Elizabeth's feelings on receipt of it; in conversation she laughed very mischievously at her husband's silliness, styling him, in that little drawling voice, '*Poor* Francis!'

Merriment continuing, she retorted with *Vera*.

In 1921, when it was published, *Vera* was the talk of the town, as *Cakes and Ale* was to be ten years later. By this time I had spent a fortnight at the Châlet Soleil and heard a great deal about the author's life with Earl Russell, of whom she spoke with ironic distaste. She had been, she said, completely deceived in his character, mistaking his rather brutal bluffness for manly independence. I did not understand how this could be, because although we both felt warm regard for Bertrand Russell, I found Francis, who liked me and at our club bore down upon me, beaming, repugnant. However, entries in Elizabeth's diary proved that she did experience attraction. The opening pages of *Vera* may provide a clue.

The book is not quite a good novel. Some of it is nudged into shape, and to that extent it is sentimental. In essential passages, however, those forming the portrait of a tyrannical husband, there is no sentimentality, but unerringly cruel moderation. Russell must have recognized scenes which had really occurred, described from an angle so unkind to his obtuse self-love as to be infuriating. He was angry enough to threaten legal proceedings against *Vera*. That was stupid. Elizabeth remained, as she had done after the birth of her son, 'imperturbable, calm and childish as ever!'

She said to me: 'It's so *silly* of Francis. If he does sue me I shall simply go into the witness-box and say: "Of *course* it's not Francis!" ' Francis must have guessed this. He took no proceedings.

Here, then, was a woman of personality who in the years I am describing had great private influence. I have always suspected that it was her advocacy that led Middleton Murry, then staying at Randogne or Montana-Vermala, to write an undeservedly favourable review in *The Nation* of a novel of mine called *Coquette*. This review, which said, I think, that I showed capacity for improvement, whereas Lawrence was standing still, roused fury among Laurentians, by whom (to do Murry justice) it was misrepresented as a claim that I was better than Lawrence. That would have been absurd and Murry did not say it. As to Elizabeth's influence, I have no information: I know only that she was capable of speaking about me, whom she liked, in such a way as to bias Murry's always fluid judgment.

Elizabeth was afraid of one person only, her cousin Katherine Mansfield, who spent some time at the health resort Montana-Vermala, immediately above Randogne. Elizabeth wrote: 'I was very shy always of her, afraid of her while intensely admiring.' She lived to find herself described in Katherine's printed *Journal* as having 'a vulgar little mind'.

I picture the two together (I never did see them so); Katherine very dark, still, enigmatically silent, hardly opening her mouth when she spoke in that low murmur; Elizabeth, so much more experienced in polite sophistications, drawling naughtily, and being confronted by unreceptive blankness. You remember how Walpole found Elizabeth's silence the most terrible of her moods: well, for once it was she who was disconcerted. She saw in Katherine her own blood; she drew extraordinary inferences from Katherine's marriage with Middleton Murry, whom she described in his relation to Lawrence as Judas, betraying the master 'with an oily kiss', and, finding no warm response to impulsive affection, marvelled at her cousin's inscrutability.

It confused her, representing defeat. When she saw herself dismissed as 'a vulgar little mind' she became introspective. 'One has so many sides and it is possible K.M. drew out the vulgar one. Awful thought—for her I mean.'

Did Katherine bring out the vulgar side? Was it not equally true of *her* that 'one has so many sides'? This is the impression I gain from Anthony Alpers's biography. Another impression is that Katherine, like Elizabeth, could and did remain 'imperturbable, calm and childish as ever', and, whatever her age, presented a 'seventeen-year-old appearance and simplicity—

rare and fascinating combination of dove and serpent'. To me, the relationship of these two women is a fascinating theme for speculation; truly a challenge to the novelist. If I live long enough I may accept the challenge.

Nobody knew what passed in Katherine's mind. It was egocentric; and it had two chief preoccupations, Art and her own unmatured childishness. Elizabeth's childishness did mature; but it was there all the time, in the absorbed realism of her mind. Katherine's mind remained unaffected by her experience. She never grew up. She pretended a great deal to herself, especially about Art. She was prevented by ineradicable conventionality from being whole-heartedly bohemian. Elizabeth, comparably egocentric, but rather in the way of self-indulgence, learned sympathy with others. She wept real tears; her sentimentality found release in cruelty and the bold exploration of young men's natures; but she was not, I think, conventional.

Nothing, as far as I could tell, shocked her. When two nuns visited at the Châlet Soleil during my stay, she spoke kindly of them to me, but thoughtfully remarked of the elder: 'Not *quite* a virgin, I think,' while other allusions, expressed in a babyish drawl and in reciprocal and appreciated candour, showed that she had coolly considered and approved my sexual attractiveness, at that time under discussion in London.

I must not be misunderstood. We were always 'Lady Russell' and 'Mr Swinnerton'; but she was calmly outspoken, and as I also am said to have a candid mind we exchanged private views of a good many people, including myself and my friends, from intimate angles. My recollection is of great sympathetic understanding, unalloyed by that softness which some (not myself) call charity, but equally free from superiority or the sly viciousness of female gossip. She spoke freely of Middleton Murry; never of Katherine Mansfield, who was too dear to her for discussion with a stranger.

I dwell upon this relationship of Katherine Mansfield and Elizabeth Russell, because it has a place in my underlying chronological scheme. Katherine Mansfield had been associated during her literary life with the world of 'arty' people and small or restricted artistic periodicals, from *The New Age* and *Rhythm* to Murry's *Athenaeum*. Elizabeth Russell's fortune lay among the genteel, among prosperous journals for women; her last book, after being serialized, was made a Book of the Month choice in America. Katherine died young, and was exalted; Elizabeth lived to be over seventy and to look back with regret upon her own work. Re-reading in age her novel of 1905, *Princess Priscilla's Fortnight*, she exclaimed in her diary: 'It has talent—a natural gift, lamentably without any real thought or knowledge.... Plainly my things are nothing at all —nothing, nothing.'

She would nowadays be dismissed by the intellectually smug as 'commercial'; but the word was never used of her while she lived. Manners were better then. She herself practised towards other writers the tolerance natural to her generation. She took pleasure in the smartnesses of Michael Arlen; but she listened also to the queer brilliance of her nephew, Sydney Waterlow, and perused with interest what was being extolled by the coteries.

Her admiration for Lawrence was fervent. She enjoyed Rose Macaulay, read Dorothy Richardson without comment, found Virginia Woolf 'thickly starred with beauty', admired E. M. Forster while lamenting his insensitiveness to women, thought Aldous Huxley very talented but sometimes 'silly', and drew the line only at James Joyce.

Hugh Walpole lent me *Ulysses*—I didn't get far. I see it is a wonderful thing, but nothing will induce me to read a thing—anything—even God's first novel, if it bores me. *Ulysses* made me feel as if I were shut up with a lunatic who was doing what the courts call 'exposing himself'. I got as far as the detailed account of the man's morning (?) visit to the lavatory and then boredom so profound fell upon me that I went to sleep. Monarch [Sydney Waterlow] raves about it. 'Marvellous—literature will never be the same—

completely revolutionising,' etc. He too sends me to sleep by the excess of his eulogies.

These words, indicating it will be said the end of an era of respectability, were addressed in 1922 to Middleton Murry. By that time Murry had ceased to edit *The Athenaeum*, which had been incorporated with *The Nation* in February, 1921, almost exactly two years after he took over the editorship.

Athenaeum and *Adelphi*

•

6 MURRY was the son of a hard-working couple who let lodgings and lived very thriftily. His grandfather was a publican. Having won a scholarship to Christ's Hospital he went on, again by scholarship, to Oxford, where his fellow-students included Joyce Cary, Arnold Toynbee, and, most importantly for Murry, Michael Sadler (later Sadleir). Through contact with a French acquaintance, he visited Paris in one of the vacations, and there tasted the pleasures of life among artists which he enjoyed ever afterwards. He was among the earliest Englishmen to be affected by the Post-Impressionists.

His first editorial venture, as I have told in *Background with Chorus*, was *Rhythm*, a large quarto monthly periodical printed in big type with a symbolic design on the thick grey or blue cover, in which he was financially assisted by Sadler and in which he ambitiously tried to be as Continental as possible. This was especially so with the illustrations, where he was helped by a highly original Scottish artist, J. D. Fergusson. Contributors, including myself, were unpaid. One of them was Walter de la Mare.

The editor further broadened his literary and artistic friend-ships by writing to men he admired, and by frequenting a celebrated second-hand bookshop in a court off the Charing Cross Road which was kept by a shrewd little rebel named Dan Rider. Rider, small, dusty, quietly obstinate, included among his patrons (sometimes, I think, his beneficiaries) a remarkable collection of men, ranging from Jo Davidson, the American sculptor, to Frank Harris, then in the last days of literary dictatorship. Hugh Kingsmill, in his book about Harris, gives a brilliant sketch of Murry and Katherine Mansfield worshipping Harris, and being utterly cast out by him because Murry, with great simplicity, had praised John Masefield, whom the Master did not approve. The encounter was poignant, and the description, which is very malicious, must be exact. It is certainly revealing.

Rhythm became *The Blue Review* in May, 1913; and *The Blue Review*, which was to contain *causeries*, French fashion, by Lawrence, Cannan, Walpole, and myself, died in August of that year. Both Murry and Katherine Mansfield were then lost to my sight until after the War; and I rely for what immediately follows upon F. A. Lea's excellent biography of Murry.

At the outbreak of war in 1914, when he and Katherine Mansfield were consorting intimately with D. H. Lawrence, he was one of a number of sensitive and highly intelligent men (including Lawrence) to whom the War was a dreadful irrelevance and military service a spiritual as well as a physical impossibility. I was not among these men; but an almost fatal illness in 1914 made me for several months an invalid, and I took no part in the War. I therefore have no right to condemn, and do not condemn, those who felt that in no circumstances could they undertake military service.

The Government of the day, when introducing Conscription, made what allowance was possible for dissidents. It could not publicly depart from the principle that every citizen ought to serve the State in time of war; but it inserted saving clauses in the Conscription Act, whereby men in certain occupations, or with conscientious scruples against killing, could be exempted. Much was left to the discretion of tribunals formed to consider such cases, and some of these tribunals were ruthless towards pacifists; but the aim of the Act was to get fit and willing soldiers, so that scholars and artists were often allowed to continue in civil life.

Among the artists were both Lawrence and Murry, with

Lawrence suffering the most stupid persecution because his wife was a German, and Murry, aided by a friend, finding work in the Ministry of Information. At the Ministry he increased his literary and artistic acquaintance, as he did even more influentially at Garsington, the home near Oxford of Philip and Lady Ottoline Morrell. The Morrells were persistent defenders of culture and opponents of war, whose circle of visitors is amusingly pictured by the Georgian poet, W. J. Turner, in the discursive miscellany entitled *The Duchess of Popocatapetl*. Turner's portrait of Lady Ottoline was kinder than most of those strewn, when peace returned, through contemporary fiction and poetry; for the lady, besides being a character for Lawrence, was a butt for wits, who all proved that no emotion is more evanescent than gratitude.

Murry and Katherine Mansfield both holidayed at Garsington, where they met the intellectual *élite*, and, as honey-bees, were strongly affected by the experience. Katherine Mansfield could not change; but Murry, so much more plastic, learned a new philosophy. Early days in Peckham had long been abhorrent to his memory; he had escaped from them with relief to school and University. Enthusiasm for art and artists had made him a rebel against convention; and as in early days all his reactions were emotional the attachment to Lawrence resulted in violent infatuation with genius, discipleship to genius but inevitably (as Lawrence prophesied) betrayal of that genius.

Lawrence found himself an alien in the Morrell world. Some members of it horrified his puritanism as blackbeetles horrified his nerves. Breakfast with Bertrand Russell and Keynes, when both, in Keynes's words, 'talked *at* him' with the kindest of intentions but with the 'brittleness' of two detached intellects, sent him 'mad with misery and hostility and rage'. These men were expert debaters; for Lawrence the seat of wisdom, according to Aldous Huxley's account of a single gesture, lay in the region of the solar plexus, and he was no debater. Having the clairvoyance of genius, he realized that the deployment of pure intellect eroded his poetic vision. The knowledge caused agony.

With Murry the case was different. Peckham, *atéliers*, the old gloomy Chancery Lane flat, rebelliousness, were submerged in a wonderful experience of leisure and astringent conversation about countries of the mind. He did not belong to this life; but, while never of it, he felt capable of incorporating its advantages in a newly-opening prospect of emotional and opportunist expansion.

When the War ended, and Arthur Rowntree, most honorably inspired to serve the cause of advanced letters, bought the moribund *Athenaeum*, he planned to make it an enlightened record of aesthetic democracy at its best. He decided to offer the editorship to Murry. 'The new opening seemed to come as a godsend,' Murry wrote; and so it must have been to Katherine Mansfield and himself, who had no means beyond a small allowance from Katherine's father. At this moment, however, nobody could have been appointed who had a comparable galaxy of contributors at his call.

Now *The Athenaeum* was the oldest and most influential purely literary journal in England. It was first started in 1828, and when, a year later, it was in danger of bankruptcy, Charles Wentworth Dilke, the friend of Keats, joined with Tom Hood and Allan Cunningham in saving it. Dilke took full responsibility and control, with the consequence that *The Athenaeum* became a power. It so continued after Dilke's departure; and at a later date it prospered under the management of his grandson, the celebrated Sir Charles Dilke.

During the great days of anonymous reviewing, when the editorial pronoun 'we' could be used with majesty and extraordinary effect upon the reputations of authors and the sales of their books, the paper was subject to immense contributions from Swinburne's friend Theodore Watts-Dunton. Circulation was always small, and much of the writing was uninspired; but book-lovers impatiently awaited Friday afternoons, when the paper was published, and sliced open the folded pages with whatever weapons were available. A silent hour followed. Very regrettably *The Athenaeum* lost its pre-eminence. During the war it became so moribund that nothing but a major operation could have revived it.

Murry undertook the operation.

The friends he had made at the Ministry of Information included his first sub-editor J. W. N. Sullivan, a man of vigorous mind and scientific understanding with the delightful boyish determination to proceed across England at a hundred miles an hour on his motor-cycle (he certainly did over ninety; but whether he managed the hundred before his too-early death I do not remember). The friends he had made at Garsington were also available, though I think they were employed with rather less free will. They were the Cambridge intellectuals who quickly became known far and wide as 'Bloomsbury'.

I suggest 'with rather less free will' because according to my recollection, which in the absence of Murry's unkept letters I cannot confirm, one of the reasons he gave for urging me to write for *The Athenaeum* was that he needed every possible buttress against people whom he called 'them'. It must be borne in mind that 'they' were a phalanx of intimates, whereas he and Katherine Mansfield were solitary adventurers. Furthermore, responsibility for success was his; and finally he may have felt that, like himself, I had 'risen from the people'. This was silly. My parents and grandparents thought themselves royal in their craftsmanship. He seemed to have shed the writers of *Rhythm* days, who perhaps had moved on to other activities; and his main contributors, apart from Katherine Mansfield, who reviewed new novels, included Bertrand Russell, the Stracheys, the Woolfs, Roger Fry, Clive Bell, T. S. Eliot, E. M. Forster, and Adrian Stephen. I cannot help wondering what these people, so confident in their own intellectual strength, really thought of Murry.

My own feeling was one of some reserve. I had great affection for Katherine Mansfield, whose nature I did not grasp (Murry himself, says F. A. Lea, knew nothing of her early exploits until he read about them in Anthony Alpers's biography); and at that time I respected Murry's seriousness and sincerity. I thought him, however, too fluent and not tempered enough to be a reliable critic. This opinion remains. I have not read his books on Shakespeare and Keats, and may be unjust. I know that Quiller-Couch took a kinder view; for once, when Arnold Bennett's yacht was in Fowey harbour, and Bennett and I expressed what Wells described as our common cynicism, Q. became warmly partisan. I imagine Murry could comprehend the sensuous flow and imagery of Keats, but I cannot link him with the noble directness of Keats's Letters or the tragic insight and merriment of Shakespeare's plays. Though Shakespeare may be the academic philosophic commentator's dream, he remains, as Matthew Arnold said, 'free'.

The new criticism I demanded was with us in *The Athenaeum*. That is why the paper has such interest for students. The new criticism worked for the destruction of pre-war standards. The method of its exponents was selectively to attack, first the Victorians, and then dead or moribund Edwardians who, having done pioneer, imperfect work, could be guyed or disparaged at will. Subjects are always ready to hand for the bold. Lytton Strachey found them in Thomas Arnold and Cardinal Manning; T. S. Eliot in William Archer, the uninspired translator of Ibsen, and in Gilbert Murray, whose translations of Euripides had been a great wonder to non-Grecians. These were serious and long-considered expressions of antipathy. Murry had not soaked himself, as Strachey had done, in detestation of the Victorians; nor, like Eliot, made an anxious pilgrimage in search of ultimate truth. He was a sporadic evangelist.

In those early *Athenaeum* days he represented the effects of successive enthusiasms for Lawrence, Dostoevsky, Hardy, Santayana, and others who appealed to his emotions. His immediate targets were close at hand, first of all in the ageing *causeur* Edmund Gosse, who still, at seventy, kept pace with the vogue; second upon J. C. Squire and the Georgian poets. The poets were an active and arbitrarily united band of practitioners; Squire was a robust, influential rival in the journalistic field, who had been literary editor of *The New Statesman* from its beginning and I think literary editor during the war of *Land and Water*. He about this time founded *The London Mercury*, a monthly review. Of Squire, Murry wrote privately to Katherine Mansfield:

There's no doubt it's a fight to a finish between us and them. . . . It's a queer feeling I begin to have now; that we're making literary history.

In *The Athenaeum* he wrote of the Georgians *en masse*:

There is nothing disturbing about them; . . . they are kind, generous, even noble. They sympathise with animate and inanimate nature. They have shining foreheads with big bumps of benevolence . . . and one inclines to believe that their eyes must be frequently filmed with an honest tear, if only because their vision is blurred. They are fond of lists of names which never suggest things; they are sparing of similes. If they use them they are careful to see that they are not too definitive, for a definite simile makes havoc of their constructions, by applying to them a certain test of reality.

From the Georgians in general he passed to Squire himself, who was regarded as ringleader of the Georgians and, in words written by Walpole to myself, 'the wisest, broadest critic we have'. I recorded the attack to Walpole:

They tell me that Murry has demolished Squire's poem *The Moon* in *The Athenaeum*. I have not seen this; but it has caused a good deal of mild excitement, and I suppose Murry and Squire cannot now fail to be declared enemies. It is a great pity. I haven't tried to read *The Mercury* lately, but it seems to be a recognized thing that it is dull. Harold Williams came in the other day to see me, and was almost indignant at the bad writing in the *Merc.*, including something of Squire's own.

Walpole retorted:

I'm in the opposite camp from you over the critical journals. *The Mercury* No 2 seems to me very good . . . I find Murry simply ephemerally petulant—not a critic at all, and so are all the Pound-Sitwell-Bell creatures. . . . *The Athenaeum* seems to me and to most of the people who write to me a gloomy pretentious affair written entirely by cranks (save yourself). What I should feel did it not denounce me and what you'd feel *did* it denounce you, dear Frank, I can't say. We're no different from all the authors that have ever been.

We were no different: it may be our epitaph. But having spent a holiday free from what I called 'the little squibs and squabbles of London cliques', I decided that 'individuals are the things to go for', and continued:

I think that is really my objection to the Squirearchy— that Squire and Shanks and Turner are setting up to be a solid body to influence opinion. I don't really care what they say, because although I like Turner, and think Squire very able, I do not think Turner a very sound critic and believe Squire to be too much influenced always by personal feeling. Shanks does write bad criticism, and he is so superior and authoritative that he isn't readable. He seems to be the weakest of the bunch but I don't dislike him personally. On the Murry side you are, I think, a little wrong. I think Huxley extremely good. Also, at times, Eliot. I admire, but dislike the Bloomsburyites. Katty M. amuses me. She, however, wrote a very sniffy review of *September*, so I have no reason to be influenced by any favourable treatment. Murry certainly asks me to write for him as often as I can; but then Squire also asked me to write for him, and the only reason I write for Murry and not for Squire is that I think Squire's moral and personal prejudices are a danger to current literature, so far as the press treatment goes. Certainly Squire's puffery of his friends got quite scandalous, and I'd rather not be puffed in the press.

Unknown to me at this time was the fact that the Squire-archy would shortly pass into shadow, and that their sin of 'setting up to be a solid body to influence opinion' would in retrospect appear not much more objectionable than the busy work in earlier generations of the Langs, Gosses, Nicolls, and Shorters. There was always puffery and detraction in the Press, mostly by individuals, sometimes by groups. If one did not belong to a group one called it a clique. If one did, I assume—for I have never belonged to a clique—that one was supported by intense moral righteousness.

Meanwhile I wish to mention that Murry's second assistant-editor, following J. W. N. Sullivan, was Aldous Huxley, whom I thought 'extremely good'. The fruit of his work for *The Athenaeum* may be read in the volume of essays *On the Margin* and, especially, the novel *Point Counter Point*, published in 1928, where he assails his former editor as a hypocrite above most other hypocrites, mocks his style, his cult of Katherine Mansfield, and his innumerable infidelities.

He was a man of middle height with a stoop and a rather slouching gait. His hair was dark, thick and curly, with a natural tonsure as big as a medal showing pink on the crown of his head. His grey eyes were very deeply set, his nose and chin pronounced but well shaped, his mouth full-lipped and rather wide. A mixture, according to old Bidlake, who was a caricaturist in words as well as with his pencil, of a movie villain and St Anthony of Padua by a painter of the baroque, and a card-sharping Lothario and a rapturous devotee.

Huxley saw Murry at close quarters, and Burlap, in *Point Counter Point*, joins other local literary and artistic figures who are portrayed with similar irreverence. I have forgotten the originals of these others; but must testify to Huxley's laughing, disgusted perception that Murry was auto-intoxicated, and in the habit of mystically identifying himself with whatever saint or genius was his latest enthusiasm. To the last he believed in his own sincerity.

'St Hugh, of Lincoln,' remarks another ribald observer in *Point Counter Point*, 'that's who you are, Burlap. He was a child, you know, a pure sweet chee-yild. Such a dear snuggly-wuggly lovey-dovey little chap. So wide-eyed and reverent towards the women, as though they were all madonnas. Coming to be petted and have his pains kissed away and be told about poor Jesus—even to have a swig of milk if there happened to be any going.... Coming to pray, but staying to share madonnina's bed.'

T. S. Eliot, whom Murry wanted for his assistant, and who contributed to *The Athenaeum*, has no unseemly ribaldries about his one-time editor. With some dryness, he once referred to Murry's 'erratic and intuitive nature', and this, as a comment on Murry's editorship, is entirely satisfactory. It explains why, today, Murry is ignored by what is called The Establishment. He was emotional, not authoritarian, in spite of his declaration that 'there must be authority'. Nevertheless his paper can be read as much more than a period piece; it really was, as Murry impulsively believed, history-making.

Like all purely literary journals, it failed to attract advertisers, since publishers cannot afford to be disinterested patrons, and rich industries have other fields for publicity. It therefore lost money. When the paper was merged with *The Nation* Lawrence wrote to S. S. Koteliansky, a Russian disciple whose ardour for Lawrence was only equalled by his detestation of Murry, whom he called 'a gheat scarndyel':

I hear the Ath lost £5000 a year under our friend the mud-worm. I hear he is—or was—on the Riviera with K.—who is doing the last-gasp touch ... K. also announcing that the *Rowntrees* couldn't bear her writing. Ah, me, we have become important. Two mud-worms they are, playing into each other's long mud-bellies.

Katherine Mansfield died in 1923: Murry, editing her letters and journals, and writing books about Lawrence and Shakespeare, continued his intellectual pilgrimage until, forsaking

Art, he discovered even remoter countries of the Spirit. Meanwhile, returning to his old ambition, the editorship of a quasi-French review, he had produced *The Adelphi*. This monthly periodical began with unexpected prosperity. He re-enlisted Lawrence, employed Koteliansky, persuaded unattached writers, including Arnold Bennett and myself, to contribute brief marginalia, and had H. M. Tomlinson, whom he came to know well as neighbour in a coastguard's cottage on the Chesil Beach, as one of his associates.

Before long, the enthusiasm which led outsiders to support *The Adelphi* declined. Modern readers who preferred an analytical approach to literature found T. S. Eliot's review, *The Criterion*, more to their taste; Murry himself lost the sympathy of his well-wishers, who disliked what they thought his exploitation of Katherine Mansfield, his denunciation of authors in other camps, and the unreserve of some of his contributors. Circulation fell; Murry himself hurried to the establishment of new social communities in the country; he passed, execrated by Lawrentians such as Catherine Carswell for *Son of Woman*, into a world which I never presumed to enter. Therefore I can say no more of him from personal knowledge.

George Doran

●

7 TOWARDS the end of 1919 Hugh Walpole made his first
very successful lecture tour of the United States. His
reputation already stood high in America on the strength
of two novels about Russia, *The Dark Forest* and *The Secret City*;
and his personal popularity was increased by natural *bonhomie*,
an attractive platform manner, and insatiable delight in gossip
and affection. He wrote to me:

It's all the greatest joy-ride I ever had. The lectures are
really a great success; they are thin, with nothing to them, but
I think my own amusement at them, myself, and everyone
else carries them off. It's all hanky-panky, like half the things
I do, but like the other half there's a *real* sincerity, and I do
love the chance of pushing some of the books that *I* like
down their reluctant throats. . . .

Of the other lecturers, I hear nothing of Cannan anywhere.
He rather did for himself right off by giving some lectures
in a Bolshevik stronghold called the Rand. But some of the
interviews with him have been very wise and decent—much
better than my own. Drinkwater is doing very well. He has
a beautiful voice, and having been an actor knows how to
use it. Dunsany is making a fool of himself, posing and being
always unpunctual, etc. Ibanez is quite mad, and throws his
interpreters out of the window.

I've picked up a pretty good idea of our little novelists'
popularity over here. *Great* enthusiasm everywhere about
Nocturne—the other books not so well known. Monty

74

M[ackenzie] gone right down with the last two—no real success here since *Sin*. S. Arnold [Bennett] talked about but most unpopular—a reaction I think and he wrote some articles during the war which they thought pacifist. Wells stands high but won't if the religious books go on. Cannan . . . very little read except by cranks. Galsworthy regarded like a cathedral but *Saint's Progress* not liked. Conrad more talked about than read though *The Arrow [of Gold]* has sold. Beresford read very little but *strongly* liked by his following. The novel of the moment (minus Miss Ashford) is *The Moon and Sixpence*.

Two interesting facts emerge from my telescoped quotations. One is that the names of Joyce, Lawrence, and Virginia Woolf, which very shortly afterwards displaced what may be called the reigning few (in the case of the younger men they were not so much regnant as personally known to us both) did not appear. The second is that in America, apart from *The Young Visiters*, which sold 200,000 copies, the outstanding fictional success of 1919 was *The Moon and Sixpence*, by W. Somerset Maugham.

I do not know how Walpole learned these things; but he had a keen scent, and he was meeting, besides journalists, book-sellers and publishers, large numbers of those who bought new novels to read and discuss. English novels were being widely circulated in the United States (after both wars British novelists had world-wide popularity; and in 1919 the younger American writers, Sherwood Anderson, Willa Cather, Sinclair Lewis, Fanny Hurst, and Edna Ferber, although they were challenging international rivals, were at the beginning of their careers), and if one entered an American city bookstore then and for several more years the sight of piled copies of new English fiction was overwhelming. Wealthy women would move from stack to stack, nodding at each to an accompanying assistant. Such zest was unknown in England, where lending libraries were forced into economy and ordered a minimum number of copies to satisfy borrowers who carried lists of alternative titles.

Walpole, Maugham, Bennett and I were all published in the United States—as was *The Young Visiters* and as, later on, was Aldous Huxley—by one who played a considerable part, not in the movement of taste, but in the promotion of public reputation and sales on both sides of the Atlantic. This was George H. Doran, an Irish-Canadian by birth, whose splendid carriage, hospitality, and publishing aplomb were renowned.

Other men in the book trade had judgment and more consistent success; Doran had genius. He saw opportunities; he took them. He wanted others to take them. It was an exasperation to him when they would not do so. 'But I want you to feel as confident as I do,' I heard him say to his adviser at that time, Eugene Saxton. Saxton, bald, pale, cautious, and full of taste, made his slow reluctant answer: 'I can't do that, Mr Doran.' A long silence was followed by a resigned shrug. 'All right.' An enthusiasm had missed fire. Only to myself, who remained in the room afterwards, did he ejaculate an irritable compliment to Saxton's integrity.

I sympathized with both men. Had I not, as a publisher's reader in England, felt enthusiasms and reluctance? Saxton was one day older than myself; Doran ten years. It is not easy for a subordinate to resist his employer, or to over-persuade his employer, about some book which perhaps he alone has read, knowing, as he does, the uncertain fates of books. It is not easy for an impetuous man of genius in publishing to endure the scruples of one whose judgment he respects.

Doran was a master of gesture. If one expressed a wish for the almost impossible, it would be arranged overnight. 'Would you like to meet So-and-so?' The meeting would occur. A celebrated actress felt curious about a suppressed book; I had a copy, sent to me before the suppression; would I lend it? I imagine the grand nonchalance with which the book was presented to the actress, who of course was not asked to return it. Merely a part of the Doran service!

We all, then or later, owed much to this generous and flamboyant man, who regarded his authors as his children and took incredible pains to win friends for them and influence people on their behalf. Doran had begun commercial life, he once told me, by selling newspapers in the streets of Toronto; but his first real employment was as office-boy to S. R. Briggs, of that city, an ex-wholesale lumber dealer who specialized in the publication of religious tracts. The work in Briggs's office was unending, and the rewards were small; but the experience was priceless. It made Doran wise in the ways of men who turn their faith to good account.

Wearied, but eager for wider scenes, he travelled to Chicago, where he joined the firm of another religious publisher, Fleming H. Revell, a connection by marriage of Dwight Moody, the evangelist. Revell three times refused Charles Sheldon's novel, *In His Steps: what would Jesus do?* because he thought it too revolutionary. The book was produced by another firm, was never copyrighted, sold in millions all over the English-speaking world, and I read it as a boy in a paper-bound edition which cost a penny. The author, of course, received nothing from his grateful readers: he was what is nowadays called a 'dedicated' or 'committed' man, as well as a modest one, and presumably did not resent the rejection of his book.

Revell had greater daring on the Stock Market, to which in a boom period he introduced the young Doran, who on paper made by one transaction some two hundred times his year's salary. The boom collapsed; the paper profits disappeared; publishing, which has sometimes been thought a form of gambling, appeared thereafter attractively stable. Doran decided to remain with books.

Not, however, with religious books. He might rejoice in the spirit of Revival, and he instructively saw the novels of Ralph Connor attain for a time the immense sales of books appealing to the simple in faith; but he preferred secular literature. Making a financial arrangement with the London firm of Hodder & Stoughton, he started in business on his own account; and one of his early purchases, perhaps recommended to him by that grey eminence of the English trade, Robertson Nicoll, was *The Old Wives' Tale*, by Arnold Bennett.

Doran bought English sheets of this book for sale in America. A friend who afterwards became a G.O.M. in the American literary scene, but who was then a New England bookseller, Frederic Melcher, warmly recommended *The Old Wives' Tale* to his customers; they in turn recommended it to others; and the book was a great success. Doran saw, and took, his opportunity. He remade *The Old Wives' Tale* in America; he acquired Bennett's other novels; he invited the author to visit the United States; he organized a lionizing reception for him at the end of 1911 which those who saw it, forgetting that the same thing had been claimed for Wilde's triumph nearly thirty years earlier, said could be likened only to the reception given to Dickens in 1842.

As a result of this enthusiastic welcome, Arnold Bennett became Doran's favourite author; and because he found that Bennett thought well of my early novels he made a contract with our agent, Pinker, for three which I was to write. The books were failures; but when *Nocturne* arrived he persevered with it, paying a smaller advance, of fifty pounds, and enjoying a welcome surprise. After the reception given to *Nocturne* and its successor, *September*, I was high in his favour. I never, of course, had the popularity of Maugham or Walpole; yet this seemed to make no difference to Doran, who included me in all his famous parties.

The company at those parties, invariably amusing and sometimes impressive, was deliciously fed. The host, brimming with flattery, and moving among his guests with rapid grace (his movements were full of this light-footed grace), head thrown back and fine leonine eyes flashing above the small white beard and moustache, surveyed and relished the scene as if everybody present was his charming friend. They were all his friends. They came because they wished to come; not one thought merely of his dinner or of some anticipated advantage. It was an honour to be asked, and a pleasure to attend.

Doran, as I have said, had remarkable address, remarkable quickness of mind, even more remarkable confidence in his talent for managing and cajoling other people. The talent was unquestionable, and to my knowledge it produced ironic—not sarcastic—response in only two or three of his authors. One was Arnold Bennett, another was E. V. Lucas, upon whom he lavished the greatest consideration. It was true, also, of my wife, who, when we had lunched alone with him one day, exclaimed wrathfully as we left: 'He hasn't said a single sincere word all the time.' This last, I think, was because Doran did not really like women, although to the male eye his manners to them were perfect.

I more than once admired the way in which he accepted failure. Sometimes it was with no more than a slightly ridiculing expression, as if he whistled a sceptical tune under his breath, sometimes with an elastic turn to new hope and a new approach. If one said 'No', he did not produce further argument. Like Browning's boastful hero in the epilogue to *Asolando*, Doran held that

We fall to rise, are baffled to fight better.

At the end of his gallant life, after dangerous illness, and after all his publishing triumphs were over, he entered any room (I have been told) like a conqueror, gracious and compelling as ever. His last letters to me, written when death was very near, had all the old buoyancy, and expressed affection, which I am sure he felt, and deep respect, which was the only sign he gave of ultimate and conscious defeat.

Let me give one amusing example, and only one, of this remarkable man in more ephemeral defeat. When, at his request, I arranged a meeting for tea with Daisy Ashford, he peremptorily changed the venue, which we found crowded, took charge of the occasion, and was in his finest mood, paternal and considerate. But he found Miss Ashford, who was very shy, rather less obviously juvenile than he had expected. 'Tell me, Miss Ashford,' he said, unexpectedly, 'how old are you?' Miss Ashford demurred, much as Elizabeth Bennet did under the demand of Lady Catherine de Bourg. Doran persisted: 'Come, I'm old enough to be your father. Tell *me*. Frank won't listen.' Still Miss Ashford, and again, under further pressing, would not yield. In one more instant the matter would have become embarrassing to us all, had not Doran swiftly, with a mixture of graciousness and irony, accepted the refusal as final. 'Suppose we say "thirty", and make our own deductions!'

Other defeats were handled in similar style. Doran concealed, from even those whom he regarded as his closest English friends—Bennett and Lucas—everything that was amiss or intricate in his financial affairs; and we received no communication whatever concerning what proved to have been his elaborately-arranged absorption by the Doubledays. Rumours flew to us from other quarters in New York; Doran's letters gave no hint. We exchanged our news in London, smiled, speculated, and waited. At last I received a private communication, which Bennett (who received no similar communication) described as 'very clever'; and Doran himself crossed the Atlantic once more, suave, confident, abounding, to report that we had changed our American publishers and that the advantages to ourselves would be manifold.

Not one word was spoken about his silence; for we also had tact. He renewed his old intimacies; he learned, as was his wont, the fascinating details of what literary men and women in London and the English provinces thought of each other; he visited his fellow-publishers; he arranged for Jo Davidson, the American sculptor, to make busts of the twelve writers—all men—whom he thought most typical of the English scene; he behaved as though he were in complete control of every resource, with no troubles, but only joys in store.

Well, that was true. We suffered no loss of consideration. But Doran remained in the consolidated organization for only a comparatively short time. Illness drove him to the restorative climate of Arizona, where he stayed until his wife's last illness took him North again. His last years were spent in Toronto.

Doran was never the obvious business brain-sucker. He might say 'Shall I take So-and-so?' but in general it was his habit to communicate as openly as his friends, and in the smallest of his parties he would repeat apparently without reserve conversations in which others had interestingly disclosed facts and fantasies about themselves. He was absorbed in publishing, and about his rivals said no disparaging word. When with authors, he led them to talk; and he knew well that the talk of authors, when not about themselves, turns very often to the discomfitures of other authors. Accordingly he was well nourished, on his London visits, with gossip.

When he repeated this gossip, as he did sparingly, he showed great understanding; but what passes at a convivial meeting ('convivial' must not be misconstrued; as I travel back in memory to those days I realize that practically all the writers we knew were markedly abstemious) looks different if it is put into print. When Doran wrote his outspoken autobiography, *Chronicles of Barabbas*, in 1935 some of the writers whose personalities and private affairs were summarized in it received shocks. The shocks were so great (it must be said that Doran's memory was sometimes at fault) that the possibility of an English edition of this book, which E. V. Lucas had agreed beforehand to publish, caused a commotion.

Under several threats that legal proceedings would be taken in accordance with the British Law of Libel, which is severe, Lucas cabled to Doran that violent cuts would have to be made in *Chronicles of Barabbas*. Doran cabled back: 'I will allow nobody but Frank Swinnerton to cut the book.' Lucas called me in; and as a result of the discussion which followed, in the course of which Lucas muttered with deep and bitter irony, '*You're* not malicious,' our friendship, although we had met before, really began.

E. V. Lucas

•

8 FRIENDSHIP with Lucas, though it could be both fluent and free, called for tact. While on the surface equable, he suffered from sensitiveness which could twist a chance inattention into a deliberate affront, or an ironic comment into an accusation. Personally a wit, he belonged, I always thought, to the days of the hansom cab and the historic Café Royal; and it was unquestionable that he remembered those days, or believed he remembered them, with affection.

He had been 'reader', not indeed for John Lane, the publisher around whom Beardsley, Richard le Gallienne, and Max Beerbohm revolved, but for Grant Richards when that bold fellow went into business at the end of the 'nineties; and he claimed to have brought to the Richards list authors as diverse as Richard Whiteing (*Number 5 John Street*) and Ernest Bramah, who wrote *The Wallet of Kai Lung*. The Dumpy Books for Children, which included the immortal *Little Black Sambo*, were also made while he was with Richards.

Lucas spoke slowly, hardly moving his lips, in a deep voice like the meditative song of the bumble bee. His manner was benign. A smile, indulgent yet thoughtful, hardly ever left his face, which coarsened as he grew older and, now that I come to envisage it, had no great range of expression. He had an extraordinary gift and longing for personal affection; and it was at the same time necessary for him to go his own way in perpetual solitude. I think he preferred unexacting male to more demanding female company, not because he disliked women, but because men would eat and drink with him and

82

go away without disturbing his peace of mind. He was not possessive, though I am sure he knew the emotion of jealousy. His friendships included appreciative contacts with Barrie, Bennett, and Wells, whom he enjoyed in small doses. These men never, to my knowledge, attended the feasts he gave at the Orleans Club in King Street, St James's.

At such feasts he provided (or when I was there he provided) roast saddle of mutton to eat, champagne to drink, and as after-entertainment the most astonishing conjuror I ever saw, a genius who baffled everybody present with his impenetrable craft. Lucas, at the head of the table, listened darkly but un-frowningly to all he could hear, sitting with almost sack-like relaxation, and making no attempt to lead the talk or stimulate the vivacity of his companions. His feasts were thus static, resembling casual assemblies around a long club table, where men exchange anecdotes, but not ideas.

The guests were usually other men of letters rather than imaginative writers (he did not love 'the adroit novelists of talent, calculating the risks and being as candid as they dare'), with some actors, lawyers, and at least one or two publishers for good measure. I even, once, saw a literary agent; but he must have been there as a friend, for Lucas was too detached to mingle business with pleasure.

His friendships perhaps explain a discrepancy between his reputation, which in the literary world was considerable, and his actual performance as a writer. A disapproving rival once accounted to me for this reputation and its rewards in press cordiality by saying resentfully (this was long before I met Lucas), 'he knows everybody in Fleet Street'. It was probably true; but he was neither a pusher nor a wire-puller. He was first of all a friend, punctilious in every detail of personal relationship, so that if one had been his host, even for lunch, there was always, the following day, a note of warm thanks. A short note, of course; when it was thought possible that after his death a collection of his letters might delight the world, they were found too meagre for the purpose.

At a little distance from friendship, but below it, came his work as publisher, as bookman (that extinct species), and as biographer and editor of Charles Lamb. His acquaintance with half- or wholly-forgotten literature was wide; he had read in poetry and *belles-lettres*, and zestfully remembered, more than the majority of professors digest in a lifetime. But he was not a scholar; he was a taster of good things, what George Saintsbury, speaking of himself, called 'an intelligent voluptuary', and his aim was to share pleasure, not to teach.

His anthologies, *The Open Road* and two volumes of ancient and modern letters called *The Gentlest Art* and *The Second Post*, are beautifully adroit, and it is a pity that the day for them is past. On that day men used to go for long country walks with a book stuffed into one pocket of a Norfolk jacket and a packet of sandwiches in another, while concealed about their persons they carried a flask which held a not necessarily alcoholic beverage. Sitting by tranquil waysides, they would eat the sandwiches, drink from the flask, and lie back drowsing over a Lucas anthology, or perhaps *The Compleat Angler*, Ben Jonson's *Discoveries*, or Selden's *Table Talk*, until they were ready for another ten miles on their feet. Publishers used the word 'pocketable' in advertising new editions of such books, the disappearance of which word being a sign that times have changed. What happy, careless, noiseless times they were! Lucas, belonging to them, and being a publisher, was able to benefit all bookish pedestrians, and the number of copies of *The Open Road* scattered among English homes from 1899, when it was first published, until after 1918 must have been incalculable.

One of Lucas's colleagues on *The Globe*, where he wrote 'By the Way', a column of short humorous paragraphs full of quips and puns, was C. L. Graves; and in collaboration with Graves, whom I never saw (he was for a number of years assistant or literary editor of *The Spectator*, and was the first man in the world to discover from *The Possessed* that Dostoevsky was a humorous writer), Lucas wrote a number of squibs which had great vogue between 1901 and 1914, when such things became obsolete.

The first of these squibs to attract attention was *Wisdom while you Wait*, a skit on the elaborate publicity introduced into England by the American promoters of a new edition of *The Encyclopaedia Britannica*. The collaborators, copying an American humorist, used all sorts of old wood-blocks and engravings which they pretended to have extracted from something called the *Insidecompletuar Britanniaware*, and amusingly mocked every grandiose claim of the original. Other, similar, booklets followed, including a skit on the popular Press called *Change for a Halfpenny*. It was all fooling without serious aim, and extremely like mid-Victorian numbers of *Punch*; but it made people laugh, as the mid-Victorian *Punch* did, and it set a fashion. A shilling was easily coaxed from the pocket of a city or suburban homegoer; the two concoctors had fun in doing something easy; they became famous. Graves's wit was both lighter and sharper than Lucas's. He was a very accomplished man.

The anthology was Lucas's *forte*. Owing to the fact that as a boy he was apprenticed to a Brighton bookseller who had a gigantic circulating library dating back to Regency days, he was familiar with hundreds of neglected or unread books. He shared his knowledge. He was eager to share it. Long before I ever knew him, being *in extremis*, and capable of only the simplest reading, I wrote suggesting that as Brabourne's edition was inadequate he should collect and re-edit all Jane Austen's letters (this has now been done to perfection by R. W. Chapman). He replied that he had no time for such a task, and as I had mentioned that I was very ill he recommended as ideal reading for a sick person Fanny Kemble's *Record of a Girlhood*. It was a good deed. Those who know this book and its successors will realize how good it was; those who do not may be glad of Lucas's tip. As he once said, 'The books I like best and can return to [are] the books with the best bedside manners.' Fanny Kemble is not only delightful in herself, but she leads on to other writers who are soothing to convalescents, among them her correspondent Edward FitzGerald.

Lucas's association with Charles Lamb began by chance. In young manhood he was nominated by his ex-schoolmate and

continuing friend Wilfred Whitten as the man to write for the
Society of Friends a biography of Bernard Barton, the Quaker
poet who was a friend of Lamb and whose daughter was
astonishingly left to the care of FitzGerald. Not knowing what
to do with this unfortunate girl, FitzGerald married her, with
the result that they were estranged for life. Lucas met Mrs
FitzGerald in the course of his research into Bernard Barton's
affairs, and in the same course had the thrilling experience of
shaking hands with at least two people who in their day had
shaken hands with Lamb. He should have been inspired.

Indeed, he was to some degree inspired; for as one thing
naturally leads to another (sometimes it is a good thing; more
often a bad one) he was offered a commission to prepare a book
called *Charles Lamb and the Lloyds*. It was not a good book; and
when permission to use the letters written by Lamb in Macdonald's edition was refused, and J. M. Dent, thinking to by-
pass the law of copyright, bought the originals from which he
printed, there was unfortunate copyright litigation, in which
Lucas was indirectly involved. Subsequent to the publication
of *Charles Lamb and the Lloyds*, but before the litigation, he was
invited by Methuen to write an introduction to a new edition
of *The Essays of Elia*. He thus became an accepted 'authority'
on a greatly loved writer.

My friend P. P. Howe, who in the matter of Lamb's contemporary, Hazlitt, was letter-perfect, scoffed a little at Lucas's
performance; but whether this scoffing arose from loyalty to
Hazlitt or from the scholar's disdain of an amateur's impre-
cision I cannot say. My own scepticism in the same field dated
from the time when, aged twenty-one, I plumed myself upon
knowing more about Lamb than anybody except William
Macdonald. I shall not dwell upon it here.

Lucas was born at Eltham, in Kent, one of seven children in a
Quaker family of which the mother was deaf and the father 'a
lonely and censorious man'. He read with most relish in modern
French literature (modern, that is, in the age before the Second
World War), where he sought a wit not then to be found in

current English. And although his lesser commentaries on life
and travel often wanted force and originality, and his novels
had neither shape nor importance, the harsh justice of his mind
was shown in the essay *Swinburne at 'The Pines'*. There was no
more scathing picture of that curious *ménage*. A similar visit
was briefly described by Max, and Richard le Gallienne threw
fantastic light upon Swinburne's naughty evasion of his
mentor's rules for sobriety; but Lucas was not surpassed. Had
he written a whole book in the manner of that essay he would
have stood before the world more nearly as he was.

He did not write the book. To have done so would have
been to desert pleasant ways and damage the reputation he
preferred for good-nature. He ate and drank and talked. When
I knew him it was his chief wish to make and keep friends. If he
liked a person he would go to extreme trouble to please that
person, even (to my distress) putting morsels from his own
plate on the plate of his guest, toasting him, and teasing him
occasionally by the humorous depreciation of other friends—
in my case, Arnold Bennett. If he did not like a person, or
found him a bore, he shunned him altogether. He would sometimes endure the company of inferiors for the sake of their
affection or their enjoyment of food and wine. Even then he
demanded that his palate should be cajoled. At lunch he drank
Pouilly and soda-water; at night, always, champagne.

As a publisher's reader he was second only to Edward
Garnett; much less serious-minded and paternal than Garnett,
much more catholic in his acceptances, less of a zealot, and
always willing to recommend for publication meritorious
writers whose work he did not personally admire. Methuen
had a very long list; and the only novel in it which could be
described as 'unpleasant' was Lawrence's *The Rainbow*, which
Algernon Methuen would not defend under threat of prosecu-
tion. I do not know how far Lucas was concerned in this
venture. I do know that he had a thoroughly good record as
adviser, was very wise, shrewd, and far-seeing, and that he
would not have sacrificed Lawrence if any other course had
been possible.

His unhappiness lay deep in temperament. Writing of him in

1909, Arnold Bennett said: 'Mr Lucas is a highly mysterious man. On the surface he might be mistaken for a mere cricket enthusiast. Dig down, and you will come, with not too much difficulty, to the simple man of letters. Dig further, and, with somewhat more difficulty, you will come to an agreeably ironic critic of human foibles. Try to dig still further, and you will probably encounter rock.' It was not rock; it was a dark and viscous ego. He was too intelligent not to realize that he lacked the genius to invent and the courage to be, in print, as pungent and terrible as he was in mordant reverie. He never forgave himself for the failure.

Outwardly he was a warm, sentimental lover of dogs and cricket; less sentimentally of literature. Inwardly he was what he showed himself in *Swinburne at 'The Pines'*, a hater of people like Theodore Watts-Dunton, who insist on managing other men for their own good. He detested 'managers' and parasites. He was also impatient of slow-thinkers and the respectable. Having seen the rise and fall of generations and reputations, he was sceptical of all who were extolled. He had no living heroes. Carrying in his heart all the unhappiness and pessimism of the disappointed man, he could not bear to read the unhappy and pessimistic works of those who parade their dejection. 'I still want books to be cheerful and amusing,' he once wrote; that is, he needed anodynes. George Meredith was his favourite English novelist; his poets were the pre-Georgians. Hence, in the post-war years, a sign of the times, his loss of fame; but in the earliest of those years he had great influence as one who could back his judgment by publishing what he thought good.

Maugham and Walpole

○

9 I HAVE suggested that Lucas's feasts were unlike Doran's parties. These were given long before 1935, when the *Chronicles of Barabbas* was published in the United States. They were of three orders. If he felt personal regard, they were small, not more than three men besides himself being present. No business was explicitly talked; he and his guests were happy and at ease, referring sportively to other men as they might have done to amusing dogs in the family circle.

The second order, entirely social, with general conversation, brought together perhaps a dozen fluent talkers from Wells to Max Beerbohm or Edgar Wallace. At one of these parties dramatic critics were discussed. Bennett produced his solitary grievance, which was that A. B. Walkley, of *The Times*, always laughed heartily at a Bennett play and always hurried away to write contemptuously about it. Maugham remarked drily that he remembered one dramatic critic advising him against playwriting because he had no sense of the theatre, to which Max mildly replied: 'You must remember, Willie, that when I said that you had only written *A Man of Honour*.' And C. B. Cochran claimed to be the only person present to have been kissed by a dramatic critic. This statement caused a shiver of horror, especially when he named the critic as Hannen Swaffer. It appeared that he and Swaffer had quarrelled, but that seeing him saluted one evening at the Savoy by some famous French actor, Swaffer could not resist the opportunity of an emotional reconciliation. To remove our horror, Max told us stories of dramatic critics belonging to a still older semi-civilization than our own.

The third order was that of the banquet. It was held in one

of the larger rooms at the Savoy which are named after Gilbert and Sullivan operas; and the company, though predominantly male, was mixed. Ambassadors, peers, millionaires joined the writers, who, you may be sure, basked in the bright lights and luxury before returning to the tortures of authorship. This order I should describe as superlative social publicity.

To myself, the Doran parties gave almost unalloyed pleasure. I am not really a social person, and my notion of the best entertainment is a single companion who knows more than I do but is pleased with me. Then, indeed, I can contribute to the common cheer. But I liked the parties, at which I could listen to people whom otherwise I might not have met—for example, Dr R. W. Chapman, the Johnson and Jane Austen scholar, Philip Gibbs, later my close friend for life, and P. G. Wodehouse. Doran was on good terms with them all, whether he published their books or not; and one never knew who would be one's companions at table. He gave great thought to this point. If he found two men growing friendly to the neglect of their neighbours, they were separated at the earliest opportunity.

During several of the banquets I met, but did not sit next to, a man whom I discovered to be a distinguished surgeon named Ivor Back. He was, as I remember, solid and dark, with the air of being well-nourished; and he had very bright and disrespectful eyes. He was also a racy talker without illusions or moral refinement. This man had a curious habit. He approached me, pointed to his chest, and said: 'Back. I met you at Willie Maugham's.' When he did this for the third time, I retorted: 'I remember you perfectly; but as I've never been to Willie Maugham's——' I did not finish the sentence. A small voice said, over my shoulder: 'You m-must come.'

I thus first met Maugham, slight, dark, quiet, composed; the most succinct talker I ever knew. He was not abrupt; he merely wasted no words. It is a rare gift, which may be inferred from his more characteristic works. As I am normally ebullient and (the reader must be aware) discursive, it is my illusion that Maugham and I accord well. There are certainly no barriers to understanding. He admired my short novel *Nocturne*; but when he read it he did not know me. When we had talked for a little while he coolly remarked: 'You're a ve-very dangerous man,' and moved away.

His book, *Cakes and Ale*, published in 1930, takes me to a period which I have not reached, chronologically; but it has its place at this point in *Figures in the Foreground*. Opinions regarding this book, on the grounds of taste or basic philosophy, may still differ; of its brilliance in execution no novelist could feel any doubt. Not only did it scathingly portray a literary *arriviste* who was also superficially a hypocrite; it offered, as companion-portrait, that of an octogenarian poet-novelist named Driffield. This companion-portrait provoked indignation, as the portrait of the *arriviste* provoked behind-the-hand merriment. It was proclaimed by the knowing as a truly malignant attack on Thomas Hardy.

Maugham said he knew nothing of Hardy; it was a coincidence that his old man was a twice-married novelist-poet to whom, on his eightieth birthday, admirers made a pilgrimage, and whose novels utterly bored Willie Ashenden; but the denials were disbelieved. Nobody thought for a moment that the novelist-poet might equally have been George Meredith. Talk spread; *Cakes and Ale* became the most famous novel of the hour. It is still the book that contains Maugham's favourite character, that of Rosie the good-hearted slut; it is still his most significant novel. The neolithic cave-dwellers would recognize it, if they had literary friends, and give it their breathless attention, as the Wedding Guest gave his to the Ancient Mariner.

Hugh Walpole, having been to the theatre one night, picked it up just as he was going to bed. He instantly identified Alroy Kear with himself, and was swept by excitement into a wild attempt to have the book withdrawn. Any legal proceedings, of course, were out of the question: he assailed the publishers.

Now the club to which he and two members of that firm belonged was temporarily closed, and my own club was giving its members hospitality. I, having called on the publishers that morning upon other business, was offered a lift to the club, and as we drove I was told the whole story. Whether I had then read the book I do not remember; but as Maugham's books were coming to me regularly I think I must have done so.

We found Walpole striding about the great columned and tessellated hall of the Reform Club in terrible agitation. At sight of me, the normal radiance of his greeting was replaced by a hot angry flush. Every suspicion he had ever formed of my natural mischievousness was confirmed. I believe he thought I was an emissary of the Devil; and of course he could not know how much of the matter I had learned, nor how far I might be in Maugham's confidence.

He bore threateningly down upon me, crying passionately: 'Look here, Frank; you're not in on this! I won't have you——'

I pacifically interrupted, and went upon my own business. I did not see him again that morning. Never afterwards did either of us refer to the encounter. I pressed no sympathy; I offered no advice. But Alroy Kear must have inspired many of the nightmares from which he regularly suffered.

After *Cakes and Ale*, then, Maugham's reputation as a novelist had no immediate parallel. Within a few months of its publication all active novel-writers were considerably his juniors. He went alone about the earth, to the East and the South Seas, still trying to 'become the creature of the moment, clear of all ties', observing and transcribing the hypocrisies of the good, and receiving little generosity from the more puritan critics who, in Walpole's phrase, 'are angry if *such* an ingredient is not there and ecstatic if *such* an ingredient is'. The ingredient missed in Maugham's work was a dogmatic philosophy or what is sometimes called 'a metaphysic'.

Maugham never had this particular ingredient. He had other ingredients, which included (referring once again to Walpole's list) personality, narrative power, sense of character, and—Walpole had not thought of this—wit. He was also, with deviations into sentimentality which made him exaggerate to the diminution of veracity, a realist. You might think, from his own account, that he pursued still the fame and income he had desired when, in young manhood, he abandoned the vein of *A Man of Honour*.

This was not the whole story, however. In fact it was the story he told after the event, when fame and wealth, which he did not very much desire, although both became him, had arrived. What he really wanted, once he had been disillusioned, in spite of wide social and personal contacts, was what Gauguin had wanted—freedom. He was naturally lonely, self-contained, troubled by a hesitation in speech which others noticed less than he did (an experience in boyhood was responsible for his belief that this was not the case), and very secret indeed. He never said more than he meant to say.

In this last respect he differed from his contemporaries. Wells, forced in childhood to take off his cap to the gentry and for all his brilliance constrained in titled company, united a love of the human species and a desire for its social and political betterment with the childish mischievous impulse to put out his tongue at dons, generals, and quidnuncs. His mind and affairs, though not revealed with precise candour in *Experiment in Autobiography*, were open; and with a single companion he would often 'tell all'. Bennett, deeply reserved and instinctively magnanimous, could be flattered into weakness. He did not love money, as is even today basely alleged; but he had been born poor, and as he said: 'Once poor, always poor. There are times when I can't bring myself to take a taxi.' He was surpassingly candid. When asked about the fortunes of a new play, he would answer: 'It . . . is a failure.' Of myself, to another friend, he said: 'I . . . tell him everything.'

Walpole was boisterous, laughing, copious, vain, and—not schemingly, almost naïvely—ambitious; but he disinterestedly gave time and praise and (in private) money to unsuccessful writers, and for all the vagaries which carried him from one rising star to another until he reached Virginia Woolf, he retained to the last a devotion to old friends such as myself. The real unease of his mind was caused by memory of what he might impulsively have blurted out just now or at some previous time. He was likely at some point to shun; but he had already ebulliently told.

Maugham differed from these three men. The anxiety to shake off domestic and social shackles is evident not only in

The Moon and Sixpence but in *The Breadwinner*, a play where the central character, a stockbroker, allows himself in this pursuit to be 'hammered' on the Stock Exchange, to his own relief and the consternation of greedily selfish wife and children. Not for him, and not for Maugham, was magnanimity an ideal; for both there was satisfaction in the turned worm, the man sick to death of his family and its demands, who was going to do, at last, exactly what he wanted to do.

This, as you can see, was an anti-social proposition; and *The Breadwinner*'s verbal felicities did not hide the fact that the characters in it were seen by the author as typically unpleasant. Shaw would have made them all preposterous, and sent the audience away sure that there was much more in the play than met the eye. Maugham shrugged his shoulders. As he said in *Of Human Bondage*, 'There was neither good nor bad there. There were just facts. It was life.'

In the same way he demonstrated in *The Circle* that even the sight of two battered relics of an old elopement and divorce did not prevent young loves of the day from repeating the folly of their predecessors. The implication was that, being fools, men and women could not learn; and nothing was to be done about it. There was no metaphysic in either *Cakes and Ale* or *The Circle*. Nor, perhaps, were there 'just facts'. What was deployed in both, I think, was an arbitrarily selected instance. If it offended, one blamed the author for having no message of hope to give the world.

I suggest that the ground of Maugham's undervaluation as a writer, and of hostility to his view of human beings, has been moral rather than aesthetic. The Pecksniff lurking in all prigs is outraged. To them, as to the poet Longfellow,

> Life is real, and life is earnest;
> And the grave is not its goal.
> Dust thou art, to dust returnest,
> Was not spoken of the soul.

The absence of soul from Maugham's work is still remarked and resented.

Walpole in America and Home Again

•

10 ALL this time I have left Hugh Walpole in America, from which country he wrote that 'I'm very happy, very well, making lots of money and friends'.

He went on to say that he had read, since his arrival, only three English novels. They were *Night and Day*, *Legend*, and *If all these Young Men*, by, respectively, Virginia Woolf, Clemence Dane, and a white hope of the immediately post-war period, Romer Wilson. Of the first he observed that it 'ran pleasantly but is surely not a masterpiece'. This is the first reference in our letters to novels by Virginia Woolf, and the fact that Walpole used the phrase 'surely not a masterpiece' suggests that the exaltation of that author had already begun. It is an interesting sidelight. His letter was dated January 4th, 1920.

Walpole proceeded, later in the month, to refer in a silly passing injustice to the fickleness of the American public. He amplified his view by saying:

> Of the writers here Booth Tarkington is the most human, Hergesheimer the most interesting. However what Conrad said in the summer, that 'it is easier to have an intellectual friendship with a Chinaman than an American' is perfectly true. The whole of this country is run for the shouting, pushing, rude, vulgar, good-hearted lower-middle class. Everything! Press, books, theatre, politics, comfort, and all. So you get immense vitality and nothing else at all . . . All the same, their kind-heartedness is astounding. It beats every other country.

I, in return, wrote from Portugal, which I was visiting in company with Arnold Bennett. This visit was undertaken because Bennett, a sick man, was having serious trouble with his wife Marguerite, who, being lonely and an egotist, had not the skill one expected in a Frenchwoman to cajole, and was reduced to anger by the adoration given to Arnold by his friends and the consequent neglect of herself. This anger led to explosions, very painful to those who witnessed them, and really very pathetic to anybody who understood the two temperaments.

One day, when Edward Knoblock and I had been lunching with the pair, we walked away together, and spoke of Bennett's serious ill-health, which was being increased by scenes in which his obstinacy was as notable as his patience, and Marguerite's aggressiveness as great as her unhappiness. To my surprise, Knoblock said that unless I did something quickly for our friend, he would die.

The suggestion seemed extraordinary, because Bennett's attitude to me was avuncular, and I could not see myself as one predestined to save his life. Nevertheless, that was what Knoblock demanded that I should become. I promised to make some plan: and being, like Frederick in *The Pirates of Penzance*, a slave to duty, I shouldered the responsibility. Being alone with Bennett a few days later, I spoke to him as a father. I said:

'You ought to get away, by yourself, for a real holiday.'

He gloomily replied: 'I know. It's no fun going alone.'

I said: 'I'll go with you.'

He got very excited.

'Would you go to Portugal, I say?'

'Yes.'

'Oh, but that's . . . fine!'

He took a brochure from his pocket; and we looked at it together. When I said 'O.K.' he rose from the table and went along the Reform Club dining-room to the head of the Booth Line, who was lunching at another table. The trip was arranged on the spot.

It was then I who had serious trouble with Marguerite; but

lacking the impediment of speech which always put Bennett at a disadvantage in argument, I soothed her. I promised that in a month's time she should have once again, and rejoice in, a healthy and affectionate husband. Her resentment at my peculiar power over this supposedly dominating man vanished. And I kept my promise.

From Portugal I wrote to Walpole:

> We have been in Havre, in Oporto, in Lisbon, in Cintra, and here, Mont Estoril, which is called the Portuguese Riviera. We walk, drive, read, talk, gamble, etc. Arnold is in the best form, and very delightful all day, saying the most stuttering and shattering things every hour . . .
>
> Portugal is the most peculiar place. I can tell you that much. Its ways and doings are perpetually astonishing. Here, on this 'Riviera', the plans to sweep the South of France bare of its pleasure seekers are advanced but not so advanced as to make the district impossible. There are villas that combine Moorish qualities with some of the most barbarous impromptu that you could imagine. The roads in and outside Oporto are grotesque. The roads here, on the other hand, are excellent. Wherever we go we come upon strange people who fall to our honest charm and frequent our society when we choose. And in fact we're both enjoying the whole thing, from the nine days' sea voyage to the prospect of another fortnight on land and the sea journey.
>
> You'll have heard, I expect, that Mackenzie goes presently to the South Seas with Eric Brett Young as his companion; that Lawrence and Francis Brett Young are in Capri; that the *Mercury* continues its able course etc. . . . Arnold sends his love and says it's about time for you to come home, as you are being forgotten by the public, though certainly not by your friends.

In reply, Walpole mentioned that he had met and liked Siegfried Sassoon in New York and was shortly to see St John Ervine, whose plays *John Ferguson* and *Jane Clegg* had made a

tremendous impression upon American audiences. The Er-
vines immediately became his friends. Of the London literary
world he said:

I thought Lynd's article on Donne jolly good in the
Mercury but Shanks's criticism maddens me—he knows
nothing about the novel at all and is as patronizing as an
Archbishop. He and the Mansfield ought to be put in a bag
together and despatched to China. Once there they might
produce a pallid offspring, child of Pomposo and Madame
Blavatsky.

He then returned to England, to Polperro, in Cornwall,
whence he wrote:

Your bloody rudeness in not answering a letter I sent to
you a week ago (especially as it contained a serious invitation) confirms what I hear as to your present haughtiness.
Nevertheless I bear no malice but hope that next Tuesday
is all right for you to lunch with me . . . How good *The
New Statesman* is just now and how dull my old friend *The
Ath.* God bless you and help you to mend your manners.

My reply:

My bloody rudeness was concluded yesterday when I
wrote to you. But even then I think I must have taken your
invitation as not quite serious, and I'm sorry for that. In
any case, I could not have come; but it was very nice of you
to ask me. I am pleased to hear that I have got haughty.
When we meet you must tell me who says so. I will then
tear his tripes out.

Next Tuesday will suit me very well. Come and take
me out to lunch . . . I shall have no money and a meal will
be a salvation. Also, I expect, my hauteur will be a little
reduced by hunger and I may be almost human.

By the way, Harold Williams turned up last week from

Russia, after terrible experiences. He and Mrs Williams are lunching with me today. Tell you all about it.

It is quite true that the *New States.* is as bright as the *Ath* is dim . . .

Well, dear Hugh, I feel quite amiable towards you, from my Olympian peak. Just a little condescending to all the world, perhaps; a little disposed to stoop in order to see my fellow-creatures crawling by. But *que voulez vous?* When one's head is so suddenly as large as mine one tends to live in a world of one's own.

Walpole's items of news at this time were that he was meeting Walter de la Mare at Fowey, and that he had met Squire during a weekend at the Desboroughs'.

He was abysmally solemn and at dinner not long ago he said loudly that he would never go to *The Beggar's Opera* because it was indecent! Talking of solemn people I've got very much to like Drinkwater lately—solemn of course but large and generous and kindly—no smallness in him anywhere. I like Ervine too, and even W. L. George. In fact writing men just now are very jolly.

A slight breeze arose between us at the end of 1920, when he announced that as a result of my disgraceful secretiveness regarding an episode in which he did not know that I had been made ridiculous I was no longer a friend of his. I was able to explain all; and the breeze died at once. I shortly afterwards —November 22nd, 1920—reported my literary activities. To make the Mackenzie pun intelligible I should explain that Edward Shanks, who dispraised me in print, and for whom Walpole expressed a Pickwickian hatred, had just published a not very good novel called *The People of the Ruins.*

For my own trumpery business, I have wrote ½ a novel. Not a Cornish word in it, though Mackenzie sent a message to say it should be called (as I was staying at Ruan Minor)

The People of the Ruans. I have done 45,000 words; but what words I can't recall, and what calibre of words I can't judge. The story is squalid, and will lose me all my readers. They will say, as a lady once said of *Resurrection*, 'I shouldn't have thought Tolstoy would have *written* such a book!' Did I tell you of a man who read *Nocturne* and said to a friend 'If I hadn't known the author was a man I should have thought the book had been written by a woman—and NOT A VERY NICE WOMAN!' I suggest that the words in capitals should be written on my tombstone.

Well, dear Hugh, never let these dark days depress you. Right will always triumph, and the M.C.C. may yet win a Test Match on a slow wicket. Fogs will pass and suns will shine; and you will read this book of mine; and say: 'I quite must draw the line. At books like water without wine; and sans a single person fine. The men are fools, the girls are kine. I really quite must draw the line. He's nothing but a nasty——'

I went to the Forum Club last night, and they said you had been coming. Gilbert Frankau (Peter Jackson: Cigar Merchant, 26th thousand, as he seems to call himself) opened the debate. Then a weird crew—S. Kaye-Smith, G. B. Stern, Hamilton Fyfe, Victor Bridges, Alec Waugh, Mary Webb (Good God, what a woman!) and others. As one anonymous spectator said, 'all stars'. I made Frankau very indignant by making fun of him.

Still in the same vein I finished my novel (it was called *Coquette*, and was about a girl who had sat at table in a country hotel with my mother and myself, whom I had christened 'the white-faced cocket', and of whom I had heard further details from a subsequent visitor to the hotel, Francis Brett Young).

You will be glad to know that I finished my insufferably bloody novel last Monday, and the typescript went in last Friday. What the book is like it would be hard for me to say. In my opinion it is one of the worst. Do I hesitate even over the qualification? I do. If I were as modest as I seem I should say it was *the* worst ever. But do not let me prejudice you against it. I do myself no good by my candour. Arnold, who has not read a word of it, is already telling people that it can't be any good, because, apparently, I have said so, and I can't lie, besides being the best critic in the two hemispheres, etc. . . .

I have been to certain theatres—always with a realization that I must deeply, if unconsciously, have sinned. I must be very wicked indeed to have to see such bad plays. I sat in Nora Ervine's box for *The Wonderful Visit* (Don't suppose that this sentence follows inevitably from its fore-runner!) and was pointed out by Basil Dean as the author of the play [a dramatization by St John Ervine of Wells's novel]. Could you imagine anything more unlike, physiognomically, than Ervine and myself? Think of an audience desiring to do homage to that plump and healthy person, and casting astonished eyes upon my meagre and repugnant wickedness! They must have thought: 'That mephistophelian reprobate write this beautiful play? Never!' And they were quite right. Instinct again. It is the final judgment. However, I had the pleasure of sitting in a draught behind Marguerite and Nora, and vainly trying to succour an aggrieved lady who sat in another draught, gave her last 2/- to an incompetent attendant for the stifling of the draught, and refused my proffered sixpence for the linkman on the ground that she had forgotten the number of her car. An eventful evening—Arnold riding about in his four-wheeler, Marguerite plunging off in search of him, and Nora (my other charge) clutching me and wailing 'Don't leave me, Frank,' while Gip Wells hunted for *her* vehicle. I got home breathless, having seen nothing of the play.

Walpole replied:

I'm delighted the book's finished. I expect Shanks is wetting his pen. He manages to irritate me with his sublime patronage more than all the others put together save Becky

[Rebecca West] whom I wish he'd elope with and the boat sink crossing the Channel!

In another letter, written in the summer of 1921 from Lady Russell's châlet at Randogne, he announced:

> One humorous thing has occurred. As perhaps you saw, Murry treated me to almost two pages of unmitigated abuse in last week's *Nation*. Then suddenly he and Katherine take a châlet in Montana! Not that it matters. He's honest and quite detached but of course its not a *good* basis of friendship if someone loathes your work and says so at the top of his voice. . . .
> I liked greatly your review of Lawrence in the *M.G.*—very true.[1] K.M. says that it is a filthy rotten book and D. l. Mare's *Midget* no good either . . .

I sympathized with the Murry dilemma, told him that my book was out in the United States, where I was being compared with Homer and Shakespeare, and said I was reading *The Memoirs of a Midget* with 'a good deal of pleasure. . . . It is a bit dull, and yet it has real charm, and a number of rather beautiful quiet things'. I also spoke up for Rose Macaulay's *Dangerous Ages*, which 'many people dislike'. Walpole, still gossiping from Switzerland, told me that H. L. Mencken had made an onslaught on me in America. 'He's a fierce fellow, Mencken, fiercer than funny but very limited in his tastes.' He then praised enthusiastically the book called *Coquette*, and I referred to an ordeal I had endured on Arnold Bennett's yacht, when Bennett solemnly read the book through. This,

1. A review of *Women in Love* which said that although the book was 'full of absurdities', and Lawrence, 'obsessed by gloating, malignant cruelty', used 'goaded and extravagant language' when he described the 'incessant sensual tortures' of his characters, 'no writer of today has such an electrically vivid power to imagine a scene'. In the chapter called 'Water Party' 'there is an imagining so superior and a beauty of such rare and sustained quality, that it deserves very high commendation indeed'. 'If much of the redundant emphasis of the minor and almost caricatured portions of the book could be eliminated, how extraordinarily noble and beautiful would the remainder seem.'

for me, was an amusing, alarming experience. I reclined in a chair on the deck (I think at Fowey, where Quiller-Couch dined with us) exquisitely idle after a period of strenuous overwork, while the reader, his spectacles far down his nose, was screwed up with my wretched book in a sort of deck-house. From time to time he rapped the window of the deck-house with a ring which he always wore—a beautiful ring with a square translucent golden-brown stone—and when he did this I was forced to rise and receive a rebuke for some error of style or grammar. Fortunately I am used, as a writer, to rebukes, and I remained calm.

I had a further rebuke, apparently, from Shanks in *The London Mercury*, which annoyed Walpole so much, he said, that he 'flung the thing across the floor'. He continued, saying that he had

> read nothing else save *Vera*, which is awfully clever but ill-tempered I think and *To Let* the best thing Galsworthy has ever done. Otherwise *Aeschylus*, finding my Greek much better than I thought.

And now came a real crisis. I wrote at length about Walpole's new book, *The Young Enchanted*, singling out characters and details, and concluding:

> I think this is what is wrong with the book (together with its too-great explanatoriness, which is like Boy McCormick saying that he was on the point of beating Kid Lewis when the sponge was thrown in—vide *Weekly Despatch* yesterday): it is spoilt because you have turned your back from time to time on your priceless gift. With the technique of a STORY, and the general framework of a STORY, you have tried to combine a psychological novel, a pamphlet, and a survey of manners and literary cliques. The survey is superficial, the pamphlet is superficial, the psychology is much too easy. But the story-telling is splendid. If it were all story, with everything else *implicit*, it would be perfectly O.K. Story-telling is your gift—not a knack or a deliberate trick, but

a real and priceless gift. . . . Do, for God's sake, write a story
by itself—no philosophy or caricatures of literary persons
or apostrophic remarks about romance and 1920 and young
enchantment. It is the reader who is to be enchanted . . .
If you would write a story nobody would bother whether
you were an artist or not. They would say 'Praise God for
our Hughie!' I swear this is true. I write in affection and
sincerity. . . . Don't be angry. I'm not being paternal. I'm
speaking with the voice of God.

To which Walpole, with great good-temper, replied:

My dear old God, I can't write much to you now because
I'm sick and in bed but I am touched at your having read
the book all through and taken trouble to write me so interesting a letter. I don't agree with all you say of course
and personally believe I'm a better creator of character than
a story-teller. You and Arnold write now so like one another
that you might be one and the same person. But what seems
conventional and sentimental to you Mighty Two in One
may not seem sentimental to other mightinesses—does not
seem so in fact. *That's* the trouble.

It was about this time that, largely through Walpole's enthusiasm, the Society of Bookmen was formed. I wrote on
April 13th, 1922:

A remarkable work seems to have appeared here from
the pen of one Brimley Johnson on the subject of you and
Mackenzie and Cannan and me, and one or two more. I
haven't seen the book itself (which I judge must be pretty
bad); but the young fellow appears to have praised me pretty
highly, with the result that all the reviewers, in retaliation,
are ticking me off. . . . I went to the last meeting of the Society
of Bookmen, and at dinner sat between [W. B.] Maxwell
and Micky Sadleir (I always feel that his book ought to be
called *Privileige*). Maxwell and I had a nice talk—our first.
I like him very much, though I don't think he makes a very

good chairman. Micky seems very concerned about some article which Mencken has written abusing him and me.

Later:

I have been doing a little laborious writing on a book which, though I hesitate to abide by our common decision to avoid self-depreciation and describe it as splendiferous, is possibly not so intolerably silly as my present opinion leads me to suppose.... I've got my little car here, and am invited to take it to Land's End and a mile and a half beyond, by Bertrand Russell; and to Weymouth and over the stormy seas by one who signs himself 1910 (M.C.M., at least). Or perhaps M.C.M. stands for 1900. I'm never sure. Or perhaps M.C.M. stands for Montague Compton Mackenzie. I'm not taking either step, as mountains intervene.

In spite of these pessimistic words I did go to visit Mackenzie on the Island of Herm; one result of the visit being that I arranged a grand reunion between these old rivals. To call it a reconciliation would be too much. The meeting took place at Walpole's house in Regent's Park; and as we approached our destination Mackenzie prophesied that the door would be opened by a butler, who would say 'I'm sorry; but Mr Walpole was lunching with the Duchess of Wrexe, and is not home yet.' Sure enough, the door was opened by an extraordinarily old butler, a sort of Firs (in *The Cherry Orchard*), who quavered: 'I'm sorry; but Mr Walpole was lunching today with the Countess of ——, and is not home yet.' We entered, roamed the room where tea was laid, and were still giggling over the confirmation of Mackenzie's prophecy when we found that Walpole was with us.

This did not ease the early moments; and both boys at first addressed their remarks to myself. However, after an hour I judged it right to leave them together. Next day I had a note from Walpole.

Thank you so much for yesterday. You did it beautifully. Difficult at first. I was nervous, so was Mackenzie. But excellent afterwards. He seemed to me delightful and utterly unlike the long-haired egotistical image I've been cherishing for years. Proof of which I have this morning purchased *The Altar Steps* and paid for it with my own money. Now there's only one person left in the world whom I detest. [A lady, no longer living, of whom he was mortally afraid as a dangerous gossip.]

Following this exploit he went again to the United States, reporting from Vermont on October 15th, 1922, that Americans, politically, were inclining more and more to 'intervention in Europe'. This meant, of course, peace-time intervention, following a period of isolationism.

In literature the old favourites on the whole remain, Arnold strong after *Prohack*, Wells very strong on the Outline [of History] (read simply everywhere). Of the younger men you and I are the best known, I think, but Lytton Strachey the God of the moment everywhere.

In a later letter he lamented the deaths of Alice Meynell and Katherine Mansfield, commended the American writer Thomas Beer as 'slow at first but one of the best and most intelligent fellows in the world', and highly praised Francis Brett Young's new novel, which I cannot identify. But what will be thought of the contradictions in his next potted survey of reputations? I quote the passage, not because it has any critical importance, but because its assembly of names highlights a single moment in taste, before that 'authority' which Murry had demanded three years earlier had begun to take charge of opinion. Those who find it unspeakably jejune should remember how the next fashion, and the next, and the next, have whizzed past in a world so distracted by events as to confuse nervous impatience of the past with the most erudite of fine taste.

Conrad immense—worshipped but I suspect not greatly read. Wells and Arnold terrific slump—so much so that there has been simply no attention paid to *Men like Gods*.

All his standing is on the History and as all the Professors are teaching all the Pupils that it's Bunk opinion is changing about that too. Of the next generation you, I, Lawrence, and Sheila Kaye-Smith are quite alone in having both sales and healthy critical approval. Lawrence of course beats us with the Eccentrics but we are more steadily and generally popular. . . . No English critics have any position here—not Gosse, Saintsbury, Squire (absolutely none), Murry. Strachey worshipped, Aldous Huxley much liked. Sabatini a great popular following. Merricks, Marshalls, Hutchinsons fading. De la Mare only poet known widely. Shaw adored. Dunsany was until he lectured. There! That's the real truth with no prejudices nor eccentricities. No new books of interest. I've been reading old ones. I thought *Lady into Fox* wonderful. . . .

Authority: The First Phase

•

11 IN THE year 1918 I became, at Arnold Bennett's insistence, a member of the Reform Club. There I hobnobbed almost daily with Members of Parliament, economists, barristers, political journalists, and of course the great Liberal editors, J. A. Spender, A. G. Gardiner, and H. W. Massingham. The contacts, since all these men were my seniors, and the talk at our table or in an overflowing corner of the smoking-room upstairs was very good, were extraordinarily educational. I heard what men 'in the know' really thought about the state of the country and about political leaders; and when once acclimatized I held my own in their discussions. Indeed, I formed close friendships with some, including Gardiner and Arthur Clutton-Brock, who wrote many of the front-page articles for *The Times Literary Supplement*.

These front-page articles had considerable influence on literary opinion (I do not know whether this is the same today, and I do not wish to suggest that it is not); and Clutton-Brock, who had wide acquaintance among bishops and adored the music of Mozart, was immersed in aesthetic theory. I presume that his theory, or theories, must have been superseded; for I do not find his name in modern books, and suspect that his mind was too original to commend itself to the authoritarians. This is a point to which I shall return in a later chapter.

I was also fascinated by the tall, gaunt, quiet, smiling, and very wise J. A. Hobson, who astonishingly had greatly influenced the mind of Lenin, and was considered unorthodox by those pinned by temperament to figures. He, too, was an original; a really great man of strikingly luminous intelligence and the utmost kindness. In proof of this latter trait I will mention that when we once talked together about economics a cheeky fellow-member, indicating myself, interposed: 'Swinny doesn't know anything about economics, does he?' Hobson, smiling seraphically, replied with exquisite tact: 'At least he's asking all the right questions.'

Since these men cannot be said to have influenced the change in literary fashion—their taste had been formed upon the Classics, and they looked with irony upon upsurging rebels from Eton and/or Cambridge—it would be improper to dilate here upon their interesting and attractive personalities, or on what I remember of their opinions. Being Victorians by birth and maturing, they found Lytton Strachey superficial; having their memories charged with mighty lines of the past, they felt distaste for the poetic wits; and Massingham was so little impressed by Virginia Woolf's *Night and Day* that he wrote derisively of the number of times the characters in that book had tea. He paid the price for his derision, of course, when *The Nation* was merged with *The New Statesman*; but the fatal words had been printed. Therefore I fear it must be said that the great Liberal editors had lost pace with the literary times.

They had also, without knowing it, lost pace with the political times; and it is for this reason that I now mention their eclipse in the post-war world. Liberals had ruled the country since 1906, when they enjoyed overwhelming victory in a General Election. Again returned to power, with a reduced majority, in 1910, a Liberal Government, despite malcontents such as John Morley (who said, privately, 'Asquith's jockeyed us') and John Burns, declared war upon Germany in 1914. During the War, in the way of governments, it was split by conflicting ambitions; and the Old Guard, which I knew, was ousted by the New, as represented in the House of Commons by David Lloyd George and his followers. I once saw Lloyd George at this time in the smoking-room at the Reform Club.

He did not once look towards former associates; but he was aware of them all. Never, otherwise, have I been led to imagine the shining of eyes in the back of a man's head. During the Old Guard's supremacy, J. A. Spender, as a fellow Balliol man, was in the confidence of Asquith and Grey, and spoke of public affairs with authority. Gardiner, reaching the editorship of *The Daily News* by way of journalism in Essex and Lancashire, had believed strongly in Lloyd George's genius; but belief had yielded to such distrust that continued editorship of *The News* under a proprietor for whom George remained a Beacon became impossible. He was retired.

All these editors, in fact, Spender, Gardiner, Massingham, Donald (of the *Chronicle*), and, a war later, Garvin, ended out of their editorial chairs. That probability is, in the modern cliché, an occupational hazard of editorship. In office they wield unlimited power; out of it they are lost. Having known the five men, I can testify that each retained to the end the exceptional qualities of character which had carried him so high. But the incessant movement of time, of circumstance, of opinion, and of ownership is inescapable.

As I say, the War gave its death blow to Liberalism. The enemies of that belief in what used to be called free competition launched their strength against it. Being attackers, they had all the weapons. The Old Guard could not grasp the fact. When Elizabeth Bibesco, who was Asquith's daughter, wrote a new and very brittle little novel, the story was told that Asquith, after reading the book, put it down with the words 'Another nail in the Asquith coffin!' I asked my friend Vivian Phillipps, who was Asquith's P.P.S., if the story was true. The reply was: 'Quite untrue. He doesn't know there *is* an Asquith coffin.'

I often think of this reply. Those whose day is done are the last to realize it. Their best friends, as the horrible advertisements say, never tell them.

Thus it was with the Liberals. They had not noticed that Murry's slogan, 'There must be authority,' was being whispered and muttered and shouted all over the world. They repeated the words 'Never again'. They spoke of the League of Nations as the ultimate instrument of Justice. But the Peace Conferences had been a scramble for loot; political observers, knowing the mood of returning soldiers, and fearing either chaos or a Communist régime in every one of the combatant countries, were anxious. When the United States withdrew, the doom of the League of Nations was certain. Well, then, 'we must have authority', not in the Arts alone, but in the management of peoples. Hence Communism in Russia, Fascism or Nazi-ism in Germany, Italy, and Spain. Dictatorship was in the air.

In Britain the Conservatives are the Liberals of other countries; but Britain had, at first, a strong Labour representation in the House of Commons, and by the end of 1923 a Labour Government. It was there, certainly, on sufferance, or as a stop-gap, or as a stalking horse; but its very existence was a sign that in future the two confronting parties would be Tory and Socialist. The Liberals, and the liberals who stood for peace and goodwill towards men, were 'out'. Even the least political-minded of writers saw this. They saw something else, too; that with the breaking-down of conventions he who would capture the popular mind must invent something which at least looked like a new fashion.

The fashion in London had already been indicated; it was for highly fastidious and in particular satirical writing; it was for an aristocracy of the intellect. Young men were in the habit of saying that they cared only for 'the first class', and the first class was apparently recruited only among members of that band of Apostles from Trinity College, Cambridge, who had succeeded to the 'effortless superiority to other men' which previously had been the prerogative of old Balliol scholars from the sister University.

This effortless superiority was reinforced by a Feminism which, having newly won the Vote, needed a woman writer as symbol of woman's equality with man. Virginia Woolf's *A Room of One's Own* was just such a pamphlet as the women needed. It was a key book, beautifully written, and expressive of that terrible predicament in which wives who wrote found themselves. Male writers were assumed to enjoy full liberty; those who were female had the household upon their backs. In order to do their best work they must have independence. This is a fallacy; but its enunciation in *A Room of One's Own* carried Virginia Woolf from private to public fame. When George Moore gravely nominated her as the next G.O.M., he meant to ridicule Mrs Woolf as he had ridiculed Hardy and Henry James; but the gibe missed its effect. Moore showed by it that he was behind the times. This was proved also by his inability to write new novels upon modern themes. He was forced to re-hash his old ones and re-tell ancient stories.

Something else was happening. Until the end of the War, and as the letters I have quoted from Walpole have shown, English novelists enjoyed a celebrity in the United States out of proportion to their quality. This was because, from the days when Washington Irving imitated Lamb and Fennimore Cooper was inspired by Scott to write romances of which one at least, *The Pioneers*, is magnificent, it had been customary for American readers to rest heavily on foreign authors, of whom the English alone did not need to be translated. There had been exceptions of genius (Motley was a great historian, and his *Rise of the Dutch Republic* has no parallel), who ranged from Herman Melville and Louisa Alcott to Henry James, and from Edgar Allan Poe and Bret Harte to O. Henry; but although Dreiser had warm admirers in Europe Americans felt their home products to be only rarely of international acceptance.

Now all was changed. With the turn of the century, after a spate of historical and sentimental tales of good average quality, several men and women were creating a new and obviously characteristic literature. The first of these, after Dreiser, was Upton Sinclair, who stirred the world with his realistic story of the Chicago stockyards, *The Jungle*. He was followed by other realists, who all astringently portrayed the American scene, from Edgar Lee Masters, whose *Spoon River Anthology*, for all its crudity, was new and seminal, to Willa Cather and Sinclair Lewis. Emily Dickinson, on the one hand,

and Robert Frost, on the other, worked with originality in not-too-revolutionary verse-forms; and after the return of American soldiers from Europe there was produced a vigorous new fiction which in its consequences shattered the sedateness of that produced by the milder English climate. While the professors still looked to France for new ideas, and concentrated upon Proust, or to Ireland for extraordinary works which they could analyse for ever, a splendid rush of new novelists brought ruthless energy into the field.

This writing made comparable English writing seem tame. It had a tremendous effect. Our young writers, greatly stimulated, began to pepper their work with coarseness and expletives. They could not really challenge the Americans. All they did was to diminish the importance of the English schools. We had nobody to stand in fiction, for energy, against Sinclair Lewis, John dos Passos, Scott Fitzgerald, William Faulkner, Thomas Wolfe, and, rather later, John Steinbeck. With the eclipse of the Georgian Poets, we were at the mercy of eccentricity and pastiche arriving from across the Atlantic.

The authoritarians closed their ranks. They were willing to experiment; in fact modernity was one of their shibboleths; but they saw in all this tumult a danger to the finest standards. They remembered that an Englishman of Victorian days had written a book called *Culture and Anarchy*, in which he claimed that

> The whole scope of the essay is to recommend culture as the great help out of our present difficulties; culture being a pursuit of our total perfection by means of getting to know, on all the matters which most concern us, the best which has been thought and said in the world; and, through this knowledge, turning a stream of fresh and free thought upon our stock notions and habits.

Their conception of culture was not at first a wide one. It was something intensive, arising from a former association of bright wits at Cambridge University, especially those which had been gathered at Trinity College. They owed to two or three seniors, for example to Bertrand Russell and G. E. Moore, much of their intellectual direction; but were members of a Society of long standing at Cambridge, known as the Apostles, which had the most exacting aims. This Society was described in the last century by an earlier member, Dean Merivale, the historian, as having

> a common intellectual taste, common studies, common literary aspirations, and . . . we soon grew, as such youthful coteries generally do, into immense self-conceit. We began to think that we had a mission to enlighten the world upon things intellectual and spiritual.

It was from association during the War with ex-members of this Society, and their temperamental allies, that Middleton Murry owed his development from earlier enthusiasms. His parents—he never forgot—had been hard-working and undistinguished poor; he still had no income but what he could earn by writing; he was among Apostles of good or moneyed family. They were, in a sense, aristocrats by birth (what Oscar Wilde called people 'of culture and position'), they naturally accepted the rank of an intellectual *élite*.

I wish only to mention this point. When I did so twenty-eight years ago I was accused of venom or conscious inferiority, from both of which faults my friends will absolve me; and I now want to develop a small distinction of, I think, some interest. It is that certain writers of great gifts and workaday experience but no academic training found themselves regarded as outsiders by a small and highly intelligent body without practical knowledge of their fellow-creatures.

> As cause and consequence of our general state of mind (wrote Maynard Keynes) we completely misunderstood human nature, including our own. The relationship which

we attributed to it led to a superficiality, not only of judgment, but also of feeling.

When Lawrence pointed to his solar plexus as the seat of wisdom, he was challenging this aristocracy of intellect. His hatred of the intellectual approach was instinctive. It was also disconcerting to the apostles of culture.

Four Journalists

•

12 LET me illustrate this matter by reference to four journalists whose experience was unlike that of the Apostles. They were Robert Lynd, James Bone, H. M. Tomlinson, and Philip Gibbs. Not one of them received or expected recognition from what Gilbert called 'the high aesthetic band'; yet all were such individual observers and recorders of happenings in their age that they strongly influenced men and women outside the academic orbit.

When together, they met as familiars, but not as a proselytizing body. Indeed, when the first three, with a fourth, my beloved friend Horace Horsnell, were in Madrid as a party, and drinking well and happily out of doors, one of them said candidly to another: 'You and I are the sort of men our mothers used to warn us against.' The words illustrate what seems to me to be the poetry of humour.

All four, with Horsnell as a fifth, were gifted men whose knowledge was first-hand. In their company flying time was endless; brains were stimulated to greater liveliness, greater penetration; wisdom prevailed. They did not argue, they pooled. Whether speaking or writing, their aim was to catch and tease the humour of like minds. As a consequence, their best work was spoken; but each of them produced at least one book which, meeting with approbation on its first appearance, is still read and will be long remembered.

Lynd, who for some years was literary editor of *The Daily News*, came from Belfast. Over the signature Y.Y., in *The New*

Statesman, he wrote light essays on subjects ranging from aunts to bed knobs. For *John o' London's Weekly* he wrote short discourses on books and their writers to a model designed by the original editor of that journal, Wilfred Whitten. Some of these essays were afterwards collected; and a selection from them can be read in the miscellany included in Everyman's Library with an introduction by Desmond MacCarthy.

The kind of essay Lynd wrote appeared in newspapers or weekly reviews from the eighteen-nineties onwards. G. S. Street, for example, who became the Official Examiner of Plays in his mature years, Arthur Symons, G. A. B. Dewar, and others contributed examples of it to *The Saturday Review*, where they were known as 'middles'. Over the pseudonym *Alpha of the Plough*, A. G. Gardiner wrote similar examples for several years in *The Star*. As 'turnovers' from the last column on page one to the first column on page two in *The Globe*, an old and respected evening newspaper, they represented some of E. V. Lucas's earliest work. Chesterton, Belloc, and, even more lightly, A. A. Milne all took pleasure in expressing the whims and fancies of laughing minds. And from time to time Lucas in his capacity as editor for Methuen arranged the publication of small volumes brimming with those fancies.

The form was first popularized in the early eighteenth century by Steele and Addison, with encouragement from those greater wits, Swift and Arbuthnot. Johnson, Goldsmith, and Hawkesworth all variously illustrated public and domestic manners and taught good morals through the same medium. The essay grew longer with Lamb and Hazlitt (and Coleridge in *The Friend*) who went deeper and expressed creeds as well as whims. It was solidified by Macaulay, who wrote what were not so much essays as opuscules. And as the nineteenth century waned it lost gravity again and rested upon smiling, quickly-forgotten half-nonsense. The exponents of this type of essay made no appeal to Virginia Woolf, who thought them triflers, as they intentionally were. *Tremendous Trifles* was the title of one collection by Chesterton; another, by Belloc, was called *On Nothing*; *Not that it Matters* was a third, by A. A.

Milne. How unpretentious both matter and manner seem today!

An encourager of the essay was Wilfred Whitten, that friend who had secured for Lucas his first commission, and so led him from Bernard Barton to the Lloyds and Charles Lamb. Whitten, whose reprint of J. T. Smith's famous *Book for a Rainy Day* contains a mass of notes fascinating to the browser, was a great dabbler in old books. He was also a colleague on *The Academy* of Lucas, Arnold Bennett, Lionel Johnson, and other bright boys of the nineteen-hundreds; and when that highly-amusing paper, in which Bennett's *The Truth about an Author* was serialized, came to its inevitable end, he moved as acting editor to a new venture, *T.P.'s Weekly*, a popular literary journal for the eager mass of book-readers, which was supposedly directed by T. P. O'Connor. *T.P's Weekly* published good work in its day, and much good advice for seekers after not-too-abstruse culture; but in the sequel it was sold to Harmsworth, and Whitten started his own paper, giving it as title the pen-name he had used in *T.P.'s*. So *John o' London's Weekly* came into being. There, in every number, as something distinct from reviews and comments on new publications, appeared an article by Whitten about his favourite reading. There was nothing quite like this article in current journalism, and it was particularly enjoyed by the frequenters of literary byways. Whitten's copy—for he belonged spiritually to the bohemians who postpone work as long as possible—was often late in reaching the office, where an anxious sub-editor was only relieved from desperate anxiety on press day by a telegram announcing that it had been begun. I believe it always arrived, until Whitten's death in 1942.

Then for the first time in *John o' London's* history a successor had hastily to be found. All rejoiced when Lynd, who had exactly the right touch, was appointed; and Lynd continued for seven years, although increasing ill-health made it latterly such a torment that he sent his articles in fragments, and sometimes, if he quoted from a book, tore out the relevant page from lack of strength to copy a long passage. Even in such conditions what he wrote was full of charm. When he died in 1949 the shock to his readers was almost as great as it was to his friends.

H. M. Tomlinson once said, in one of his letters (when Horace Horsnell was very ill, and Lynd in spite of his own dying condition asked what he could do to comfort our exhausted friend), 'he and Sylvia are as fragile as two lilies in a frost'. It was true. Buoyed up as they were by extraordinary courage, both Lynd and his wife lived in constant weakness. When one of them was a little better, the other became the invalid; and when I visited their home in Hampstead they seemed—but this may have been my imagination—to take turns in drinking from a bottle on the mantelpiece. The bottle contained, not, as some may suppose, good heartening Irish whiskey, but Easton Syrup, a tonic so powerful that once, when in a condition of debility I took what must have been too large a dose, I felt myself walking a foot from the ground. Neither of the Lynds gave any sign of such levitation. They went on talking blithely as before.

They were always blithe. Lynd himself was at ease in every company. He was sure enough of himself as a man to need no bush and no 'line' to make his presence felt. Those who met him abandoned their own pretences and defences as soon as he looked at them. I never knew a man who did not brighten at the sound of his name. If one said: 'I saw Lynd——'one's companion asked eagerly: 'How was he?' as if his well-being were the most important thing in the world. That, in a profession full of jealousy, was testimony to his charm.

Besides charm, he had immense unparaded knowledge of literature, and stern knowledge of Ireland, which he expressed in a book on that country. His humour was of the ironic rather than the effervescent order, very quiet and very dry. He did not ridicule; he had no intellectual vice.

He was tall, and his lean shoulders were much bent. Above them was a thin dark face, in which sensitiveness and reflective amusement were both apparent under a sort of flounce of almost black, wavy hair. His brow, according to my recollection, was capacious. His voice was low and rather hollow, without resonance. And—it is a scarce and under-estimated quality—he was humane. As he said in one of his essays, 'perfect manners in literature are rare nowadays. Many authors are either pretending or condescending, either malicious or suspicious.' His own manners, as man and writer, were perfect.

He escaped the disagreeableness of the uneasy by being, at all times and in all company, unaffectedly himself.

I am naturally [he said] a stay-at-home, and the only home in which I have lived all my life is my body. Born under Saturn, I have nevertheless been happy enough never to wish to change it for a better. If I have wished to be a better man, I have still wished for the new spirit to inhabit the same body, for, though it is a body that no man could be proud of, not being built in any of the noble styles of architecture, I am used to it and am bound to it by all manner of sympathies. Not that I have looked after it as well as I might have done. I have allowed it to sink into dilapidation and disrepair, so that it already resembles more than it should a piece of antiquity. But even the crooked man with the crooked cat probably lived happily enough in his crooked little house, and would not have left it without compulsion.

Having reached this understanding with himself (and of himself) Lynd was free to observe the world with critical detachment. He had no hope of changing it; he even thought it might be a better world than puritans imagined. But he suffered from no flabbiness of mind; he was never a coward nor a compromiser; the kindness he expressed in print was the kindness of his heart. Hazlitt said a familiar style was one of the hardest things in literature to master. This is true only as a retort to those disdaining it as something beneath their own exhibitionist vanity. It is not true of Lynd's writing, which is that of a man who found life more amusing than self-display, and the enjoyment of it better than more conventional disgust.

His most serious literary study, included as a whole in the

Everyman's Library selection from his work, was *Dr Johnson and his Friends*. Considering that it was written in 1927, before the publication of the works and papers discovered at Fettercairn House and Malahide Castle, this shows a remarkable grasp of Boswell's character, as it does of the personalities of Johnson, Goldsmith, Reynolds, and the rest of that extremely vocal circle. True, the book talks of them all as men, and does not analyse their printed works; but accurate knowledge of the works is implicit in every comment, and as he was not writing a professorial history of eighteenth-century literature, or a still more professorial thesis for a doctorate, he did the world good service.

There was one publication which Lynd never achieved. He was to write for the English Men of Letters Series a volume on Robert Louis Stevenson intended as a counterblast to my own much-abused study of that author. If it had ever appeared, the book would not have been abusive. He would have made all temperamental allowances for Stevenson, and would have produced a classic estimate.

You will have noted my claim that Lynd was familiar with eighteenth-century literary figures. At the beginning of the twentieth century that was not unusual, I think perhaps because both were periods of agnosticism and social theory. Encouraged by our elders, Leslie Stephen and Austin Dobson, we read Locke, Godwin, and Bentham, when we were not reading Richardson and Fielding (although when he reconsidered Richardson Stephen found him quite as repellent as Zola). It was a fashion, like any other.

This may be why, when H. M. Tomlinson was writing a *causerie* in *The Nation*, of which paper he was for a while literary editor, he was accused of being no *litterateur*. The critic said:

> You never devote your page to the influence of the Pleiades. You never refer to eighteenth-century literature. You never look back on the names familiar to all who read

Latin. What is interesting to truly curious and bookish people might not exist for you.

That was incontrovertible. Tomlinson had not the scholarly mind. He was an observer. He had reflectively read many books, but they were not the books used by men living in libraries. His interest was in the 'whys' and 'hows' of life itself, in every aspect of nature, in the thoughts and experiences of travellers and comparable meditatives as they elucidated for him the mysterious universe. He might have been considered as a sort of modern Sir Thomas Browne or Robert Burton, but for the fact that his education, unlike theirs, had never compassed the dead languages. It was empiric.

I once described him as the Hamlet of journalists, a phrase which he appreciated; but I cannot and do not wonder that when Maynard Keynes found money to support an unremunerative *Nation*, on condition that its policy was changed, Tomlinson disappeared with his editor, H. W. Massingham, from its columns. The new direction, largely drawn from Cambridge and Bloomsbury, did not want a Hamlet among its contributors, any more than it wanted a Thomas Browne.

Tomlinson was born a real Cockney—much more real than Max Beerbohm, who so described himself because he came from Kensington, or than William McFee and myself, who hail from Wood Green. His father was a foreman in the East India Docks, and his first impressions were of masts in Blackwall Reach. Real Cockneys, however, have compensations; Tomlinson could travel easily to Epping Forest, in neighbouring Essex, and for this reason his physical life was influentially associated with local equivalents of the sea and the jungle. Boyish imagination did the rest.

In the eighteen-eighties, when he roamed the docks and glades and riverside streets, the State was not deified; men knew that if at long last they became unemployable their one refuge, a deadly shame to the respectable poor, was the Workhouse. The Workhouse, like unemployment, lay at the back of their thoughts; twin terrors. This knowledge, gained in childhood, produced Tomlinson's loyalty to the poor; the loyalty was not sentimental, as genteel critics supposed, but was charged with an irony incomprehensible to those critics.

The books in his youthful home ranged from the Bible to Cook's *Voyages* and the works of Artemus Ward; and the boy found his way through Dickens, Stevenson, and Carlyle to the writers who were chiefly to inspire his manhood thoughts—Emerson, Thoreau, and Whitman. It was a strange conjunction; for I do not need to tell you that the Cockney, having no provinciality, and no acquaintance with dons or Apostles, has little reverence for his betters or for gravity. He has never learnt to assume what Leonard Woolf calls the 'defensive carapace' necessary to all Public Schoolboys; he has never acquired the Public Schoolboy's sense of superiority to the under-privileged. He needs no carapace, and his inborn sense of superiority to all men arises from the immensity of London itself.

London [said Tomlinson] is numerous towns and they have little knowledge of each other. Poplar had never heard of St John's Wood. Not only that, but one of our streets would not know what the next street did; it might be as sundered as forbidden territory. A boy, before his initiation, would loiter there at his peril. He was a foreigner, though only from round the corner. Here and there in the parish were corners and byways avoided by all except the doctor and the venturesome, where a policeman's helmet might be seen in the gutter on the morning following Saturday night. There it stayed. Nobody would touch it.

This was the background. When Tomlinson's father died, the boy had at once to leave school in order to earn money. His wages (like my own at fourteen) were six shillings a week, and his office was in Leadenhall Street, at the heart of the City of London. He was often sent by the firm aboard ships which lay down the River Thames, and his longing for travel to distant parts of the world was nourished by all he saw and did. He could not yet indulge the longing. He was tied to daily work as office boy and clerk. He had no influential friends, had missed the possibility of a scholarship through the need to earn, and was without resource.

Only later, after youthful marriage, did a violent scene with his employer send him hunting for other employment, into by chance what a later friend, Philip Gibbs, called The Street of Adventure. He impulsively walked into the office of the halfpenny Radical newspaper, *The Morning Leader*, asked to see the editor, Ernest Parke, and was at once engaged as reporter. His first assignment was to sail with a fleet of trawlers on the Dogger Bank and tell what he saw; his second, to cover Naval manœuvres. The Navy did the honours. Tomlinson responded. He was triumphantly at sea.

Parke, a good editor, prided himself upon quick decisions. He liked Tomlinson's conscientiousness and Tomlinson's thoughtfully-phrased work. When he heard that a ship drawing twenty-three feet of water was to travel up the Amazon and to the Madeira River, which was five hundred feet above sea level and two thousand miles within the heart of South America, he sent his incredulous junior straightway upon that voyage, also. By this decision he made a happy man. Tomlinson found in the journey all he had been seeking—romance, the answer to every boyish dream; and the articles he sent home became the basis of an afterwards famous book, *The Sea and the Jungle*.

The Sea and the Jungle was published in 1912, when the author was thirty-nine; and if his had been a different character, and there had been no world war two years later, it would have made him a fashionable writer.

He was never destined to be a fashionable writer. Readers of his novels, *All Our Yesterdays* and *The Day Before* will know what his attitude to warfare was. He thought it insanity. Yet he was sent to the Western Front as a war correspondent, and he wrote his best about what he saw there, and was deafened for life by the noise of heavy artillery. By one of the uncanny chances affecting unprofitable newspapers the radical *Morning*

Leader had been absorbed by the more moderately Liberal *Daily News*, and instead of Parke Tomlinson had A. G. Gardiner as his editor. Gardiner greatly admired Tomlinson as man and writer; but he once told me that Tomlinson's despatches from the Front were too depressing for the *News's* readers; they gave a picture of war which, to a people standing in great need of some daily victory, was too darkly-hued with the writer's horror. Other men could brighten the colours; Tomlinson could not do so.

This was one of the crises of his life. It meant that he was thrust thenceforth into a kind of journalism—I have told already how he was rebuked by a reader of *The Nation*—which was not wholly congenial; and when *The Nation* was swallowed he had no regular 'platform'. Fortunately his novel *Gallions Reach*, which he called to me 'a Treasure Island yarn', was greatly praised, and gave him a new prospect. Less fortunately *All Our Yesterdays*, which followed, showed that so far from being a born novelist he was dominated by three non-fictional elements, those of poet, journalist, and, most inopportune of all, quietist philosopher. As he wrote in a letter to myself, 'Plato has been the ruin of me'. Only in his last book of all, *The Trumpet Shall Sound*, were the three elements fused. I quote a letter of 1940:

> As you know, I've got my own notions of novel writing. There is the cinema technique, the flash on and off of significant episodes, the use of the time-space theory, which is now a commonplace on the 'screen'; and there is also the illumination of ideas through showing the drift, the apparently casual drift, of human 'progress'. Yet, as you are well aware, the world is what it is through, not fate, but the unconscious desires of men.

This latter 'illumination of ideas' is what he sought to express in his own fictions. He had no instinct for dramatic situation, although he could relish it in Shakespeare and Hardy; being a Cockney, he could not take some provincial setting and people it with living characters. If he yarned, it was about men he had known, or places he had seen; truth and the journalist's contact with humanity were his references. As a consequence it is as a descriptive writer that he was most distinguished. There, in my opinion, he was very distinguished indeed.

One curious episode in Tomlinson's literary life deserves mention, because it casts a light on the way things happen in the literary world and on the warfares of the period. Norman Douglas published in 1917 a novel called *South Wind*, which has ever since been admired by all who have a taste for erudite irony. Douglas, however, belonged to no set, and he was afterwards under a cloud as one who had exhausted normal sexual relationships and been charged with an offence against a boy. Italy was his beloved ground of exploration, as *Old Calabria* proves; and he lived on the island of Capri until Mussolini drove him forth. He wrote *South Wind* as an amused study of life on Capri, although he denied my suggestion that the Keith who figures in the book was a self-portrait.

Subsequently, continuing to live abroad, he wrote other books on various subjects; but in spite of their quality they were not acclaimed as they should have been, and their sales were relatively small. Richard Aldington felt strongly that there should be some public tribute to Douglas; and Tomlinson was asked to write this. He refused, thinking himself unfit. Douglas himself, however, intervened, saying that he would only agree to such a tribute if Tomlinson wrote it. 'I saw no help for it then,' wrote Tomlinson to me in after years; 'and went to it.'

Now it so happened that in 1925 a book was published called *Memoirs of the Foreign Legion*, by M.M. [Maurice Magnus]. It was not a particularly good book; but it contained a long introduction by D. H. Lawrence, who, while admitting that Douglas had 'never let me down', produced one of his caricature-portraits in which he described Douglas as mean, greedy, and offensive at table. Douglas, taken aback by the portrait, replied in a pamphlet entitled *D. H. Lawrence and Maurice Magnus*, with a mild defence of his conduct and attitude towards

Magnus. So matters stood, there being some disagreement about the relative quality of attack and defence.

Six years later, in 1931, came the tribute by Tomlinson. It began in the most challenging manner by saying that 'Classification has its disadvantages'.

Because of it, a contemporary novelist, let me say D. H. Lawrence, will be called a 'master', and 'the greatest of modern writers', and will be even gravely contemplated as a momentous advent, the most poignant expression of soul since nobody knows when; one severely analytical critic thought that Christ would be the nearest comparison. D. H. Lawrence, known as a novelist, in consequence received a wide and fixed attention, an attention both serious and fervid. His name is able to evoke the same mystical homage and fierce opposition as Gandhi's. On the other hand Norman Douglas, who has given us some of the best narrative prose we have had this century, has had scant consideration except for his dubious gift for throwing from innocent words shadows with apparently accidental yet embarrassing outlines, and as that happens too often in his books for accident to be more likely than devilment, it has attracted some peculiar and expectant notice. No critic, however, has declared the body of the serious work of the author of *Old Calabria* to be worth more than a severely brief if favourable expert opinion, though beside it Lawrence's *Sea and Sardinia* is mainly the captiousness of an avid adolescent with a queasy mind.

I do not think it is at any time good criticism to praise one writer at the expense of another; and this attack on Lawrence came when Lawrence was being hysterically exalted. It was therefore inopportune, as well as impolitic. Looking back upon the episode in 1937, Tomlinson remarked: 'The critics *flew* at it. It did Douglas not a penn'orth of good and me harm.'

Yes, it did Tomlinson harm, because from that loyal and unguarded moment his own work was dismissed as trivial by what I had demanded as the 'new criticism'. Enemies gathered about him for the first time. Not until he was eighty was he again highly praised in the press; and then, of course, it was too late. His strength was exhausted. Almost his last letter to me, undated, and for the first time unsteadily written, said:

I'd much prefer to talk to you than to write. The last is labour, and the other is fun. We hope Mary, and all of you, are now untroubled by any of the 1000 various ills to which we are heirs. You have been in mind a lot, lately, but far off. Never mind. We know you, and are sure of your bright eye and understanding.

And in the last of all, accepting an invitation to lunch in town which he has to attend by taxi: 'We two only. I want to look you in the eye.'

This is a book of personal gossip, and not a critical study; so I shall say nothing in detail of Tomlinson's work, and attempt no analytical valuation of it. I want only to say here that if those who attacked his rueful story of the inter-war period, *The Day Before* (they surprisingly included Hugh Walpole), had heard his innocent voice, which was quiet and rather hoarse, with, nevertheless, a curious fluty note, they would have discounted the ferocity of the words I have quoted. Being a Cockney, he had no sympathy with Lawrence's immoderate angers. Since Douglas was equally unspectacular in style, and, whatever his faults, an original, Douglas was his man. Some have questioned Douglas's scholarship. Tomlinson was aware only of the rich, naughty irony conveyed with such stealth that more superficial minds either missed or resented it. Lawrence had savaged and caricatured Douglas: was he to be allowed to do this as a privilege, without counter? But Douglas was what Lawrence called himself, 'a giraffe'; so was Tom-linson. They were two giraffes, in fact, for whom the tide of opinion made no allowance. Whether that tide will turn, I cannot say; if it does, we shall be back at George Sainsbury's dictum, 'the one question of criticism is, "Has the man done what he wanted to do, and done it well?" '

My third journalist is James Bone, who when asked to name his place of education replied 'Glasgow'. Bone died in 1962 after celebrating his ninetieth birthday, when, besides receiving a telegram of congratulation from the Queen, he was given a luncheon and praised as highly in the American press as in his own paper *The Manchester Guardian*, now, to my regret, *The Guardian* only. He, too, was one of those quiet originals who thought less of their superiority to other men than of service to his paper and his readers.

His book, *The London Perambulator*, is a classic of wisdom and easy narrative. It is also an illustration of the fact that while London is overwhelming in its production of poets, the prose writers who have celebrated its marvels, always excepting Dekker and Lamb, have reached the capital from elsewhere. Leigh Hunt can just claim to have been born in its environs. Johnson, Dickens, Neil Lyons, made it their home as in these days Gerard Fay is so wittily doing. The explanation is simple. Henry James, another sojourner from elsewhere, said:

Many may call London dreary, stupid, dull, inhuman, vulgar. But I take it as an artist and a bachelor; as one who has the passion of observation and whose business is the study of human life. It is the biggest aggregation of human life— the most complete compendium of the world.

I notice this fact, that the true-born Londoner, although he may be curious about other cities, and certainly takes pride in the city of his birth, does not as a rule take seriously the lesser local prides which give provincials intense concern. As a child and a choir boy from the age of six I walked backwards and forwards to the church of St Mary, Aldermanbury (which has a bust of Shakespeare in its garden), through Smithfield and Newgate Street and Cheapside; as a boy I trudged through the City streets delivering copies of periodicals published by Hay

Nisbet & Co.; at various times from the age of four onwards I have lived in Clerkenwell and Bloomsbury and made excursions to many suburbs; but of London as a whole I know almost nothing. The place is too large for comprehension by the unleisured many.

Its size was no handicap to James Bone, who came from a travelling family. His brothers were Muirhead, the artist, and David, who commanded a great liner and wrote one novel of quality, *The Brassbounder*. These two were as different as possible from James; but unity prevailed among them, and they associated as often as their occupations allowed. In latter days, when their wives and Muirhead were dead, James and David even set up house together in Surrey, to which county writers and seamen appear to gravitate. It was always a noble experience to talk with them; David hiding his humour behind the dignity, almost solemnity, of a commander, James with the twinkle of a man to whom the world, as Stevenson said Sainte-Beuve thought it, was 'a single great book'. 'It seemed all one to Sainte-Beuve,' said Stevenson, 'whether you should read in Chapter XX, which is the differential calculus, or in Chapter XXIX, which is hearing the band play in the gardens.'

It was David who, when an ignorant intellectual, having misread the title of his novel, sought information about the moulding of brass, roared out: 'I'm a seaman; not a bloody printer's devil!' It was James who invented the tale, which has gone round the world, of a cat in Charing Cross Post Office that obligingly licked stamps for the customers. James also told how, having picked up in the gutter one night the London correspondent of a distant newspaper and taken him home in a cab to an ungrateful and suspicious wife, suddenly thought: 'Good heavens! In that state he can't have sent off tonight's letter!' Busy with kindness, he wrote at speed, and despatched, a substitute letter.

The man came to him forty-eight hours later completely bewildered by word from his editor that no fewer than *three* letters had turned up that day, all so excellent that it had been hard to decide which of them to print. The first was the man's own, sent before carouse disabled him; the third was the work of yet another benevolent friend, who had seen the correspondent reeling. I hope, indeed I feel sure, that Bone's was the winning entry.

It so happened that I was responsible for the publication by Chatto & Windus of David Bone's post-war history, *Merchantmen-at-Arms*, which had magnificent illustrations by Muirhead. One day the brothers crowded into my little office like the Three Musketeers in Henry Hamilton's melodrama, looking in their several ways like schoolboys out for a holiday. They sat beaming at me as we all talked at once. Finally they asked me to dinner that night. I was engaged. Their smiles yielded to concern. One of them, probably Muirhead, said mournfully—half reproachfully: 'You don't often get a chance of dining with all three of us at once.' All nodded in apparent melancholy. Of course I cancelled my engagement. We dined at Simpsons, in the Strand, my recollection being that over a dozen people sat round as happy a table as I ever saw, and that every one, except myself, was a Bone. Surrounded by Bones!

One other dinner I remember was that given to celebrate Tomlinson's seventieth birthday. Those who were to propose the hero's health were James Bone and myself, and we accordingly flanked Tomlinson at a table spread between two other long tables. But in fact everybody spoke. Everybody insisted upon speaking. Far down one of the long tables sat David; and he spoke. He had pronounced only four or five droll, weighty sentences when a note from James was passed to him. He paused, gravely said: 'I take no notice of notes sent by young brothers,' and continued speaking. As he finished, he remembered the note. 'Now let's see what my young brother said.' The note was opened. It contained the words: 'Speak up. We can't hear you.'

When William McFee visited England some years ago, he stayed with the brothers at Farnham, and as he was anxious to see me he wrote asking me to telephone if he might come over to lunch. James answered the telephone: 'We'll come, too,' said he. In consequence David, ever the commander, took entire charge of the proceedings. McFee, hampered by deafness, could be communicated with only by the written word. It was David who brought the magic slate from which words were obliterated by the movement of a shutter; it was David who wrote the messages; it was David and James who did the talking. McFee found himself back at Farnham having exchanged not a single word with me. This was the true Bone touch; and it was delightful.

Last among my journalists who also by writing books influenced their age comes Philip Gibbs. He died in 1962 at the age of eighty-four, having grown more and more frail as the months passed, with ever-increasing and alarming difficulty in breathing. There was never any failure of memory, and to the end his talk was a stimulation to all who heard it. He was not a wit; he spoke (in what he described as 'my sepulchral voice') with a fastidious drawl which was not in the least affected; his manners were perfect; and he could draw from every allusion some episode—always an amusing episode—of the past which was as fresh in the last months of life as it must have been when it occurred.

His was the well-filled mind of the ever-observant journalist. He recalled how once, at a royal occasion, he slipped under a rope which was being stretched to separate distinguished guests from the herd (a French ambassador being less adroit than he), and found himself walking with Queen Alexandra. The Queen, assuming him to be at least a diplomat, entered into conversation, was enchanted at being able to hear his resonant voice, and, on a later occasion, greeted him as an old acquaintance. He remembered how the wife of an improvident man educated all her children by means of superlative, supposedly secret, begging letters to her husband's friends. He described his own ingenuous, ingenious part in the siege of Sydney Street; and how as a very young man indeed he over-reached Arnold Bennett in a matter of price; and how he was engaged and dismissed as literary editor of *The Daily Mail*—'You're sacked';—and how on refusing to commend the Baconian theory for another journalistic boss he was again 'sacked'. He also recalled a remarkable occasion when, at the time of the Crippen Case, in company with J. P. Eddy (afterwards Recorder of West Ham), he talked and listened for days with Miss Le Neve, who was found not guilty of complicity in the murder of Belle Elmore.

Memory of those days never left him. He conceived great respect, even admiration, for Miss Le Neve, and was particularly impressed by the fact that although suffering from strong emotion, and even weeping as she spoke, she could not restrain laughter at recollected absurdities. He told me this whole story during a long taxi-ride which we took together to Waterloo Station. It was enthralling. It lasted throughout the journey, at the end of which I found that the taxi-man, too, owing to an open window and the penetrating power of Gibbs's voice, had been enthralled. He glowed with excitement, almost with affection, as he received his fare. He said breathlessly: 'Thank you, sir. And I 'ope you 'ave a *very* 'appy journey!' No better testimony to Gibbs's superlative story-telling gift could have been given.

In print, this great gift was dimmed. Gibbs typed straight on to the machine, the letters of which, owing to partial blindness, he could not see. Speed, facility, and avoidance of the disagreeable gave his novels great popularity with running readers but made them colourless and even sentimental. The value of these books, as I have already suggested in *Background with Chorus*, is that they concern themselves, impartially, with events recent in the hours of their composition. And I say 'hours' because Gibbs would often, as he grew old, lament that he had no theme for another novel, and three weeks later, when asked if he had found one, would gaily answer: 'My dear feller, I've written half the book.' He claimed no importance for anything he did except the war correspondence of 1914–18; yet the books were widely read to the last, and they may be significant to future generations wanting to know what topics mattered most to normal people at particular moments in our age.

Pursuing accuracy, Gibbs flew in his late seventies with test pilots, or travelled headlong (as he had done all his life) to distant places where things were being made or done to change the face of civilization. So parchment pale that one dreaded lest he should become transparent by the next visit; looking like the ghost of a strikingly handsome old actor with his hat very slightly cocked down towards the blind eye, he would scramble across ditches while one watched him in trepidation. 'My dear feller, I couldn't *see*!' he would explain when rebuked for recklessness. But he had not fallen. His feet were always on the ground, and his interest in life and current literature never faded.

He did not greatly admire some modern writers; yet he conscientiously read them. In calm accents he would say, of one, 'The first book was moderately good; the second inferior; the third no good at all,' and of a much extolled work by a young woman, 'It's really the filthiest book I ever read.' No moral indignation marred the judgment; I do not think he could be shocked; his views were not amplified, nor Olympian, he merely stated his natural reaction as a professional.

Always in search of essential facts, he would summon, and question, those who had taken part in actual events. He was doing this to within a week of his death. From his twenty-first year he had talked with innumerable distinguished persons, from General Smuts to Sir Winston Churchill, from French and American generals and diplomats to every odd customer and almost every child whom he met on the lanes about his home in a Surrey village. All were free of his company; all trusted him; all nourished his mind.

One story which amused him in the last years was the sequel to a lunch with Lord Samuel at a Chelsea restaurant loved by Gibbs. The two men had lingered over coffee until the other patrons were gone; and at last Lord Samuel also went, leaving Gibbs, as host, to the waiter. A stranger, the only other person remaining in the restaurant, paused at Gibbs's table on the way out. He had recognized Lord Samuel, who at ninety-odd years of age looked much as he had done half a century earlier.

'What an extraordinary man he is!' exclaimed the stranger.

'Most extraordinary,' agreed Gibbs.

'The finest brain—one of the two finest brains—in England,' said the stranger.

'Yes,' agreed Gibbs. 'Who is the other?'

'Yourself, sir.'

Greatly tickled, for he had been referred to in print by an affectionate cousin as having no brains at all, Gibbs answered: 'Do you know who I am?'

'No,' said the stranger. 'I said that to be on the safe side.'

Brains, however, are not the only criterion of quality. Gibbs's genius lay in something rarer still, which is called sympathy. Children appreciated this at sight, and were as happy in his company as he was in theirs. My own daughter, when two years old, and after they had played at ball together in the garden of our cottage, was one of those who took him to their hearts. As he sat indoors afterwards, talking to me, she stood by his side, and at last, in spite of congenital fastidiousness, could not resist the inclination to ruffle his hair. She never did this, or anything like it, to another visitor. It was a spontaneous movement of love and trust.

Perhaps I should say that Lady Gibbs had contributed to the atmosphere of kindness; for a part of their game in the garden had been the placing of a rather dusty tennis ball on the brim of her hat (she, meanwhile, conversing with my wife), from which it bounced very amusingly. Only at the end of the visit did we learn that the hat was a new one, worn that afternoon for the first time.

As it was with children, so it was with grown-ups. We did not ruffle his hair; he and I did not even shake hands; but when we learned by telephone of his death my wife and I were silent, stricken with a grief which has been rare in our lives.

Apostles of Culture

•

13 SHORTLY before the end of his first term at Cambridge, after impressive success at Eton, John Maynard Keynes received a mysterious visit, says his biographer Roy Harrod, from two fellow-undergraduates, Lytton Strachey and Leonard Woolf. They came as representatives of the Apostles, to see whether Keynes was worthy of election to the society. As might be expected, for he was the ablest and most brilliant of those who afterwards became known as the Bloomsbury set, he was found worthy. From that time onward he joined with the other members in discussing the universe and planning its improvement.

Young men have done the same thing through the ages, presumably before Universities were founded, but certainly from days before the Reformation. I must admit that I am hazy about what happened in pre-Reformation days; but one has only to read Erasmus or the delightfully burlesque *Epistolae Obscurorum Virorem* to feel sure that when youngsters with brains or education, or both, are brought into close daily contact their wits are stimulated to an extraordinary degree. Like the sentry in *Iolanthe*, they 'think of things that would astonish you'.

The Apostles rejoiced in these wits and the thoughts they gave rise to. It never occurred to them that other young men, elsewhere, had comparable wits and thoughts just as magnificent; it never does, fortunately, to any young man. If he is not sure of his own superiority to the rest of mankind, past and present, before the age of twenty-five he will do nothing whatever in life. He has not learnt, by rubbing against those of different upbringing and experience, how small his capacity will prove in its struggle with human ambition, stupidity, and folly; but he does learn all the arts of debate, and is ready to put every one of his seniors right upon every subject known to man.

Keynes illustrated this trait a little later, when at the age of twenty-four he was for a time at the India Office. He said:

> I am bored nine-tenths of the time and rather unreasonably irritated the other tenth when I can't have my own way. It's maddening to have thirty people who can reduce you to impotence when you're quite sure you are right.

This is the eternal cry of eager self-confident youth making its first contact with the adult world. In 1907, when Keynes wrote, older men still had rights and power. They might be stupid, obstinate, or fearful of decision; but they were seniors, and they could not be thrust aside by an impetuous, imperious child, fresh from Cambridge, who believed he knew best.

Even in earlier days, Keynes (who was so bright and quick that he often criticized himself) glimpsed a possibility which, after seeing a Shaw play in 1905, he mentioned to Lytton Strachey.

> Is it monomania [he asked]—this colossal moral superiority we feel? I get the feeling that most of the rest never see anything at all—too stupid or too wicked.

He was half-right in the feeling of mass-stupidity; his comments in more ambitious writings such as *The Economic Consequences of the Peace* (1919) show far-reaching insight into character, and it seems to me that he was justified in his impatience with the insensate folly of the human species. But Keynes was the Apostle who went out into the world, and learned from it at first hand. He did not get lost; he went before; and the others did not follow.

They stayed in their closets, continuing to meet, to talk, and to be to the end an immaculate body of adolescents. They saw none but men and women of their own social class, none who did not share their restricted but highly cultivated interests; and they continued to believe that those not in the charmed circle were inferiors to be shunned lest they spoiled the perfection of a dream. Strachey himself had what he called his Castle in Spain, a house in which they should all live together, writing, painting, criticizing each other 'without reserve'.

Of this band of world-shunners the dominant figure was unquestionably to be Lytton Strachey, that long, emaciated figure whose sprawling relaxation is so perfectly shown in the painting by Lambe which is to be seen in the National Portrait Gallery. I have written about Strachey's work in a former book, *The Georgian Literary Scene*, and I do not wish to repeat the criticism here, especially as my opinion of that work has slightly declined in the past thirty years; but subsequent reading, in the Life of Keynes by Roy Harrod, Keynes's *Two Memoirs*, Leonard Woolf's *Sowing*, Virginia Woolf's *A Writer's Diary*, and *Virginia Woolf and Lytton Strachey: Letters* has shed additional light upon a singular personality.

He was the son of a soldier, Lieut-General Sir Richard Strachey, who, having served with distinction in India, spent a sedentary old age undisturbed by the clamour of ten boisterously-intelligent children. Lytton had teased and amused his brothers and sisters since boyhood, and, thus practised, knew all the arts of caustic comment and the springing of surprise. It is said that while his manner was outwardly diffident he deeply appreciated the mystifying power of silence over more ebullient persons; and after sitting in apparent meditation among busily talking friends he would suddenly explode into incalculable witticism or profundity—I suppose upon something said earlier by one or other of his companions, but certainly with the object of disconcerting hearers. He called his grimmer silences 'death packets', which indicates their intention.

Strachey's voice was normally low; but in discussion or elaboration it would fly up to a strange falsetto which some describe as a squeak, and certain curious changes of stress, as well as the speed with which he gathered phrases, gave his speech a character which unfriendly ears found affected. The falsetto, or squeak, being infectious, became habitual with attendant males, so that it was afterwards known as 'the Bloomsbury voice'. I have heard it used by non-Blooms-buryites, always accompanied by a grimace expressing intellectual self-amusement, and whether or not it is a sign of conceit I have found it, in moderation, not disagreeable. In Strachey's case it accompanied wit.

At some time he decided, according to Keynes, that

> certain Latin technical terms of sex were the correct words to use, that to avoid them was a grave error, and, when in mixed company, a weakness, and the use of other synonyms a vulgarity. But I should certainly say that this was later [than the early undergraduate days]. In 1903 these words were not even esoteric terms of common discourse.

No doubt the decision to use them came after Strachey had completed what modern writers call the *persona* which he wished his contemporaries to accept. He was always a sick man, without physical energy, and much calculation occurred behind that inescapable languor.

The calculation was revealed in his writing, where he carefully chose incidents in the lives of four eminent Victorians, and quotations from what they had said, with the object of staining an entire age. 'Is it prejudice, do you think,' he asked Virginia Woolf, long before he produced the book which made his reputation, 'that makes us hate the Victorians, or is it the truth of the case? They seem to me a set of mouthing, bungling hypocrites.'

He thought them hypocrites, because his dream was of a literature which should 'pour from the press reeking with all the filth of Petronius, all the frenzy of Dostoevsky, all the romance of the Arabian Nights, and all the exquisiteness of Voltaire'. 'At *last* it'll tell the truth, and be indecent, and amusing, and romantic, and even (after about 100 years) be written well.' By comparison with such joys, Victorian writers did indeed seem stuffy and Victorian heroes solemn to the point of ridiculousness. They had lived among horsehair and mahogany; they had observed Sunday as a day of gloom and over-eating. They had professed to believe in God; it was their notion to lead and teach others to lead Christian lives; but for the sake of self-advancement they were ready to sacrifice in secret and for a consideration every principle they held. To Strachey, all were Pecksniffs.

When brooding in some of his silences, he saw what a splendid joke it would be to expose them, not with the hollow rant of Carlyle or the easy emotionalism of Dickens and Thackeray, but with the superlative irony, the mock simplicity, of Voltaire. The idea, at first sportively entertained, grew stronger the more it was considered. At last it took possession of his mind. Who among typical Victorians best deserved his hate? Which of them could be made most completely ludicrous?

Strachey's knowledge of the Victorian age in England was much smaller than his knowledge of the literature of eighteenth-century France; but memoirs of the chief Victorian figures lay readily to hand, full of delicious pickings for the artist whose mind, rejoicing in Voltairean anti-Clericalism, was essentially nonconformist. The Church was no longer a persecuting force; its tyranny had been watered down by the rationalism of the eighteenth century and the respectability of the nineteenth. To cry *ecrasez l'infame* would be grotesque; how much more amusing to make ardent supporters of the Christian virtues laughable. He did this with deliberate malice. He was a reformer.

Now Thomas Arnold was the man who developed what was most formidable to the rebel in our Public School system. His reputation for Christian example was so widespread that in 1914, when my mother arranged for a young girl to 'live in' as housemaid, the girl's father, a window-cleaner, called one evening to see me. He was slightly tipsy; but, saying that he knew his daughter would be safe in my charge, he concluded with a fine peroration: '*I* know a gentleman when I see one. *I* know what Arnold of Rugby means.'

Arnold of Rugby, then, meant for Strachey the acme of priggishness. Arnold would not have approved the filth of Petronius, the frenzy of Dostoevsky, the romance of the Arabian Nights, and the exquisiteness of Voltaire. Moreover Arnold's son, Matthew, had been a prince among School Inspectors, a man of strict loyalty to the Establishment, who praised Hellenism as the gospel of sweetness and light; and as Strachey, according to Leonard Woolf, concealed 'behind the gentleness, the nervousness, and the cynicism ... very considerable passions', his hostility to the Arnolds was instinctive. Thomas Arnold was his predestined victim.

Another was Cardinal Manning, who could be contrasted with a man of much finer spirit and intellect, John Henry Newman. The comparison of Manning and Newman in Strachey's essay is the most brilliant of all his performances. It almost justifies Virginia Woolf's inclusion of him in her curious list of approvable novelists—Lawrence, Joyce, Forster, Strachey, and Eliot;—when in fact Strachey's novels were daydreams which he could not write down because, he said, they were 'too *scabreux*'. Such a contrast of one man, one way of living, with all the heroic virtues of the pacifist, would have been, to one less indolent than Strachey, a splendid theme for fiction; if he had so used it, he would have become, at a stroke, the most popular novelist in England, where sympathy with the loser, or under-dog, is all-powerful. He preferred to remain safely in the study, among books. But although he preferred Newman to Manning he did not therefore write his essay about Newman. That would have nullified his hatred for the Victorians and blunted the poignard he used against Manning. Success was complete; Manning became contemptible thenceforward.

In 1943 and 1944, when Strachey had been dead for more than twenty years, two articles were printed, the first in *The Cambridge Review*, the second, by request of Wilson Harris, the then editor, in *The Spectator*. Both were by F. A. Simpson, an historian whose two books about Napoleon III (especially *The Rise of Louis Napoleon*) are among the best of all modern biographies. The writer, an English Churchman, had taken the trouble to check every strand of the material used by Strachey in this Manning essay. He showed, I think convincingly, that Strachey's bias had led him to misrepresent the crucial episode in Manning's life—his submission to Rome.

Strachey's aim was to show Manning as a man of overwhelming ambition. He accused him of changing his faith in assurance of a glittering reward, of having, while still an English Archdeacon, seen the Pope and been promised great advancement if he apostatized. 'Precisely what passed on that occasion never transpired,' said Strachey, with naughty innuendo. 'One would be glad to know what precisely passed at that mysterious interview. . . . It is easy to imagine . . .' etc. But Simpson contradicted both innuendo and 'imagining'. His explanation was that Manning was sent to Rome in May, 1848, to obtain Papal approval of a translation into Italian of Sir Charles Trevelyan's pamphlet on English famine relief for Ireland. The mission was executed. There was nothing 'mysterious' about it. In the very 'Journal' quoted by Strachey, and in a further account dictated by Manning to his secretary which was printed in a book named by Strachey as one of his authorities, appeared every detail of the audience. There was thus no ground for Strachey's charge of calculated apostasy.

I know nothing about this matter. I take the criticism from F. A. Simpson's *Spectator* article, which, if it is correct, explains why, for all his brilliance and amusingness, Strachey was not admired by men able to estimate the travesty of Victorian principles and manners. That this travesty was influential is certain. It was a part of neo-Georgian fashion; and it belonged to the same destructive order as that by which satire replaced what Wilde, a rather soiled Victorian, described with admiration as the virtues of the poor—charity, kindness, and sensitiveness.

It may be that those virtues are not virtues at all, but hypocrisies. Wilde was 'a lord of language'; and when he praised the poor he was smarting under the ostracism of his own class. 'With people of our rank,' said he, 'prison makes a man a pariah.' 'In the eyes of the poor prison is a tragedy in a man's life, a misfortune, a casualty, something that calls for sympathy in others.' Discount the comparison as one may, it is a charge of cold-heartedness against the *ton*.

Wilde felt as quick a disdain as Strachey for bad writing. He had as great a regard for what he called 'women of culture and position'. He was not ready to martyr himself for the sake of sincerity. And yet his wit was markedly free from what members of the Labour Party call 'denigration'. So was the laughter of those journalists of whom I wrote in the last chapter. They did not fail to notice pomposity and humbug; they regarded these as belonging to the nature of man, about which they had learned, not from books, but by actual contact.

I have not hidden my preference for humour to wit, 'with its faithful attendant, ill-nature'. Shakespeare and Jane Austen ridiculed; but nobody questions their sweetness and wisdom, which are qualities as rare as nectar; and nobody calls them soft. The laughter of Bloomsbury was always salted with derision. I have quoted a remark of my own to Hugh Walpole, to the effect that I admired but did not like Bloomsbury; and the chief exponent of the Bloomsbury spirit was Lytton Strachey. I wonder whether my present readers have seen the letters exchanged between him and Virginia Woolf? They were published in 1956, and they are full of interest for students. It seems clear to me that of the two Strachey was the dominant and less attractive personality. I shall try to explain this view by reference to the letters.

It is Strachey who dangles before his friend the charms of lasciviousness, the filth of Petronius, the romance of the Arabian Nights (presumably in the French translation of Mardrus, published between 1899 and 1904), and his own meditated but unwritten novel, in which the scenes are 'a little too *scabreux*', and in which even the footman and prostitutes are amazing. Virginia Woolf responds to these 'exacerbating' visions (the word is Strachey's) with a satirical reference to pure English maidens, 'among whom I have no right to class myself', and references to the unemptied W.C. in the hotel at Tarragona where she was spending her honeymoon, and in the streets the naked boys 'balancing their buttocks in the pellucid air', but such coarsenesses occur only in the letters to Strachey. Her Diary, where she spoke to herself, is the work of a different person. My suggestion is that in the letters she made a wholly feminine effort to rise to Strachey's level of free speech as described by Keynes.

They were evidently congenial to each other as talkers, and I think Virginia Stephen, as she was before marriage, besides being fascinated by Strachey's oddities of manner and startling eruptions from cryptic silence, was flattered by his friendship. When, in 1909, he proposed marriage to her she at once accepted; only to learn within a few hours that the thought of any such union had become repulsive to him. 'Her sense was amazing,' Strachey wrote to a brother. Her sense was that of an exceptional woman, proud beyond his power of comprehension, who could never have stooped to protest. This is shown by the fact that she remained his affectionate and admiring friend to the last, her final letter, written in 1928, being one of great sincerity. Their bond was playful disdain for lesser men and women; and, in both, the disdain arose from a timidity which produced estrangement from the world at large.

Many years ago (in 1938) I read some words by another writer, Christopher Isherwood, which impressed me as an illumination of this estrangement on the part of the intellectually segregated few. The passage occurs in Isherwood's autobiographical work *Lions and Shadows*, and it describes a self-conscious young man's reactions to the ways of ordinary holiday-makers in, I think, the Isle of Wight. He has been, of course, contemptuous of those ways.

But beneath all my note-taking, my would-be scientific detachment, my hatred, my disgust, there was the old sense of exclusion, the familiar grudging envy. For, however I might sneer, these people were evidently enjoying themselves in their own mysterious fashion, and why was it so mysterious to me?...Why couldn't I—the would-be novelist, the professional observer—understand them? Why didn't I

know—not coldly from the outside, but intuitively, sympathetically, from within—what makes them perform their
grave ritual of pleasure?

There is a problem here. The journalists I named were
natural 'mixers' with all types. It was their duty as journalists
to go everywhere and be in accord with those they met. When
Tomlinson berthed with the second mate of the steamer
Capella en route for Central America he was at one with the
crew. When Philip Gibbs interviewed Ethel Le Neve he took
with him no preconceptions. He felt that, as Maugham said,
'there was neither good nor evil here. There was life.' Such
experiences had nothing to do with culture in the Bloomsbury
sense; but both men were increasing their knowledge, and,
accordingly, our knowledge, of mankind and the universe.
They left to philosophers the task of generalization.

I have never underestimated the value of generalization, or
the delights of intellectual activity. Metaphysics, like Mysticism
and Mathematics, cannot be denied a priceless charm. I do
no more than indicate the problem of experience versus
non-experience. Virginia Woolf wrote in her Diary: 'I can't
imagine what goes on behind faces.' And again, 'I can make up
situations, but I cannot make up plots.'

In this dilemma E. M. Forster supplied help. He said: 'Yes—
oh dear yes—the novel tells a story . . . I wish that it were not so,
that it could be something different—melody, or perception of
the truth, not this low atavistic form.' In these words Forster
reassured all the bookish people who 'cannot make up plots'.
The term 'a mere story-teller' became thereafter an easy term
of reproach for those who, seeing life as a vast reservoir of
stories about human beings, give us our deepest insights into
character.

We are an injured body [wrote Jane Austen]. Although
our productions have afforded more extensive and unaffected pleasure than those of any other literary corporation
in the world, no species of composition has been so much
decried. From pride, ignorance, or fashion, our foes are

almost as many as our readers; and while the abilities of the nine-hundredth abridger of the History of England, or the man who collects and publishes in a volume some dozen lines of Milton, Pope, and Prior, with a page from *The Spectator*, and a chapter from Sterne, are eulogised by a thousand pens, there seems almost a general wish of decrying the capacity and undervaluing the labour of the novelist, and of slighting the performances which have only genius, wit, and taste to recommend them.

If you have little experience of life, stories do not flow into your mind. If you dwell in the study, or exclusively in the company of intellectual equals, you miss all contact with the passions and follies of those who make up your species. Are such common and distressing phenomena worthy of your attention? You have a more celestial aim, the analysis of forces, the theory of government, the construction of a universal ethic. But Shakespeare told stories (sometimes not very good ones), and made them tragically moving; Jane Austen told stories in which new chapters and new wisdoms reward the twentieth or thirtieth reading; Dickens, whom Virginia Woolf said she would not cross the street to meet, endlessly explored Henry James's 'biggest aggregation of human life—the most complete compendium of the world', and lived in an exultation of story. Do not these three alone justify dramatic narrative?

My belief is that the reason why Virginia Woolf could not 'imagine what goes on behind faces' was that her terms of reference were all literary. She saw life at second-hand, or, like the young Christopher Isherwood, from a disapproving distance which she could never bridge. She perceived and convincingly recorded the weakness of a man like Lowes Dickinson, whose book *The Greek View of Life* so strongly influenced Forster:

> Goldie depresses me unspeakably. Always alone on a mountain top asking himself how to live, theorizing about life; never living. . . . Always live in the whole, live in the

one: always Shelley and Goethe, and then he loses his hot water bottle; and never notices a face or a cat or a dog or a flower, except in the flow of the universal. This explains why his high-minded books are unreadable.

Her own vision was poetic. She had the compensations of that vision and the society of a narrow circle. Yet there must be something wrong in an intellectualism which baulks comprehension of the unintellectual. 'I can't imagine what goes on behind faces.' She knew what went on in her own mind; but she would not have crossed the street to shake hands with Dickens. 'Dickens,' said E. M. Forster, 'is actually one of our big writers.' Was not Virginia Woolf, in supposing that the unintellectual deserves no respect, making a compensatory assumption, which is really self-defensive?

As long as outside opinion did not intrude, she was happy in her dreams and in what she called 'saying some very sharp things'. 'I don't want "a philosophy" in the least.' She resented Lawrence's 'schoolboy tweaking and smacking of anyone opposed to him; Lytton, Bertie, Squire'. She resented criticism of herself—'in one's strained state any fly has liberty to settle and it's always the gadfly'; but she was an acute critic of others, dead and living—if they were outside the ever-charming circle in which, long ago, she had been treated 'like a spoilt monkey'.

That circle meant everything to her, from security to a field for her sharp sayings. She sometimes talked with visitors breathing a similarly rarefied atmosphere, such as Victoria Sackville-West and Rose Macaulay; but more robust contemporaries, who did not come as Hugh Walpole did to worship a Sybil, remained unknown. She apparently never met Wells or Shaw; she had only once a few minutes in the company of Arnold Bennett, when, according to her Diary, she and David Cecil 'teased him' very condescendingly. By this account Bennett behaved with characteristic forbearance: had he 'teased' back she would have thought it an outrage. At his death, while repeating the snob *clichés* about his vulgarity and brassiness, she could not deny a feeling of sadness and unwilling respect for his integrity. Otherwise her reference to Galsworthy as 'that stark man' shows ignorance, and other comments show that her inventiveness as well as her understanding would have been enriched by wider contacts. What a pity she could not mix with the untouchables! Arnold Bennett used to say 'nine out of ten people improve on better acquaintance'.

Instead, she remained aloof, telling herself that she must follow her own path, as all original minds must do, but filled with melancholy, 'making up' her stories while looking at the fire or sitting in a garden, picturing delightful scenes as a fanciful child does in reverie, enjoying at Rodmell, in Sussex, the sense of sanctuary but always in terror of loneliness and increased dislike of what she called hierarchy and the patriarchy. It was an interesting mind; and the strongest impression one gains from her Diary is pathos.

One of the Moral Rearmament leaders composed an aphorism: 'It is the banana wot leaves the bunch that gets skinned.' The inference from this aphorism was that we must all stick together; it is disproved by the case of John Maynard Keynes, the ablest as well as the most ambitious of the apostolic group which allowed its reasonings to be dominated by the philosophy of G. E. Moore. Having done brilliantly at Eton, he was rightly seen by the group as an intellectual asset. He was also extraordinarily independent. He therefore scoffed, later on, at Moore, as he did at Henry Sidgwick, a former idol of eager Cambridge undergraduate philosophers. He would not be bound by old loyalties; he could not remain a Bloomsburyite.

His associates watched anxiously as he strayed into the larger world of politics, finance, and public affairs. Roy Harrod says they were delighted by 'his sallies against the great and pompous', as they must have been delighted by the journalistic ventures which gave them successive 'platforms'; for the sallies were after their own hearts and the employments afforded were necessary to them in a normally philistine region. Nevertheless they were disquieted at losing his devoted attention. Virginia Woolf wrote to Strachey in 1919:

> Maynard seems much the same as ever only more and more genial, and, superficially, kind. I suppose the danger lies in becoming too kind . . . still, kindness doesn't flourish in our corner of Sussex.

There is great meaning in these sentences. First, she is writing to Strachey, and must therefore eschew kindness. Second, she is afraid of the thought which has occurred to her that Keynes, after all, was finding the world more interesting than his old friends. If for 'more and more genial' one reads 'more indifferent to us' or 'more ready to compromise with those whom we don't approve, or even with the Devil', we perceive the concern underlying affectionate words. To extremely intelligent people the spiritual corruption of politics, where expediency rules, is vile and frightening.

Keynes did not see in the corruption of others any danger to his own integrity. He did see the lack of principle as ruinous to the Peace Conference of 1919. He went farther. Owing to abnormal quickness of mind, and a rare ability to estimate conflicts of character, he dramatized the chicane of political leaders at Versailles. His portraits of Wilson, Clemenceau, and Lloyd George are superb; he saw that the consequences to mankind of what they did and failed to do would be tragic. He was powerless to influence events; his power lay in analysis. The consequences proved tragic.

Keynes read deeper than politics, into failures in leadership and, finally, into the horrifying weakness of human nature under stress. By comparison with this brilliant dramatization, the dreams of Virginia Woolf and the anti-Victorian preoccupations of Lytton Strachey seem trivial. Keynes was an economist; but although he dealt detachedly with this one aspect of affairs in which he was a master, his true interest was in life. It engrossed him. He could be 'more and more genial', and 'superficially kind'; but that was because his intelligence had altogether left the study and the debating society. He was working on the plane of tragedy. There were obviously no Gods among his Dynasts; there were superlatively crafty men outwitting a distinguished simpleton, and so fully committed to manœuvre that they sacrificed the destiny of peoples to immediate purposes. 1939 was the inevitable consequence of 1919.

Besides making contact with power, Keynes did other things which removed him from Bloomsbury. He made a great fortune by the most astute financial dealings; and he married a lovely genius of the Russian ballet, Madame Lydia Lopokova. Engrossment in great affairs, as I have said, stimulated his good humour; the discovery of one secret of happiness carried that good humour to the skies. To the joys of vivid activity was joined the rapture of wedding an enchantress. Love sustained him; activity killed him.

It is said by all that Keynes was often 'rude'; so were others of his generation, and so, with less excuse, are many of his juniors; it is a disease of arrogance in the modern age. It was exasperating to him to be opposed by men of slower wit; but very few of the quick-witted have that divine gift, patience. He wanted things done at once. He was not a self-made boss, or a bully; he saw far ahead, and he was always sure that he was right. Accordingly, although he continued to be more and more kind to his old friends from Cambridge, he knew that he had grown out of their world.

This quotation from Roy Harrod's fine biography of the man explains the fact clearly. It begins by celebrating Lydia Lopokova:

> The direct expression of feeling, the spontaneity, the inventiveness, the gaiety, the queer unusual ideas, all flowed into her speech. Her aphorisms or comments, amusing, wise, or perhaps sheerly fantastic, were her offerings to the good cheer of the company. To Keynes they were meat and drink; his amusement and appreciation never flagged. Like the others, he was an aristocrat in his tastes, caring only for the best; subject to that, he was catholic. Was Bloomsbury becoming a little stereotyped? He at least delighted in novelty

and freshness. His imagination was always ready to be stirred, even by the most absurd fancy.

Lydia's method was not really compatible with what were now the fixed habits of Bloomsbury. She might make a sally. 'Oh, Lydia, how fascinating; now do you suppose that . . .' Here clearly was material for delightful dissection, gentle mockery being piled on mockery, all in the greatest good humour; this should elicit some new defensive dictum, to be thrown into the cauldron and added to the excellent dish that was being cooked up, the final elucidation of all the fantastic consequences of her line of thought, the *reductio ad absurdum* achieved with great merriment. But Lydia had not the appetite for this. . . . The flow did not appeal to her. The mordant irony of Virginia Woolf, her mocking comment, her remorselessness in defining exactly how things were, weighed on Lydia's spirits. She found these highbrows woefully depressing as a group.

America

●

14 AT THE end of 1923 it was my turn to visit the United States and send messages from various American cities to Walpole and other friends. It may give readers some notion of those days if I quote from one budget to Walpole, written on December 16th from Cincinnati.

I have had one mad rush, ever since I got to New York. I was met by Saxton and Overton, encountered Burton Rascoe during the first hour, and was thrown immediately into a lively party of the Benéts, Donald Stewart, etc. Next day more wildness, and dinner at the Cobbs'. And so ever since. I have been to all sorts of places, have spoken at the Cosmopolitan Club, N.Y. Town Hall, Columbia Univ., Yale, Northampton, and twice in Atlanta, and once at Knoxville, Tennessee. Also after lunch at Dutch Treat, Coffee House, and ½ dozen others. Awful ordeal! And been interviewed by 500 people, it seems, who ring up while I have my bath—even here. I go on to Columbus, and back to New York. I do not know what the actual true feeling is, of course, regarding my public appearances (I expect it varies with each individual, as you must have found with your own), but as far as I can judge the results are satisfactory. I won't be too sure of that. I may yet find it all a mistake. *Felix* [*Young Felix* was the full title of this novel] has had an astonishing press, and is selling rapidly. It is everywhere regarded as my best book. That, by the way, is what Arnold says it is, but few others, I believe, in England, where it is not what is wanted. . . . You will be surprised to know that at Atlanta they consider me the most *human* author they have ever met. This notwithstanding very lively and kindly recollection of H.W. I am pleased to find that these recollections of you are very widespread. Another thing, great interest in Arnold; and *Riceyman* everywhere acclaimed. . . .

I met W. L. George in New York. Hergesheimer has asked me to visit him. Marquis has lost his wife. . . . I haven't yet met Becky [Rebecca West], but she also is due back in New York next week. A party was suggested between her, Fannie Hurst, Stefansson, and me. I told Stef. I didn't mind, but that Beck might not be all agog. When Canby mentioned *Nocturne* at a lunch there was loud applause. Damn that bk. I am very tired of it.

This letter explains how it came about that I now met many of the rising American writers. I crossed the Atlantic with Willa Cather, sitting beside her at meals and discussing literature and music, as to which she was so well-informed that two men who ate opposite to us thanked me afterwards for the pleasure they had received from our conversation.

In New York, beside the Benéts (Mrs Benét was Elinor Wylie, a poet often contrasted in those days with the widely-discussed Edna St Vincent Millay), I was unexpectedly addressed in the street by Laurence Stallings, the first of the bitterly-critical post-war novelists, made friends with Floyd Dell, whose novel *Moon-calf* was all the rage, and Mary Colum; and met Edna Ferber, Fannie Hurst, Zona Gale, Robert Frost, Robinson Jeffers, George Jean Nathan, Carl van Vechten, Ernest Boyd, and many more. All were friendly, and, to me, very likable. I did not meet Mencken, who disapproved of my books; and no meeting with Hergesheimer took place until some years later, in London. I had already met Sinclair Lewis in England. After attending my *début* in New York, the agent's manager said candidly: 'The lecture's not much; but they like you. They hate Hergesheimer and Lewis, Hergesheimer because he's so ugly, Lewis because he's so rude.'

The agent had heard the least good of my lectures, and fortunately I had three others. At the University of Illinois in Urbana I delivered all four in two days, with Stuart Sherman in the chair; and I owe it to myself to say that for the third and fourth a much larger hall than had been arranged was needed to accommodate the crowd. Moreover, the contacts I enjoyed widened my knowledge of American life and literature, which had previously been gained only from such authors as had been published—it was relatively a small number prior to 1920—in England.

These authors ranged from Louisa Alcott to Edith Wharton, from Mark Twain to Bret Harte and Stephen Crane, and from George Ade (of the *Fables in Slang*) and *Mr Dooley* to Dreiser, Upton Sinclair, Kate Douglas Wiggin, and the extravagantly popular Ralph Connor, Harold Bell Wright, Gene Stratton Porter, Alice Caldwell Hegan, and Jean Webster. Miss Alcott had been my love and model from the age of six; I had revelled in Twain, Bret Harte, and *The Red Badge of Courage*, rather grudgingly admired *Ethan Frome*, laughed uproariously at George Ade and *Mr Dooley*, been crushed by the salutary verisimilitudes of *Sister Carrie* and *The Jungle*, and despaired of a nation which could idolize the sentimentalists. I now realized that even if the new writers were not adding to the specific gravity of the novel they were courageously attacking the task of producing what was called an autochthonous literature.

Their English counterparts still enjoyed critical esteem in America. There were no figures in American literature comparable to Conrad, Wells, Bennett, and Galsworthy; and A. S. M. Hutchinson's *If Winter Comes* had swept the whole country. That book's vogue was past; and although Walpole and I commanded respect as writers and considerable popularity with the reading public (his reputation and sales being about three times my own), it was clear to me that, having now a vigorous literature of its own, the United States would no longer turn its eyes to Europe for idols.

There was another reason for a decline in English popularity. The immediately post-war years had produced a flood of lecturers from the British Isles. Monetary temptation was put in their way by agents who understood the American passion for lectures; their wartime predecessors—S. K. Ratcliffe, John Cowper Powys, for examples—had done much to plead the British cause with isolationists; and, as happened again after the Second World War, British stock stood high everywhere. I had not wanted to join the band; I refused several times; but the entreaties of my publishers, plus a wish for personal reasons to be out of England for a few months, could not be resisted. I have always been glad that I went, and that I met, in particular, so many American writers of my own age.

I could not compete with them in vigour. Although I have great nervous energy, my line has always been sympathy rather than drive. But I could and did understand what they were trying to do, and, like the journalistic interviewers, who everywhere gave me a splendid press, they realized that I was not the spoiled and condescending Briton of American legend or the rising mode. This produced an extremely good understanding, especially with Willa Cather, who had as little egotism as anybody I ever met. She was very intelligent, short, stoutly built, fresh-coloured, with a square, open, rather Teutonic face which revealed practical insight, not abundant genius. Her work was built to last, as it has lasted, without verbal brilliance or sensational success; but with a mellowed quietness of great charm; and as I recall our conversations I recollect only that she was more interested than I was in Wagner's *Ring* and that she was amused by my ruthless comments on our contemporaries, without ever dwelling upon distastes of her own. She had one such distaste; but it was characteristic of her that she afterwards confessed to misjudgment of the condemned person and asked me to forget it. This request was made from no conventional dread of being thought censorious (the American words at that time were 'picking' and 'knocking'), but because she set a high value upon candour.

Fannie Hurst was another extremely simple person. The great comb in her black hair, which suggested Carmen-like flamboyance, was the merest decoration; for she was frank and unaffected, without the defensiveness which had made some young women writers at home seem over-aware of their literary performances. I feel bound to say, however, that most of the women writers I have personally known in England since very young manhood have been wholly free from affectation. Probably those I saw as visitors to publishing offices or at early literary parties were below their best. I found some of them intolerable. Fannie Hurst had only the most natural kindness; not a wisecrack left her lips; I should never have guessed from our talks that she was one of the best-known novelists in America. *Lummox* was to be seen everywhere; my copy was given to me by Stefansson: it contains fine abrupt impressionist pictures of life in down-town New York, reminiscent of those in Stephen Crane's book, *George's Mother*.

Fannie Hurst spoke kindly of Edna Ferber, but with a smile which suggested real or fabricated rivalry. I was not well enough informed to estimate this. But there may have been some competition between them. She was much slower in manner than Edna Ferber, and her literary aims were different. Miss Ferber's verve and high spirits produced immense narrative skill and assurance. The energy of her mind has shown itself in the gallop of her printed works, rich in colour and the enjoyment of hazard, and thus suited to the spectacular drama of pioneers, new townships, and sudden wealth. She was, in fact, the predestined writer for a medium then in its infancy. We now see the effect that medium has had upon novel technique, as well as upon the careers of men and women to whom action speaks louder than words, and it is very great though not—as it was in her case—always admirable.

The Movies had arrived; not yet the Talkies. The world was still enthralled by Charlie Chaplin, Mary Pickford, Gloria Swanson, and Douglas Fairbanks; and the wholesale emigration of British writers and actors to Hollywood had not yet begun. When I went to California I was driven quickly through Hollywood; and the only film star I met was Miss Swanson, who in New York spoke not one word about the pictures which she so exquisitely adorned, but sat modestly on the floor showing beautiful photographs of her children. Vital statistics were for later particularization.

One other writer must be mentioned on account of his early performances in a fashion developed much later to boring-point, the documentary. Upton Sinclair had caused a sensation by his picture of the pork-packing industry, *The Jungle*. He had been preceded in America by Frank Norris, whose speciality was wheat, and by Theodore Dreiser with several novels on the epic scale; but he was a master of close detail and uncoloured narrative. Only a little after my visit came the huge *Boston*, in which he studied the long-drawn case of Sacco and Vanzetti. Our meetings took place at Pasadena, where, observing Montague Glass and myself enjoying great laughter at the remote end of a table almost as long as the Cromwell Road, he picked up his chair and pushed it between us, saying, 'I must be in on this.'

He had to be in on everything, because his interest (Matthew Arnold said the word 'curiosity' had been blackened by English misuse) was insatiable. One had only to look at the thin, coolly smiling, and very sharp-eyed face to realize the alertness of a mind to which the lives of public men, criminal trials, business organization, and the exchequers of every worker were of absorbing interest. That mind travelled at last to Europe and the problems of high politics with equal but less convincing accuracy, and its interest in every minute of every day never failed. Conversation which had been—for Montague Glass was a marvellous *raconteur*—purely sportive took a sharper note; but to the visitor, if not as memorable as Glass's anecdotes, it remained quite as entertaining.

It must be remembered that later writers, such as Scott Fitzgerald, Hemingway, Steinbeck, and Thomas Wolfe, had either not yet appeared or were in their early days. Fitzgerald's *This Side of Paradise* was out; but I forget whether I heard of it. I met him once in London, when his reputation was that of a brash youngster approved by a highly troubled Galsworthy; and I hope not to be thought unkind if I record our brief encounter. I had recommended Chatto & Windus to publish *The Great Gatsby*. One day, just at lunch-time, I was told that a Mr Fitzgerald wished to see the partners, but that both had already gone out: would I see him? I went from my office to the waiting-room, where a young man sat, with his hat on, at a small table. He did not rise or remove his hat, and he did not answer my greeting, so I took another chair, expressing regret that no partner was available, and asking if there was anything I could do. Assuming, I suppose, that I was some base hireling, he continued brusque to the point of truculence; but we spoke of the purpose of his visit, and after a few moments he silently removed his hat. Two minutes later, looking rather puzzled, he rose. I did the same. I spoke warmly of *The Great Gatsby*; and his manner softened. He became an agreeable boy, quite ingenuous and inoffensive, and finally asked my name. I told him. If I had said 'the Devil' he could not have been more horrified. Snatching up his hat in consternation, he cried: 'Oh, my God! *Nocturne*'s one of my favourite books!' and dashed out of the premises.

That was our only interview. An American friend thought Fitzgerald must have supposed my anonymity to have been a joke at his expense. It was not. I have not the Continental habit of introducing myself by name; and even in those days did not go about saying 'I'm Frank Swinnerton', as George Doran said I ought to do with the addition of 'Damn your eyes!' So I was innocent of all wish to disconcert one who pretended that he felt no excitement at the English publication of his novel.

I did not meet John dos Passos, whose *Three Soldiers* I much admired, and who was another of the writers who prompted Stuart Sherman to write his protest against the trend of American fiction in the 'twenties, *On Falling in Hate*. I did, however, on a number of occasions meet the ebullient Sinclair Lewis, who knew and detested the censoriousness of small-town life, the strident conventionality of business men, and the danger lest political apathy should open the door to Fascism in the United States. Lewis was an intense lover of freedom. If, as I do, you think this a quality, you will see why I think him the most important American novelist of his generation. That in the realm of art he will 'last', as the saying is, I do not believe; he was too much an echo of what a French philosopher called 'the noise of life' for that. But at a crucial moment in history he was the international voice of alarm at the social and political facts which needed to be proclaimed. His influence upon truly revolutionary writers, until the rise of Hemingway, had no parallel.

Nearly ten years ago (in 1954) I caught sight of some words in a review of a new book by Lewis which seemed interestingly truthful. The reviewer confessed that much of what he had previously read by the author had irritated him; and I thought I understood why this was. Lewis irritated many people, not only with his pen but in person. He was lean, sandy, freckled, staring-eyed (his eyes had red rims), impulsively energetic, terribly copious and without repose, given to outspokenness of a kind disconcerting to the staid, full of enthusiasm; the sort of man who, suddenly crying 'Let's go gay!' would rush to a car, whirl along at immense speed, and turn up far away at three o'clock in the morning, rousing friends from their beds for chat, whisky, and improvisation.

He could drink furiously, talk without end, impersonate for an hour, or five hours, a salesman from the Middle West, and exhaust everybody but himself. He could be an appalling nuisance. Yet he had huge capacity for respect, as for generosity. He acquired information very fast, recorded it at the typewriter, cut with the utmost ruthlessness what he had written, and, as an experienced journalist, produced criticism of his own country in such a style as to force attention from all who were saying 'Sh! Sh!' and covering their ears to escape the unpleasant.

Lewis had written several books before he found true form with *Main Street* and *Babbitt*; but once his power of mimicry and exposure had been established he was irresistible. Nor was he, in himself, what blatancy and even wild conduct suggested.

In spite of every report of maddening behaviour I never in all our meetings found him anything but honest, simple, sober, and very likable indeed. His talent was real, his mind quick, ardent, and far-flung; and at need he could be as quiet as a mouse. The stridency to which people objected was merely Lewis singing.

However, they did object to his voice. They heard the voice and disliked it; a fact which prevented them from doing justice to the song. It happens all the time as we read the writings of those with whom we are not quite in key. A few words, an opinion, a persistent trick of style, some ridicule of something we take seriously, some harshness to somebody we love; and we deliver inexorable judgment. 'That chap's a dirty dog!' 'Do you know him?' 'No, but you can tell from his writing.' I was once innocently reading an article in a French review when I came across an unexpected reference to myself. 'He has a truly detestable personality,' said the critic; *'une personnalité vraiment haissable.'*

This man had been reading one of my novels, which had been written, I thought, with impartial sympathy; and he had felt, behind the recital of distress, a being antipathetic to himself. It was candid and intelligent of him to say so; for not all critics are outspoken in just this manner. The feeling, however, expressed otherwise, is common; and once we learn to identify it we shall find antipathy grinding out hostile reviews everywhere.

> I do not love thee, Doctor Fell,
> The reason why I cannot tell;
> But this alone I know full well,
> I do not love thee, Doctor Fell.

The critic has, or should have, the last word. He should comment with detachment upon the literary quality of the book he has read with an open mind. This is not the custom. Too often, he glances at the author's name, the publisher's name, the first two or three pages, and the paragraph which publishers insist on setting as a guide to judgment. He then, unless the writer is fashionable, dismisses the book—and, of course, the author. When disparagement is most elaborate, or most contemptuous, it is least warranted. It may even betray the reviewer's uneasy sense of inferiority to the writer. In that case it is what Smee, in *Peter Pan*, called 'a sort of compliment'.

This, to me, is a most interesting topic, not as concerning myself, who am often belittled, but as concerning authors who are habitually attacked with venom. They are attacked because they disturb. Sinclair Lewis disturbed; and he made enemies by his disturbance. Bernard Shaw disturbed; and although Shaw had no personal enemies, for he did not attack persons, but always windmills, he made every dramatic critic look round for some weapon to pierce imperturbable or destructive self-assurance. The consequence was that after any Shaw first night there was an outcry, the commentators declaring that what he had written was not a play, that he was spoofing the public, that he was an impudent ignoramus. He did not mind. This heightened his offence. 'That's the worst of Shaw!' cried fiery H. W. Massingham to me one day. 'He can't get angry!'

Massingham could get angry; and he thought it one's duty to retaliate furiously upon one's opponents. He loved and admired Shaw. He would have liked to see his idol savaging the very smallest of small dogs. He did not realize, perhaps, that for Shaw the critics were attacking what he had said the day before yesterday, whereas Shaw himself, a really big dog who was laughing and chivalrous in the days when he attacked what he called 'Sardoodledom', was already engaged with the middle of next week.

In the same way, reviewers used to produce vitriol to throw at Wells, who was more vulnerable than Shaw, because he was apt to become peppery and think of insulting retorts upon his critics. Shaw only laughed, as you can read in the Epilogue to *Fanny's First Play*; Wells was hurt, indignant, and well aware of the self-betrayals of his denouncers. He hit back. Nevertheless he once said to me with rueful good-humour: 'You can't be said to have "arrived" until a new book of yours has been slated in every paper in England.' I do not know what Sinclair

Lewis's attitude was. In England he did not arouse excitement as he did in the United States.

I think he liked England, and English writers, who, on the whole, are quiet men. Indeed, it may be said that many English writers (and reviewers) are more agreeable than their books (or their reviews) might lead you to suppose. I never set eyes on D. H. Lawrence, who at times must have been a difficult customer; but I have often been struck by the fact that literary feuds are more often the work of ardent supporters than of any hostility between principals. This was so in the case of Dickens and Thackeray. Mrs Lynn Linton, who knew and felt affection for both, once wrote:

> The antagonism created by the world's fancy between them never existed in reality between the men themselves. . . . Each stood at the head of a distinct school of thought, representing different aspects of human life, and each had his followers and adherents, for the most part arrayed in self-made hostile lines, with a very small percentage of that *tertium quid*—those impartial critics who could admire both with equal favour.

She was thinking, perhaps, of John Forster, whom she never forgave for his Life of her friend Landor; but you can see the same performance at the present day. In politics, where strife is continuous, rancour is more declared than it is in literature; but it is not greater. In the literary world there have always been plenty of little men to decry their betters from conscious inferiority, or a love of mischief, or mere incompatibility of temperament. Incompatibility exists between great men, who sometimes can see the faults in each other's work and miss the original qualities; but this incompatibility is that of big dogs, not yappers.

Why does it exist at all? I cannot tell you. It seems to be common to men and animals. Even the small singing birds, or most insignificant chirpers, have sudden violent hatreds; naturalists tell us that their very songs are sweet only to human ears, since to other birds they are no more than a series of boasts and warnings. In the case of authors it may arise from some instinctive comparison: either 'There, but for the grace of God, go I' or 'What is he getting that is denied to me?' or simply, as in Sinclair Lewis's case, 'I don't like his loud, piping, or provincial voice.'

Personally, I do not care for aggressive writers—or men. I have never felt the same impulse of affection towards Ben Jonson that I always felt towards Shakespeare. I do not like Junius. I detest John Wilson Croker as much as Macaulay and Disraeli, who stamped upon or lampooned him (Macaulay for political reasons; Disraeli repaying an old score), must have done. I dislike a number of pugnacious journalists of the past, whose names are never heard today. I dislike them, as Max Beerbohm disliked Clement Scott, because they were stupid and intolerant and took unctuous pride in their stupidity and intolerance. There are two or three men today from whose work my eye slips with the greatest ease. I do not like their personalities. They seem to me much worse than stupid; and I should not be surprised if the feeling of disapproval, at least, is reciprocated.

So I come back to Sinclair Lewis. There was something raucous in his note. He was living at high tension, driven by the febrile energy of his temperament; and he was extraordinarily sensitive to his company. He found it impossible to talk to Wells, for whom he had the most eager admiration, because Wells (who called himself 'a cat-man', meaning that he preferred to walk alone) was too self-conscious to endure such explosive enthusiasm. He was garrulous to the point of boringness with Arnold Bennett. He was subdued with myself because he thought me merciless. When he 'went gay' it was because his lonely spirit could not bear itself a moment longer. I think Lewis then heard his own voice, disliked it, and knew there was no hope of changing it.

A Lively Romantic

•

15 TURNING for a while to more domestic material, I
propose to offer a last batch of extracts from the
Walpole letters. These will show what names were
current in our world in the middle-twenties, and how they
struck two contemporaries. I claim no other importance for
them.

Having returned from America in March, 1924, I married,
and fulfilled an old dream of living in the country. I had
already given up dramatic criticism in the hope of assisting my
old friend P. P. Howe, who was well qualified for it, and I had
cut journalistic work to a minimum. I continued to visit
London for three days a week, and to receive visits in the
country; but from this time onward I concerned myself less
and less with what I had described to Walpole as 'the little
squibs and squabbles of London cliques', and enjoyed a new
life of health and happiness.

In a letter written to Walpole on September 21st, 1924,
after learning that he was to write the volume on Anthony
Trollope for the English Men of Letters Series, I congratulated
him on his latest novel:

> I am glad *The Old Ladies* is coming out so soon. I liked the
> air of it in *The Criterion*, but did not read it there because you
> had told me that fragments only were to be serialized. . . .
> I've got both *A Passage to India* and *Elsie and the Child*; but
> haven't read either of them yet. The title of the latter I think
> deplorable. I also have to read *Bricks and Mortals*, by Herbert
> Tremaine [pseudonym of Maude Little], *Marmaduke*, by

Allan Monkhouse, and *St Joan*, by B. Shaw, not to mention
[Wells's] *The Dream*, which I haven't yet read. It will strike
you as strange, but I too have been reading Trollope. I have
read recently *The Bertrams* and *The Three Clerks*, and when
I am through with contemporaries (urgent ones, I mean) I
am going on to *Castle Richmond*. This of course is not for any
book about Trollope, but is merely contributory reading
towards my celebrated work upon the English Novel, which
may be expected about the year 1944 [it was never written].
I think parts of *The Bertrams*—the interviews between George
and Caroline, e.g.—absolutely first class. I'm not so sure
about *The Three Clerks*. I can't help feeling that Trollope's
wicked characters are a bit namby-pamby, like the wicked
characters in Talbot Baines Reed's school stories, who go to
low public houses and swear, but who never get what I
might call robustiously naughty. . . .

I have read the new Lawrence [*The Boy in the Bush*, by
D. H. Lawrence and M. L. Skinner]. Part of it is superb. The
rest, gobble. I had to do it—much against my will—for the
M.G.[1] I have seen Arnold a lot in the last 3 weeks, and he
seems very well, and very sublime. I ran into Forster the
other day, and we had a very amiable talk. He is a very
courteous chap. Apparently *A Passage to India* has done well,
but not as well as *The Green Hat* [by Michael Arlen]. Nothing has ever done as well as *The Green Hat*, except perhaps
Gerald Cranston's Lady [by Gilbert Frankau], and the works
of Mr Louis Golding. Have you ever, by the way, seen the
little pudding that goes by that last name? . . . I seem to have
offended —— . . . I am not offended with anybody. I am a
quiet old nacker, much given to good works, but generally
condemned. . . .

1. 'Over and over again one receives the thrill given by original insight—the
uncanny revelation of truth which comes only from the mind of genius. . . .
But gradually, after several of those savage and almost sadistic descriptions of
violence to which we are accustomed in Mr Lawrence's work, we find ourselves in the ancient nightmare of sex and unreason which before now has
spoiled some of his best books. . . . From the sure confidence of the artist's
imagination we are turned once more to the very nearly hysterical bewilder-
ments of an over-sensitive nature instinctively at war with natural behaviour.

In June, 1925, I acknowledged receipt of Walpole's Rede Lecture, published by the Cambridge University Press, called *The English Novel: Some Notes on its Evolution*. This began with a lively admission that the speaker could not define what a novel was. He thought a visitor from Mars, presented 'with a page of Mrs Virginia Woolf's *Jacob's Room*, a free verse by Miss Edith Sitwell, and one of Mr Pearsall Smith's *Trivia* would be puzzled to name the one of these three belonging to the genre of the novel'. In a rapid and very adroit survey, ranging from *Tristram Shandy* to *The Golden Bowl*, from Thackeray to Sarah Grand, and from Conrad to Romer Wilson and Margaret Kennedy, he managed to bring into one sentence as practitioners of the older technique 'such novelists as Mr Frank Swinnerton, Miss Sheila Kaye-Smith, and Mr Francis Brett Young'.

He concluded:

It is not enough for the novelist to note the tiny earthly changes from day to day that go on around him, not enough for him even to analyse the marks and scratches made by events upon his own tiny personality. Having created he must place his creations in a world that is larger than his mortal eye can scan and that has more meaning in its truth and beauty than his mortal brain can grasp.

My comment was:

Many thanks for the booklet, which I have read with much approval. I think it very good. The way you lightly but comprehensively cover the ground is A.1. As you will have expected, I began to quake a little when you came to the spiritual third dimension, but I think you got over that very nicely. Indeed, I feel that you have done something awfully difficult with such skill that only those who know something of the task will be able to realize how well you have done it. Had you given Sheila her place in front of me (*place aux dames*) I should have felt like Our Saviour upon the Cross, but now I only feel like an interloper in the

Mr Lawrence's philosophy—the powerless fist-beating of an imprisoned child —comes in where his imagination fails.'

marriage-bed of two true lovers. I feel that Sheila and Francis were made for each other. I am only a nasty common fellow in such company. However, of course you know best, and really my company is better than I have any pretension to. Far be it from me to carp at my company. It may be that Sheila and Francis will be the haughty ones, bloated as they must be with great successes.

I wrote later in the year upon a much graver matter, which in view of the assumption that all novelists live like fighting-cocks and have pockets full of pound notes may surprise. One of the authors who used 'the stream of consciousness' before anybody else in England did so was Dorothy M. Richardson. In 1915 she began to produce what proved to be a continuous novel about a girl and woman named Miriam. The first volume of it, containing an introduction by J. D. Beresford, was called *Pointed Roofs*, and the last came twenty years later, the whole series being unified under the general title *Pilgrimage*. How far Miss Richardson based her work upon diaries, if she used such things at all, I do not know; but the exactitude with which she offered Miriam's mental reactions to everything that occurred in her daily life was laughingly admitted by Mrs H. G. Wells and a friend who recognized in her pages not only the dresses they had worn twenty years earlier, but the manner in which Mrs Wells had then played the piano.

There was much more to the books than precise memory; and the novelty of Miss Richardson's technique was immediately recognized and admired. The author of *Pilgrimage* was a serious artist, of whom Abel Chevalley said in his study *Le Roman Anglais de Notre Temps*: 'De tous les ecrivains de la jeune génération, c'est Miss Dorothy Richardson qui parait aller le plus loin et le plus conscienment vers une rénovation totale du roman anglais.' He made some reservations, it is true. Nevertheless the words I have quoted explain the admiration felt by all who read the books. These have, historically, another importance; they show how, as early as 1915, one writer at least was determined to break away from convention.

I assume that admirers, though keen, were fewer than they

should have been; for in letters to Walpole which I have mentioned I wrote:

> By the way, Dorothy Richardson is apparently in such financial distress that H.G. [Wells] has conceived the notion of applying on her behalf for a Civil List pension. I feel sure that if he goes on with his scheme you would be willing to support it. Nothing has been done yet—as far as I know—but Jane Wells talked to me about it, and it seemed to me that if it took shape you would want to help.

Mrs Wells now writes saying will I write a letter to the P.M. saying how much I esteem D.R.'s work, and send it to *her* (Mrs Wells) so that it may be put with the others. Would you be willing to do the like? If so, would you write such a letter to old Stan. [Mr Stanley Baldwin] and send it along to Mrs Wells? And could you tell me of anybody else who could be profitably approached for the purpose? Mrs Wells has herself written to Arnold [Bennett], Sassoon, Galsworthy, Tomlinson, Guedalla (which you may think a strange mixture, worthy of comparison with ——'s list of famous novelists), but I wondered if you could think of people weighty enough to impress Baldwin. D.R. is absolutely broken with poverty, and this proposal is one to save her from desperate distress. I thought of asking Monty [Compton Mackenzie] to contribute a letter, and I think Mrs Wells thought Sassoon might be instrumental in getting some mandarins. . . .

Walpole wrote, as requested; but found it difficult to think of further names, as 'my more particular friends Drinkwater, Lucas, think D.R. awful (to such a world do I belong) and I don't suppose that Beresford would mean an awful lot to Baldwin'.

The application was made, and was successful. It is a sad comment on the rewards of original writing that it should have been necessary; but later experience, especially as a member of the Royal Literary Fund Committee, has shown me that severe hardship among authors who miss general acclaim, or who outlive their popularity, is a common phenomenon. Unless they make money by journalism, the stage, or in business they will find that books alone will keep them poor for life.

Prior to 1926, I had enjoyed a regular salary—which never, I think, exceeded £550 a year—as reader for Chatto & Windus. I had also written reviews and articles for the Press. My novels were selling about 20,000 copies in the United States, and I see that one of them called *The Elder Sister* had passed 8,000 in England within a few weeks of publication. So after much thought I decided to leave the publishing trade. I did so at the beginning of 1926, when my wife and I spent a daring but economical two months in the South of France, at a place called Sainte Maxime s/Mer. Subsequently, and I should explain that the reference to Arnold Bennett's costume was a small joke about the impending birth of his daughter Virginia, I wrote to Walpole:

When I went up to town to lunch with all the demnition bow-wows at the Ray Long festival [Ray Long was editor-in-chief of the Hearst magazines] I looked for you but you was not there. Arnold was, in a maternity gown; and so was St John Ervine (dressed as ordinary); and I was introduced to your friend Clemence Dane; and in the distance saw Benedick Hutchinson [Walter Hutchinson the publisher, recently married]; and sat next to Mrs Belloc Lowndes and saw one whom I took for the ghost of Van Biene [a once popular violinist], and found it was Jerome K. Jerome; and so on. . . .

Mary and I returned from France a month ago, and I have been working like a galley-slave, and am ½ through a new novel, as to which I feel the customary qualms. People stop me in the street to congratulate me on my liberation from Chatto & Windus (such people as Sir J. M. Barrie and Mr Thornton Butterworth [another publisher]). . . .

Mr Martin Secker, having had measles in the train between Paris and Geneva, is convalescent, and was *not* responsible for the further malformation of Mussolini's nose. Mr Sydney Dark says that Mr John Squire has never written under the pseudonym of 'Roderick Random'. That is all I know about the great world at present. . . .

Walpole delayed his congratulations on my freedom from the drudgery of reading manuscripts, on the pathetic ground that 'I never feel that you need congratulations from me about anything'; and then reported that he was being pressed for contributions by *The Adelphi*, *The Criterion*, and *The Nation*, which had become a different paper from the one which Massingham had edited. 'Can it be,' he asked, 'that I am becoming highbrow? God forbid. As a matter of fact I fancy they're growing a little uncertain of their young genii and gazing at people like you and me a little doubtfully.'

My reply included two admissions and a compliment:

As to leaving Chatto's, I'm glad and I'm sorry. I've been there 18 years, and I hate breaks. Also I had played a leading part in the firm's revival. But I hadn't been very comfortable there for the last year or so, and I had planned to leave when the present senior partner retires in another year. I wanted to be away four or five months altogether this year (including U.S.). So I put the matter to Mary, and to Arnold (who said he felt *here*—pointing to his breast—that I ought to clear out, and at once). There were cries of distress from all except one man, who I think was glad for me to go, though he cried also, and wrote me continuous letters; and I left. My regret was for the break. My dread is of some sudden collapse of my earning power, though I don't see how I can possibly fail to earn our keep, and my mother's keep, by writing. . . .

As to my need of congratulations—believe me, I am as hungry for them as you can be. My particular temperament is a difficult one, for I am very mercurial, and yet I strike people as being otherwise. Also, my happiness is really controlled by my affections, and if these were taken away I should have nothing to live for. I haven't, as people like H.G. and Monty have, the faculty for regarding my own amusement and self-exploitation as the greatest good. . . .

I think you are right in thinking that the stomachs of the highbrows occasionally sink as they contemplate their own works. And after all, dear Hugh, that you have a creative

faculty which is denied the sterile highbrows. They may say
... that you write badly; but they must be conscious of your
energy and your fruitfulness. . . .

A further compliment followed, together with a mild effort
at self-exculpation:

I like to think of you as sitting to John, hobnobbing with
Duchesses, and leading the fashionable life generally. It suits
you, and must be great fun, particularly as it does not in the
least represent your sort of root attitude to civilization. As I
grow old I find that I want all people to have what they
fancy. I am getting so amiable that I hardly ever say more
than a dozen malicious things a day, and as I have never
thought a malicious thing in my life ('Oh come, Frank,'
says Hugh. Well, it's true, for all that. My tongue runs
away with me. However . . .) I am gradually becoming a
philosopher.

As for Raleigh [Professor Walter Raleigh, whose *Letters*
had just been published], I just couldn't stand his letters. I
had read a few pages in a mood of appreciation, and suddenly I sat up in my chair and said 'Somehow I hate this bloody
supercilious highbrow!' You see, my dear Hugh, I was never
at a Public School or a University, and to me the pride of
erudition is something vile. Also, all contempt for others
which is based on non-comprehension. . . .

I am full of FEARS regarding *Lord Raingo* and *Wm.
Clissold*. The latter I have been nosing into, and have something more than vague fear to go on. The former is about
our friend Beaverbrook [it was not]; and Arnold is not
sound on Beaverbrook. . . .

While we were in town this week we went to our first
literary tea party (at least, Mary's first). Christ! There we met
those celebrated novelists —— and ——. My dear Hugh, we
were never as eccentric as these women novelists are! Nor as
morosely or flippantly aware of our talents. I mean we can
never have been as self-conscious. Of course, there's Francis;
but Francis is Francis. He is a school to himself. . . .

To conclude—for in mercy to the reader I have omitted many items amusing to myself in this correspondence—I quote one letter written as late as 1941.

My dear Frank, yesterday I was going through some old drawers and came on a fat bundle of letters from you to me circa 1912–1914. I read them and was delighted with their intelligence humour and friendliness. *What* good letters! Afterwards I reflected on our friendship and although we seldom see one another thought how fine a thing it had been for me. How lucky too we both have been—both with hard unhappy childhoods then living successfully by doing the thing we love to do—you with your happy marriage I with my friendships. In these letters we obviously regard Jack Murry, Shanks, and Squire seriously. What a lesson in values! But I *am* glad we have been friends for so long. I know that I have often been a comic figure to you but *almost* always a comic for whom you have had a certain tenderness.

That is all. We exchanged further letters, the last of which, from Walpole, was dated 'Feb. 8. 41'. Characteristically it says: 'I've read only one good novel this year so far—L. A. G. Strong's *The Bay*—in proof.' The letter added that he would be away until May, and suggested a meeting in that month. The meeting never took place. On Whit Sunday, June 1st, 1941, he was dead.

Reputations drop more quickly now than ever before, and the romantic or as I should like to say really creative novelist is out of fashion. Walpole is out of fashion. When I bade him in 1937 not to mind the ridicule of his knighthood, he replied, 'I'm already Bishop, Curate, Uncle, Mayor in the papers, which throws a half-light on my kindly pomposities,' and 'I'm very happy and can stand a hell of a lot of teasing.' Well, the teasing and caricature are finished. To the coteries, his is a faded name. In Public Libraries, on the other hand, which are places where books are nursed for indefinite survival, Walpole's are still eagerly read. The fact would have given him ingenuous delight.

Star Reviewing

○

16 I WISH now to speak of a phenomenon of the later nineteen-twenties; and in order to show how it arose must recapitulate a little.

When, in the year 1908, a highly original weekly, *The New Age*, under A. R. Orage's editorship, was being bought for the sake of brilliant ethical and political battles between Shaw, Belloc, and Chesterton, it included 'an occasional *causerie*' under the general title 'Books and Persons'. The signature to this *causerie* was 'Jacob Tonson'; and Jacob Tonson startled us all with bold claims for Russian novelists other than Tolstoy and Turgenev, and by cheeky assaults upon all inflated reputations and pontifical mandarins. He was not a professional iconoclast—that would have been nothing new;—he was an independent who knew a great deal about the Novel and the literary world. He wrote with emphatic brevity.

I cannot remember how soon my young friends and I (we were in our early twenties) discovered that this refreshing writer was Arnold Bennett; but the secret was soon open enough, and I learned with pleasure that certain articles signed 'E.A.B.' which I had cut, in boyhood, from the old *Academy*, had come from the same pen. I did not read a Bennett novel until 1910: I previously read an anonymous work of his called *The Truth about an Author*, buying it in 1905 for a few pence, along with three books by Henry James, when The Times Book Club was at war with publishers and advertised itself by a giant sale of books at cut prices. *The Truth about an Author* and the Tonson paragraphs were obviously from the same hand, the hand which afterwards wrote *The Card* with the object of 'cheering us all up'.

In 1917, when Hugh Walpole and I were both invited by Bennett to Thorpe-le-Soken for a weekend, we talked with great animation on Walpole's part and wit from our stammering host. In the course of this exchange Walpole spoke of *Books and Persons*, and when the cuttings were produced asked to be allowed to take them to his room. Next morning he demanded that they should be collected into a book. Bennett, still rather sceptical, asked my opinion as a young publisher; so I spent an hour alone with the cuttings. Having done this, although from morbid horror of self-advertisement I advised the omission of a favourable reference to myself, made before Bennett and I became friends, I promised to have the book published by my firm.

I spoke of *Books and Persons* in *Background with Chorus*, where I emphasized its novelty in 1908 and its less novel but still vivacious attractiveness in 1917. Modern readers cannot appreciate the novelty; all they can see is that some of the enthusiasms were facile and are now out of date. The articles had been written at odd moments for amusement, and without remuneration; they amused when more pretentious exercises had sunk without trace; glancing at them again today I found my own amusement return.

Twenty years after the *causeries* began to appear in *The New Age*, perhaps when the two men were travelling together in Germany, Lord Beaverbrook suggested that Bennett should write for *The Evening Standard* a new series of 'Books and Persons'. This was inspiration. Bennett, flattered, accepted the suggestion. Whether he then saw what a dilemma the work would present I do not know; but it is certain that *The Evening Standard's* weekly book page became one of the sensations of the day.

The dilemma was this. It is one thing, at forty, to please bright minds with cheeky nonchalance written over a pseudonym in a small journal; quite another, at sixty-one, to write publicly, under a famous name, in an evening newspaper of universal circulation. Bennett used his customary emphasis and the ranging curiosity which led one exasperated highbrow to squeal at me 'the trouble is, he's so damned interesting!' but he could no longer be the carefree *franc tireur* of 1908. Then, he was assailing academic ancients; now, inevitably, he was writing about his juniors.

Every junior (I think rightly) is allowed to deride his elders, whatever their quality; but by tradition no elder is ever unkind to youth. The famous writer's motto is, and must be, *noblesse oblige*. Bennett was a practising novelist, and therefore subject to attack by every emergent undergraduate; his work in fiction was being published simultaneously with his journalism; he was, as it were, in the arena. Had he been severe, he would have disgusted the very readers he wanted to influence, and by the young would have been charged with murder. He adopted a manner of easy benignity, using the first person singular, and avoiding altogether the analytical style then coming into vogue.

Hence the success, and for long the great influence, of the new 'Books and Persons'. Bennett, a great reader in the night, through sleeplessness, sat up in bed 'perusing' (as he would have said) new books. If he did not care for them, he said nothing. If he found them interesting, he said so in brisk sentences. If he thought a good author had written less than his best, he chided. He was never dishonest. He refused always to puff the work of his friends or their relatives. If he took the trouble to discuss much-commended writers who were less good than their trumpeters claimed, he remarked the fact with decorous magnanimity.

For this magnanimity and his tolerance of what the intolerant would not tolerate—the work of imaginative novelists—he was accused by the intolerant of 'selling the pass' to the Philistines. It was his object, not to sell or defend passes, but to spread to all the sweetness and light of his own temperament. He was an interesting writer on life and letters because he was deeply interested in both. Too modest to wish to dictate, he wrote as a judge will converse—I do not know any richer conversation—when the day's legal labour is done, with a sort of slippered ease. 'After dinner,' said Sir Robert Walpole, 'I always talk bawdy, so that all may join in.' Bennett never talked

bawdy; he always talked so that all might join in. He did this
in *The Evening Standard*.

One result of this new excitingness in book reviews was that
the sale of new books was stimulated. If a publisher could quote
Bennett as having extolled one of his products, he rubbed his
hands, and caused further copies to be bound, if not printed.
Booksellers were for the first time in history seen to smile.
Authors, on tip-toe, hoped that this week, or next week, he
would praise what they had written—and make their fortunes.
A glow of happiness and expectancy spread over the entire
literary horizon, except in one quarter, where a patch of
lowering cloud emitted a murmur as of thunder. The trouble,
said this murmur, is that he's so damned interesting.

Interestingness, added the cloud, meant compromise. There
was no compromise. Only certain writers should be praised;
the rest, if not ignored, must be 'written down'. Bennett did
not 'write down', in either sense. He was written down; the
story that he cared only for money (the fact that he was
receiving £3000 a year for his articles gave it plausibility) was
widely spread; animus, in spite of his immense generosity to
young writers, was cultivated. Traitor! 'All for a handful of
silver he left us!' Vulgar Provincial! 'Oh, luxury!' one critic
imagined him saying; 'Oh, being-in-the-swim!' He was caricatured as a fat man with a quif and a fob. Bennett remained
calm under all these affronts.

He was right to do so. During the war of 1914–18, when
space was restricted, the reviewing of books had become,
for some editors, a waste of space. Short notices of high quality were still printed in such dailies as the nobly-influential
Manchester Guardian. Otherwise only the two Sunday papers,
The Observer and *The Sunday Times*, granted plenty of it to their
literary contributors. These papers carried one regular two-
column article about a non-fiction book, and one two-column
article about half-a-dozen coagulated novels. The writers of
non-fiction articles were Edmund Gosse, until his death, and
thereafter Desmond MacCarthy, in *The Sunday Times*, J. C.

Squire and, subsequently, Basil de Sélincourt in *The Observer*. The novel reviewers in the same papers were Gerald Gould and Ralph Straus. All were competent; none could stray far from the reviewer's essential task of provisionally appraising the week's good, bad, and indifferent publications. Bennett had the privilege of writing at large about any book he liked. At large: that was the point; I think the malady.

A new fashion rose from Bennett's example. This was the employment of a celebrated novelist to write—still at large—about his contemporaries. The novelist was expected to be a genial *causeur*. He spoke for nobody but himself, uniting if he could Bennett's sense of responsibility with the art of the familiar essayist. Unlike the pre-war *causeurs*, from W. L. Courtney in *The Daily Telegraph* to Robertson Nicoll in *The British Weekly*, who had been primarily literary men, he was there because he was a celebrated novelist. He was expected to use the pronoun 'I', and to *talk* to his readers.

The first of Bennett's rivals appeared in the London *Evening News*, which was edited by a very able newspaper-man from Northamptonshire who had learned his job on *The Star*. His name was Frank FitzHugh, and I always think of him as being about seven feet in height, with a huge frame, a fresh colour, and a curious Cockney accent. He appointed J. B. Priestley. Priestley's love of books, and his ability to write vigorously about them, had been proved in many newspaper articles, books of essays, and the volumes on Meredith and Peacock which he contributed to the English Men of Letters Series. *The Good Companions* had made him one of the most successful novelists of his generation. No other man, I think, commanded equal gifts for this particular job.

About that time I was asked by the Literary Editor of *The Evening News* to contribute occasional light articles to his magazine page on subjects suggested by himself. I do not re-member what they were; but I wrote a number. One day I was summoned by telegram to ring up *The Evening News* office. The Editor wanted to see me: would I call when next in

London? I said, suspiciously, 'Why does he want to see me?' The answer was: 'He wants you to write the book article.' I said: 'But Priestley does that, doesn't he?' 'Not any longer,' came the reply.

I learned no more. I called within two or three days at Carmelite House; and the proposition was made. I said I did not want to write the book article. FitzHugh begged me to experiment for six weeks. I should have complete freedom in the choice of books, and could say whatever I liked about them. The one reservation was that I should write about no book which I did not find in the book room. Hundreds arrived there every week, and I chose about twenty as possible subjects for notice. If I did not write about the books, nobody would do so; a fact the recognition of which made me extremely scrupulous. At no time did I hear why Priestley had relinquished his task. FitzHugh, after suffering great pain for several years as a progressive illness disabled him, is dead. He was alarming in his physical strength and pugnacity, and I remember thinking one day when his arrival in the room scattered members of his staff that if I had been dependent for a living on his decisions I might have feared him. I did not fear him. He treated me for three-and-a-half years with jocular and admiring consideration, exclaiming as I arrived: 'Enter a Torch!' or 'Enter Littracher!' and once, after such a greeting, asking: 'See, when was it you wrote a good article? Oh, last week!' When, at his request, I had composed and sent in the obituary notice on Arnold Bennett, and asked if it had been all right, his answer, with a teasing grin, was: 'Yes.' A moment later: 'Very good.' Still a moment later: 'Splendid!' I believe the unavoidable cessation of his book feature caused him real distress.

I was not accused of 'selling the pass'. I wrote with candour, but without spitefulness. I enjoyed the work, and took pride in it, doing my best to give each article variety by introducing it by some general technical or aesthetic observations which one enthusiast suggested that I should gather into a book called *Critical Gambits*. The article always appeared first in the paper's Friday Lunch Edition, and when I saw Bennett, as I generally did on that day, I found that he had made a point of reading it before I met him. Any error I had made in grammar or opinion was gravely remarked; but his verdict was often: 'It was awfully . . . adroit.'

Without consultation, we had adopted the rule, which he kept to the end, and I broke only once when, under editorial command, I discussed *Imperial Palace*, of never writing about each other's work. If FitzHugh received any complaints from authors or others he presumably dropped them in the waste-paper basket; and I had only one persistent foe. This was a man who from time to time sent anonymous postcards questioning judgments, one of them bearing a cutting from the paper which said: 'Mr Swinnerton's articles appear every Friday'. To this he asked: 'That is why wise men avoid *The Evening News* on Fridays.' I noticed after a time that the post-mark on these cards was 'Hanwell'.

After a little while Bennett and I were joined as arbiters of taste in literature by Compton Mackenzie in *The Daily Mail*, and by Hugh Walpole in, I think, *The Daily Sketch*, as well as others of popular fame. I feel sure that purists must have cursed this particular fashion; for it has always been a fashion of another kind to regard the word 'novelist' as an oath of con-demnation. Forgetting that I was one of the accursed brigade, an M.P. once witheringly ejaculated: 'These *novelists*!' I replied: 'We always say "these *politicians*!" ' He was much offended. But I myself did not approve of the fashion where-by established novelists were called upon to judge all other authors.

I disapproved because—unlike Bernard Shaw, who thought every review should be signed with the name and address of its writer—I have always preferred the anonymous commentator who uses the editorial 'we' to the professional who draws attention to himself by saying 'I'. Also, I think the review of every book should be separable. The habit of finding some arbitrary contrast between one book and another—of, as it were, making the whole thing a bumping race—seems to me a bad and a lazy one. The reviewer's mind is not submissive to the author; he does each man injustice. Only a really competent journalist can escape this danger.

I speak of a fashion of the late 'twenties and early 'thirties which has continued into the 'sixties without the excuse of notable names. It was at its least objectionable when followed by Bennett, Priestley, Mackenzie, and myself, because all were established writers, successful enough with the public to be above private grudges. All were talkers. All had much to say which could find no place in their novels. None had any wish to show off. The day of exhibitionism had arrived; but it was confined to those who feared that without some additional plumage they would never be noticed.

I do not pretend that my own articles equalled Bennett's for readability, or that they intimidated the ignorant by their critical acumen. On the contrary, in each case. A writer for the diurnal Press has no time to formulate an elaborate critical theory; he relies upon experience based on everything he has read, and upon the resultant intuitions of the hour. I had, and have, considerable acquaintance with English literature, some French, and in translation some Russian. So all I claim is that editors and readers of all classes enjoyed what I wrote and came again for more a week later. 'I know,' said a young intellectual, 'that even if he doesn't like my book he'll give it fair treatment.' This, naturally, was my aim.

Now for what seems to me the fatal flaw in all such reviewing. The writer, although a 'star', has yawning gaps in knowledge. He is incompetent to deal with learned or specialist work. He therefore has either to ignore many books of great virtue or to deal with them inadequately with an admission of his ignorance. He can do the latter as an ordinary 'we' reviewer cannot do. The ordinary reviewer can fudge; the star must not do so too often or he will be exposed to ridicule. By the use of 'I, I, I' he can become the friend of his readers; but in such circumstances really serious criticism perishes.

I say that this personal approach, objectionable as it rightly is to the academic mind, was tolerable in men of mature personality. It has since those days become, not a fashion, but a habit with many who ought to be, in the words of an old reviewer, 'still carrying their L plates'.

The sickness had its origin in Bennett's elderly benignity and journalistic instinct. It was maintained by the deliberate unpretentiousness of attendant stars. These stars understood what stumblers were trying to say. They knew, and had already avoided, the stunts that clever people think clever. In dealing with the clever, being in reality so much cleverer, they acted less like critics than like tender nurses, saying with full knowledge of the pain caused to an author by printed cruelties, 'Here, but for the grace of God, go I.' Unlike Bloomsbury, they practised kindness. It is a generous trait; but in less able hands it would have nourished a rank growth of mediocrity. Perhaps it did so?

The Evening News

•

17 HAVING lamented the fashion for reviews written by men well known to the novel-reading public, I claim on their behalf that as the novelist-stars brought considerable skill to their tasks they maintained a wide interest in the novel as art. They did this in good faith, and novels continued to be taken seriously until the Second World War. During that war, owing to black and stay-at-home nights, when every kerbstone was a danger, they had unprecedented popularity.

After the war a new generation of literary editors decided that novels must be subordinated to works of history, biography, travel, and *belles-lettres*. As Jane Austen had said a century-and-a-half earlier, a thousand pens eulogized 'the nine-hundredth abridger of the History of England', while 'there seemed almost a general wish of decrying the capacity and undervaluing the labour of the novelist'. This was another fashion, to which I shall refer in my last chapter.

For the present I say only that I enjoyed being a star reviewer. I liked seeing my name in large type across a wide page and even, once, on a poster of *The Evening News*. I liked being told by journalists that what I wrote was 'damned good journalism', and seeing Squire buy a copy of the paper to read what I had written, and being approached by Edgar Wallace, who was an old *Evening News* man, with a question about something I had said that very day. But chiefly I enjoyed the opportunity of expressing what, as an individual, I really thought about books and their authors. The reviews I wrote in 1914 for

The New Weekly and from 1916 until 1928 for *The Manchester Guardian* had been signed, if at all, with initials only. However uncensored in opinion, I had been limited as to space and confined to editorially-picked individual books.

Now I had elbow-room. Being no longer engaged in the daily grind of reading manuscripts (I once calculated that I must have mastered the contents of nearly a thousand every year), I dwelt in a charming Elizabethan cottage in Surrey. The cottage overlooked a Common where, at weekends, good cricket was played, as it continues to be played, in a fine spirit of sportsmanship; and I worked as and when I liked in a garden studio erected by the previous owner, Lawson Wood. Short of complete idleness, always my dream, no greater happiness was possible.

I had other causes of happiness, both domestic and professional. Since domestic happiness is not a fashion but a blessing it has no place in a record of literary affairs; and I shall confine myself, as far as temperament allows, to the relevant. A publisher's reader, such as I had been since the year 1910, seeks quality of one sort or another in every manuscript submitted to his employers. His reports may consist of a few words or of a thousand words; but in reading he has to set all prejudice aside and base his judgment on merit, though it be merit in a form he does not like. This calls for great self-discipline.

Merit is rarer in manuscript than it is in the printed books which are said to 'pour from the press'. It is also harder to determine. When a good manuscript—I use the word because 'typescript', although more accurate, is less comprehensible—turns up, the professional reader is always cautious in elation. He may be wrong; he is advising his firm to risk money which is not his money; can the author be expected to maintain this excellence? So the problem becomes a psychological problem, fascinating but taxing. On the whole the professional reader's love of quality in others must be disinterested. He will probably not see the authors whose books he recommends. Should the author be shown the report on his book he will regard the reader as nothing more than an anonymous benefactor or curmudgeon. As Dr Johnson said of the lexicographer, this man is 'a harmless necessary drudge'. Edward Garnett remains the grand exception. E. V. Lucas and I could not escape the general knowledge that we were editors as well as writers, and Lucas was made a director of his firm. I was not and did not wish to be. I preferred anonymity.

A star reviewer, on the other hand, was not condemned to read whatever was put before him. He was expected to radiate stardom. His portrait, in my case a discouragement to readers, appeared almost every week. If he thought highly or poorly of a book he risked, and gladly risked, in praising or condemning it, not his employer's money, but his own reputation. He could lift the heart of a discouraged writer (which I think it is a good thing to do) and recommend something caviar to those who would thereupon read it because he told them to do so. He could likewise, knowing all the miseries of authorship and wounded vanity, so temper blame as to render it tolerable to a morbidly sensitive class. I did all these things. I did not puff, and I did not bait. I said that some who were much-advertised did not deserve their superlatives, and that some who were largely ignored should be given their due. Accordingly, I sometimes met men who, at sight of me, raised their fists in threat; I still, after thirty years, meet others who gratefully remember commendations of their early work; and at least one novelist, prominent today, mended his ways after a rebuke which at the time was naturally resented. Star reviewing was not all evil.

I am not myself a great believer in reviews of any kind. I have never yet thanked a reviewer for praise; nor protested against his adverse opinion. In regard to the whole body I echo the words of a Surrey bowler who was asked what it was like to bowl to W. G. Grace. He said: 'You see, sir, it's like this. When I bowls to the Doctor I puts the ball where *I* likes; and then the Doctor puts it where *he* likes.' I write books as well as I can, to satisfy myself. I know what I want to do, and I am indifferent to the opinions of those who do not understand what I have attempted. When the books are sent to a newspaper for notice, it is the literary editor's job to say whether I am sufficiently in his good graces to deserve notice, and, after that, it is the reviewer's business to express what opinions he chooses.

If he shows himself to be incompetent, his incompetence will eventually recoil upon himself; but that, I submit, is not the author's business.

Looking just now through my own *Evening News* articles, I find that I began them by contrasting two explorers, Sir Harry Johnston, the small, fearless, plump-cheeked man who, whenever he used the telephone, was addressed as 'Madam' by the unseen person at the other end of the line, and R. B. Cunninghame-Graham, who could be imagined as a Highland chieftain or a superb subject for Velasquez, and whom I met only once, at the home of Festing Jones, friend and biographer of Samuel Butler. There is a difference of approach. I had known Johnston very well, and was several times a guest at his old priory near Arundel. Therefore in writing about his brother's 'Life', then newly published, I treated him as a man. He was a prattling gossip with innumerable stories, many of them scandalous, about those he had known in the course of a long life; he was no writer. Cunninghame-Graham I extolled as a writer of rich gifts as well as an adventurous traveller. He was an original and a grandee, and in my view a writer of classic quality.

At Festing Jones's our fellow-guests were two ladies who claimed former intimate acquaintance with him. He responded with the most cordial courtesy, and was never at a loss, remembering all that they remembered and gratifying them by the most ample consideration. But at the general departure he pretended to have left his walking-stick behind. To Festing Jones, under his breath, he muttered: 'Tell me, my dear fellow, who the devil *are* these two ladies?' On being told in a whisper, he raised his head and his hand in acknowledgment, and rejoined the ladies, carrying the walking-stick, debonair as before. It was throughout a masterly performance.

In a second article I discussed a volume of essays by Aldous Huxley, which I thought suggested that 'misanthropy and agoraphobia, united', were driving the author 'into a fatal intellectual solitariness'. I quoted a passage which (written in 1929) showed the direction Huxley's impatient mind was taking:

I find nowadays [he wrote] that I simply don't want to be up-to-date. I have lost all desire to see and do things, the seeing and doing of which entitle a man to regard himself as superiorly knowing, sophisticated, unprovincial. . . . 'Be up-to-date!' is the categorical imperative whose cogency I refuse to admit. When it is a question of doing something which I regard as a duty, I am as ready as anyone else to put up with discomfort. But being up-to-date and in the swim has ceased, as far as I am concerned, to be a duty. Why should I have my feelings outraged, why should I submit to being bored and disgusted, for the sake of somebody else's categorical imperative?

I quote this as illustrating resistance to what, at the time, was a cult; that of 'contemporaneity'. This cult, extremely popular among pseudo-intellectuals, was used as a pretext for throwing overboard all respect for the older generation.

The word 'contemporaneity' has been dropped as its users matured; in its place we have a new word, 'tradition', which has attained magic as amalgamating the new with the old, and giving the very recently new a classic status. But I also quote for the sake of showing that Huxley was already moving towards the intellectual isolation which he has realized. He has carried a speculative mind far from the assumption that 'there must be authority', in which he never believed. To him, as to Shaw, 'the golden rule is that there is no golden rule'. He was always an original, not a systematizer. He is still an original, aloof from current ideas, following thought into uncharted regions for which the 'traditionalists', who need dogma, express contempt. He said, still in 1929,

How one's feet itch to kick the bottoms of those imbeciles who always agree with the old sophist [Socrates], whatever nonsense he talks!

For Socrates, substitute any leader of young minds, and you will find Huxley with a foot raised. His rejection of authority has led him from iconoclasm to what he calls 'the perennial philosophy', which is an elaboration of the Christian and highly non-conformist view: 'Blessed are the pure in heart, for they shall see God'. He has reached this point through the exercise of intellect, whereas Christ and the ancient mystics, like primitive painters, naïvely expressed pure experience; but under the Swiftian ironies of his middle years he was always engaged in simple inquiry. Whether the mysticism of *The Perennial Philosophy* represents for him the end of thought, and whether it is the ultimate truth for mankind to follow, I do not attempt to say. The fact that he has reached it brings me to something I want to add.

Huxley was never one of those who cried: 'Down with Humour!' He has too much of it in his own composition. Though he finds human beings disgusting and crowds a nightmare, he has always been free from self-consciousness. He does not condescend to 'inferiors'. Pharisaism is not in his nature. Several of those are dead who could have testified to his kindness; but Robert Nichols, who to spasmodic genius added extraordinary talkative ebullience which bored the wits, and who was described by a less patient friend as 'a sort of inspired idiot', said that the two men who had never failed in tolerance towards him were Huxley and Arnold Bennett. Huxley, equally at home with Bennett and D. H. Lawrence (he awed Wells, who saw in him a mystic likeness to Thomas Henry Huxley), brought humanity to every relationship.

As a boy threatened with blindness he had to spend many long days in darkness. His considerable height (he could not stand erect in our beamed dining-room) suggested out-grown strength. He has always needed for health's sake to live quietly in a warm climate. Yet he has worked incessantly, even when ill; and has studied, thought, and intellectually proliferated as no man poorer in learning or less gaily conversible could possibly have done. This, in my judgment, is the sign of spiritual opulence.

I first met Huxley, whose contributions to *The Athenaeum* I admired, at a party given in Hampstead by Middleton Murry and Katherine Mansfield, when K.M. was very ill and could not move from her chair as she talked in the curious undertone which charmed me to the last. When Aldous and I spoke together he said he had just completed the typescript of a volume of stories, and asked if he might show it to me. Two days later, *Limbo* was on my office desk. Its laughing, boyish quality was obvious; and besides arranging the book's English publication I suggested to Doran that if he wanted to cultivate young talent, as he did, he should take the American rights. I therefore claim to be in some degree Huxley's 'man midwife' (as the Princess de Lieven insisted upon calling George the Fourth's physician Sir William Knighton); and while not always able to follow a powerful mind through its progress to transcendentalism I have never failed to rejoice in his triumphs.

From *Limbo* Huxley passed to the Peacockian *Crome Yellow* and to ampler and still more grotesque surveys of the pretentious vagueness and immorality of contemporary pseudo-intellectuals. His types belonged always to the middle-class, and were always examples of what modern culture does to essentially inferior natures. They were often recognizable caricatures of living people, and, since recognition of their friends in trouble is one of the pleasures of the smart, brought him instant popularity with 'the little West End clique'. The caricatures annoyed those who were laughed at. By them, Aldous was considered very cheap, and really not at all first class.

His types discussed literary and philosophical problems of the day, exhibiting verbal fluency and sometimes remarkable scholarship about the past, but never showing the smallest personal interest in any generation, any class, but their own. Accordingly, all who disapproved of Huxley's freedoms denounced him as ephemeral (Edwin Muir's word was 'fashionable'); and one man, writing to me, spoke harshly of his 'Victorian giggle'. It may, indeed, have suggested a limitation in Huxley himself, as well as of his characters; for he confessed in *Do What You Will* that

My own feeling, whenever I see a book about the Future, is one of boredom and exasperation. What on earth is the point of troubling one's head with speculations about what men may, but almost certainly will not, be like in A.D. 20,000?

Three years later, in 1932, he wrote *Brave New World*, a book about the Future.

This book gave Utopians a great shock and created a new fashion of its own. It was satire unleashed, which showed that Huxley, who had known Lawrence well, and had severely handled Swift's foulness, had not failed to learn from Swift's ferocious genius, as well as from Lawrence's talk. *Brave New World* was the fruit of laughing impatience with both contemporaneity and the dealers in Nowhere. It was also a sign that Huxley, having socially liberated himself from the London cliques and immoralists, had entered an atmosphere altogether more rarefied. He was still on the unending pilgrimage towards light.

He is not, temperamentally, a novelist. When, in much later years, in the person of a character named Mr Propter (*After Many a Summer*, 1939) he expressed his views on the novel, he was as contemptuous of that form as he had been of Utopias and the men who wanted to be up-to-date. He dismissed

all the innumerable anecdotes and romances and character studies [which have] no general theory of anecdotes, no explanatory hypothesis of romance or character, . . . no coordinating philosophy, . . . and no principle of arrangement more rational than simple aesthetic expediency.

No novelist by temperament could have written such words, which are those of a man obsessed by matters more abstruse than Art. Huxley, by then, although still writing fiction in which human foibles were ridiculed from Olympus, had embraced Mysticism. He was to produce in 1946 an elaborate series of extracts from mystics of several countries and several centuries. As this book, however, belongs to a period, and a fashion, in advance of what I am now discussing, I shall not discuss it.

I ask the reader to remember that I remain, for purposes of narrative, in the nineteen-twenties. Since those nineteen-twenties another war has been fought; many critical dogmas have been circulated; political, theological, metaphysical, and psycho-analytical judgments have become a part of mental training. In the 'twenties the seeds of war had already been sown, the judgments and dogmas existed in embryo; but one wrote without satirical intent of the novel as The Novel. The impulse to write novels came directly from the sensibility of men and women to whom, as to the Grimm dwarf quoted by Conrad, 'something human is dearer to me than the wealth of all the world'.

Just as Jane Austen felt able [I wrote in introducing an anthology of Modern Fiction] to write and publish without reference to the French Revolution and the Napoleonic Wars, just as Walter Scott could use his knowledge of former times to entertain generations apparently convulsed by the overthrow of Napoleon and the tumults of Reform, just as Anthony Trollope could placidly record the doings of Barsetshire while a whole world was agitated by the Darwinian theory, so many of our living novelists have been able to avoid rivalry with the newspapers and the bulletins of learned societies by the exercise of a similar prerogative.

This prerogative is none other than the use of the creative imagination, to which they have added a steadfast belief in the interest and importance of individual characters, and a perception that Freud's tragic philosophy is not necessarily, as some enthusiasts have supposed, the last word in explanation of human activity. While the mathematical school has suggested that a man is but the sum of his impressions and memories, a sensitized nonentity with a stream of consciousness; while the political school has declared that art must lecture the world in favour of Communism or Fascism; and while the very modern discoverer of Sex as Everything has learned a whole vocabulary of scientific slang with which to spatter his pages, the born novelists have continued to tell us what happened once upon a time to Brown, Jones and Robinson, and to explain how it happened to them, and why, when all is said, human beings suffer and rejoice less on account of political and economic conditions, less on account of repressions and complexes, than because they are fundamentally irrational, passionate, and egocentric.

Other views are current today. I speak of the past. And in consulting the cuttings of my *Evening News* articles I meet on every hand illustrations of the fact that the more everything changes the more it remains the same. H. W. Fowler had republished a volume of essays first produced twenty-two years earlier, and he quoted some of the reviews it had received in 1905. One said: 'he is merely shallow and oh! so banal and trite'; another that 'he has a cultured mind, a pleasing wit, and a dainty fancy': a third that the book was 'a true autobiography of a second-rate soul', and a fourth that it revealed 'a happy knack of quotation and allusion which cannot fail to recommend his lightly touched pieces of self-portraiture'.

Elsewhere I record the condemnation by a reviewer, unnamed, of an author, also unnamed, belonging to the 1884 vintage. This author, said the reviewer, 'has no interest for this generation'. Also the severity of a highbrow who, addressing myself, dismissed the writer of a poor biography with the words: 'One feels—it's a horrible thing to say—but one feels that he hasn't had a classical education.'

The reviewer's generation has had its say and, I fear, its day. Speaking for that generation the reviewer could not foresee that he too, at forty-six, if he produced any works at all, would be at the mercy of comparably severe juniors. It was a time when young men spoke of 'my generation'. Generations, owing to the partial loss of one of them in the War, had become sharply divided. A gap had been left which could only be bridged by some such contempt. I suspect that the condemned novelist may have been Francis Brett Young; but have no notion at all about the biographer. My record is simply that, on being asked by the highbrow what I thought of him, I replied: 'He's clumsy.' The reference to a classical education, which was not tactful to myself, who had not even been to school, followed. There was no difference of opinion; the highbrow's comment was not meant to be offensive to me; I quote it only to illustrate a pride in culture which I first noticed in the nineteen-twenties. I had not met it in my seniors, perhaps because, of them, only Belloc and Galsworthy were University men.

Do not forget that the world had been overturned. And Dean Inge had said of it: 'This is a world in which everybody is wanted, but nobody is wanted very much.'

Meanwhile, like the novelist who had no interest for that generation, I was forty-six and therefore presumably *vieux jeu*. But, like the younger generation, I had digested *The Interpretation of Dreams*, *Creative Evolution*, *Sex and Character*, and *The Nature of the Physical World*; and, unlike the younger generation, to whom these writings were intoxicating, I resembled the eldest Oyster in *Alice Through the Looking Glass*:

> The eldest Oyster looked at him,
> But never a word he said:
> The eldest Oyster winked his eye
> And shook his heavy head—
> Meaning to say he did not choose
> To leave the oyster bed.

I had no pride of culture (it would have been ridiculous); I was neither a highbrow nor a spokesman for 'this generation'. I absorbed but did not parade. The writers who, according to the cuttings, chiefly took my eye between October, 1929, and February, 1932, were old and young. They ranged from George Moore, Bernard Shaw, and Bertrand Russell to Evelyn Waugh and Roy Campbell. They included Kafka, who in the impressive translation of *The Castle* made in 1930 by Willa and Edwin Muir was to become the very latest and most admired thing in modernity.

Yes, but another symptom of the hour should be recorded. I received a circular, accompanied by what the sender described as a 'questionary', from the editor of a French literary review. The circular announced the birth of a new 'mouvement' in letters, to which the name 'Populism' had been given. New writers, it said, are 'too often busy describing the idle rich people and the smart set. They ignore the more vigorous, healthy, and perennial part of the nation, viz., the popular classes.'

Distinguished French novelists, continued the circular, were going to write very plain, decent novels, dealing with the life of the common people. In this way they hoped to effect what they called a 'reaction' against bad taste, mannerism, and excessive psychological analysis. They also hoped to interest the public in truthful rather than bizarre stories. The circular and 'questionary' invited my encouragement of the scheme.

Unaware that this language would become more familiar as the Communist cause advanced, but well aware that the 'mean streets' school popular in the eighteen-nineties had been followed in this century by gritty but realistic tales of common people by Bart Kennedy (a precurser in style of Hemingway), James Blyth, and Horace W. C. Newte, and in the United States by Dreiser and Upton Sinclair, the claim seemed peculiar. Nevertheless this circular now has its significance in the history of literary fashion, especially as the outstanding French novelist of the age was unquestionably Proust.

Other writers to be dealt with in these articles were John Masefield, Walter de la Mare (*On Desert Islands*), Salvador de Madariaga, William Faulkner, Michael Sadleir (his book on Lytton), Edith Sitwell, Edmund Blunden, L. A. G. Strong, Norah Hoult, Dorothy Sayers, Thornton Wilder, A. P. Herbert, Ford Madox Ford, Henry Williamson (who had already published *The Pathway* and was retracing his steps through the childhood of Willie Maddison in revised versions of *The Beautiful Years* and *Dandelion Days*), Francis Yeats-Brown (whose *Bengal Lancer* was one of the hits of 1930),

Wyndham Lewis, Ezra Pound, John dos Passos, Oliver Onions, Winifred Holtby, Norman Collins (as critic), and Drinkwater (as biographer).

If it is suggested, in face of these names, that the period was barren, and that apart from two or three outstanding men and women none have any 'interest for this generation', I can only suggest a little assiduous homework. Too much writing-off of unread authors takes place today. Not all of those I have named have figured in professorial surveys; but professors cannot read or mention everything, and if they are pursuing a very thin line of 'development' to the exclusion of all other lines whatever they may be dating themselves, and not establishing a canon. It was a professor, a very extraordinary professor (in fact, George Saintsbury), who referred to 'that basest of limitations, the single appetite for modernity'. Our professors must think again: 'contemporaneity' is 'out'; 'tradition' is 'in'. Before long, we shall be back in 'the main stream of English literature', which is something different from the tempting runnels and backwaters of professorial whim.

George Moore, who had somewhere in that malicious composition a vein of strong sense, made a couple of interesting pronouncements to Geraint Goodwin. The first, a technical criticism of *Tess of the D'Urbervilles*, does not concern me just now; the second is the point I made earlier:

It is true [said Moore] that not every writer can write a novel, just as it is true that every novelist is not always a writer. People never seem to realise that there is such a thing as narrative gift—the power to tell a story. But now, because the novel is so popular, everyone with any power of expression, poets, essayists, historians, and almost everybody who has ever held a pen—clerks for all I know—seem to think they know how to write a novel. Of course it is absurd, and what surprises me is that they never seem to realise what the technique of a novel means. . . . Look at that chap Lawrence, a man of plenty of talent. He has written at least one good book, *Sons and Lovers*, but even there he did not know how he was going to end it. Of course, if I were to quote other instances, I should have to say the writers did not know how they were going to begin.

There spoke the proud craftsman, the novelist to whom Balzac, who was called by Lawrence 'a gigantic dwarf', was the model for all to follow. His own early books were never available at the Select Libraries, which he called 'the symbol and glory of villaism'.

> The villa made known its want [I quote now from *Confessions of a Young Man*], and art fell on its knees. English fiction became pure, smutty stories were to be heard no more, were not procurable. But at this point human nature intervened; poor human nature! when you pinch it in one place it bulges out in another, after the fashion of a lady's figure. Human nature has from the earliest times shown a liking for smutty stories; smutty stories have formed a substantial part of every literature.

Moore in time ceased to write realistic fiction or smutty stories. He turned to reminiscence, to the revision of his first books, and, at last, becoming barren, to an ironic re-telling of the life of Christ and to pictures of ancient times. In connection with this last phase, I have something to add.

I reviewed in August, 1931, the ordinary edition of *Aphrodite in Aulis* (it had been published earlier in a form for bibliophiles), contrasting Moore's style with Dreiser's as it was exemplified in an autobiographical work called *Dawn*. I said:

> The contrast between the two books is extraordinary. Mr Moore's suave simplicity, with its air of saying no more than 'the fat cat sat on the mat', its sly mischief, the occasional absurdity (as when the characters, wishing to agree with each other, say 'Thou hast said it'), and its constant beauty, is enchanting. Mr Dreiser's graceless sincerity, without music, without 'allure', is as unimpressive as an inventory.
>
> Mr Dreiser's genius consists in truthfulness, in power, in determination.... In my opinion [he] is only seriously a bad writer when he tries to be a good one....

If one turns from *Dawn* to *Aphrodite in Aulis* the change is so marked that one instantly smiles. For whereas Mr Dreiser writes:

'In many cases where death or non-employment interfered with the completion of an agreement, it seemed to me a shame to take the money, to come week after week and collect with threats or sour looks for something which had been amply paid for——.'

Mr Moore's lisped limpidities run:

'The hot morning had hushed the thrushes in the groves, the larks in the sky, the linnets in the bushes, and drawing their hats over their eyes after the meal they would have dozed if the chortling and the scratching of the cock had not kept them awake. We might quiet him with some crumbs thrust into his basket, Biote said from under her hat; or maybe he is thirsty, Kebren, go to the brook for water.'

Mr Moore has been perfecting this style for many years. . . Behind the innocent words is a terribly acute brain, gentle lightnings from which play incessantly upon the page. However quick one's own mind in accepting implications, Mr Moore is always there first. But whether he is laughing or serious when one overtakes him I have never decided.

. . . The reader is soothed and charmed. He yields to illusion. Insensibly, he believes himself to be—save at times, when a character says something in a modern way, such as 'How difficult everything in life is!'—in the world of the ancients. It is an amusing experience.

A few days after the review appeared, I happened to visit Charles Evans, of Heinemanns, who had published *Aphrodite in Aulis*. He greeted me with relief; for Moore had just been on the telephone, complaining of 'that fellow—he's a well-known novelist', who in order to traduce him had invented the phrases 'Thou hast said it' and 'How difficult everything in life is!' pretending, as was quite impossible, that he had used them.

Fortunately I found the passages at once in another copy of *Aphrodite in Aulis*. Evans then told Moore, who, more indignant than ever, refused to believe him. When confronted with the passages in print, he declared that they must have been inserted by the compositor. Alas, it was shown that they had been in both the typescript and Moore's corrected proof. He was thus reduced to reviling his typist, who of course had no defence.

The explanation of both banalities was simple; as was Moore's refusal to accept blame for them. Though given to laughter at other men, he felt only reverence for himself.

I never met him. I saw him only once, at a theatre on Sunday night, when I think the play being privately acted was one by Conal O'Riordan. For some reason Moore, who was to occupy a box, arrived at the opposite side of the theatre; and the assembled audience had the unexpected amusement of seeing a drooping bottle-necked man with what Wilde called 'that vague formless obscene face' under white hair travel slowly across the stage as if he had been engaged to speak a prologue and pass from sight. When at the end of the journey he disappeared, only to waver into the proper box, all present breathed deeply in relief.

His recognized disciple was Charles Morgan, who after experience as naval officer and prisoner in the War of 1914–18 wrote a striking novel called *My Name is Legion* and then (it seemed to me) in later books over-did the theme of adultery. He wrote very smoothly indeed, sometimes with beauty; but was attacked and parodied as a novelist and disparaged as a critic by those who detested his moderation and his prose. I think the reason may have been that the prose, instead of being (as his play was called) a flashing stream, was so smoothly mellifluous as to bore his adversaries. If that is so, admiration for George Moore's later work was his ruin. But Moore himself remains a delightful theme for memory, less as novelist than as autobiographer and the subject of long fascinating stories of meanness and eccentricity related by James Stephens and others. That is, he was a character; and as a character has importance to all who collect impressions of notable men.

Three Rogue Poets

•

18   I HAVE been speaking of one small aspect of the 'twenties. I have done this for the reason that other and more partisan writers have taken no heed of it at all. Partisanship, that is to say, has been busy since 1920; and many unfortunate writers have had their heads pressed under the waters of oblivion in the hope that they would sink. Maugham was one of these writers.

It seems possible that others experienced misfortune because they obstinately followed their own stars, disregarding the times, and failing to observe one important element in modern literary reputation. This is publicity. If a man or woman is not seen, or photographed, or boosted by either a claque or an advertising agent, he or she ought not to grumble at neglect. Quality alone, so great is the number of living authors, will only be established if one book, or several books, can make the writer a subject for discussion.

With the older generations, of Shaw, Belloc, Chesterton, Wells, and Bennett, that was easy. All were public figures. They wrote controversially upon many subjects, and were encouraged to do so by editors who knew their readiness to express opinions on politics, history, morals, or religion—four subjects which always produce heat—and who believed in seasoning mediocre periodicals with what little girls, when skipping, used to call 'salt, mustard, vinegar, PEPPER!'

Shaw was regarded as a tremendous self-advertiser. When anything astonishing happened in the world he was rung up on the telephone by journalists; and he always had something vehement and amusing to say about it—without payment. Wells was detested by thousands of people who thought his opinions abominable and were angry at his ubiquitousness. Once when I was staying at his house he was delighted by the receipt of a letter which said: 'For years I have been trying to find a paper you didn't write for. I thought I had found it in —' (I forget what the paper was; something like *The Cabinet-Maker's Journal*). 'But now you have turned up even there!' Wells laughed very mischievously, and said: 'Now *what* paper can I write for that he's likely to turn to?'

Belloc and Chesterton were prolific journalists, Chesterton with a divine gift for what was thought to be paradox, although more often than not it was truth in delicious colours; and Belloc with a wealth of preposterous assertion about the world's past which made him loathed by every Professor of History in the land. Bennett was less hated; but what were called his 'pocket philosophies' encouraged the invention of discreditable stories about plans made early in life for marrying a French wife, writing pot-boilers until he was forty, when he would produce a masterpiece, and grow fat and wealthy. Men who pretended to have known him found that after the success of *The Old Wives' Tale* they could dispose of such articles to the innumerable cheap journals of the time. His quif and his fob and a peculiarity in the shape of his mouth were a godsend to caricaturists; a love of the theatre made his presence at first nights familiar, and stories of frilled and even coloured dress shirts abounded. These stories, like those about his planned life, his gaping love of luxury hotels, and his avarice, were all untrue. But they made him 'news'.

After the 1914–18 War, editorial policies changed. Belloc's great prestige as a weekly commentator on the War naturally passed; Shaw was called by A. P. Herbert 'a septuagenarian chatterbox'; Chesterton died; Bennett was used by the highbrows as a symbol of the vulgarity which they sought to destroy. They all remained public figures, because they represented original mental activity regarding affairs in which ordinary men were passionately interested. The new generation of writers, apart from J. B. Priestley, had no such knowledge of affairs, and did not wish to engage in public political argument. Had it done so, it would have found editors reluctant to print any longer the polemics of amateurs. The word 'expert' was first heard.

In 1933 I was asked to contribute an article to a new journal edited by George Jean Nathan, Ernest Boyd, Theodore Dreiser, James Branch Cabell, and Eugene O'Neill. It was called *The American Spectator*, and it was to be very outspoken. I chose for subject something much in the minds of the five editors; and I reprint it here as a part of my book because it has chronological interest. The article was called *American Authors and English Reviewers*; and it said:

A number of American writers are under the impression that English reviewers deliberately belittle American books. This is a mistake. Such writers are often exasperated to find that a favourite author, like wine drunk with relish in its own land, does not travel well. But there is a considerable misunderstanding of the point of view of literary critics in England; and this I will endeavour to correct.

In the first place, literary reputation in England is largely social. I remember being told by Gilbert Cannan that when he was at Cambridge University he heard reports of a wonderful youth who was at Rugby (the public school), and who was coming to Cambridge later. When Cannan had left Cambridge, and was in London, he heard of a wonderful young man who had arrived at Cambridge and was shortly expected to reach London. The young man—in each case it was the same young man—was Rupert Brooke. He finally reached London with a reputation already made.

This is a simple instance, but it will show what I mean. If a young man whose father has been wealthy enough to send him to a first-class English public school shows any kind of literary talent, news of it travels fast. He goes to his university double-starred, and at once enters the literary sets there. In due time he descends upon London with an immediate right of entry to literary sets in the capital. His reputation has preceded him. If he has talent, the path to a restricted fame is wide open. If he has little talent, but an eye to the main chance, he attaches himself to somebody rather more talented, and achieves a minor literary job. A little money will always help him into the publishing trade, where his previously formed literary connections will be of use.

If our young man has genuine talent, the flying start he has received will carry him quickly to eminence. He can then be prosperous, if he wishes, or he can be very refined, very fastidious, very costive, and extraordinarily respected. If his social manners are good, so that he is seen everywhere, and is welcomed as a rising star in the best drawing-rooms, he will be assured of great contemporary fame. And all the friends he has made through his early life at his public school and university will instinctively rally to their distinguished colleague, both in society and in the press. They will know him and admire him; but they will also be influenced by a desire for reflected distinction, and will praise him with loud hymns.

This praise is not disingenuous. If a man has been educated according to an established convention, if he has been taught by the same masters, the same tutors, the same professors, he will sympathize with work coloured by that convention and by the set of ideas with which he is familiar. He praises whatever is acceptable to him; and if he has pretensions to aesthetic judgment will find appropriate superlatives without strain.

Not every young man, however, can prosper in this way. A young provincial, for example, who comes to town with no reputation at all, and who wishes to be a leading writer, has a longer apprenticeship to serve. His name is unknown; he has no family connections or social prestige; he is a sort of literary poor relation. He is the boy who gets the small type notices in *The Times Literary Supplement*. He is the boy who sometimes gets no notices at all in the critical press. It is to nobody's interest to bring him to the surface and spread the good news of his arrival in town. This is where the writer with the ready-made reputation scores.

Now, my suggestion is that when an American writer sees in the English press some unpleasant or extremely sharp notice of an American book, he jumps to the conclusion that another insult is being offered to the Stars and Stripes. Nothing of the sort is intended. But the author of an American book, like the English provincial author, has no social reputation by which he can be ranged and judged. Nobody knows him. Nobody has watched him grow up. Who is he, anyway? What has he done?

Well, he has written this book, you say. True enough; but in England fourteen thousand new books are published each year. Is it not clear that when a reviewer who has been properly educated has attended to the claims of his own literary class, and the people who cannot be ignored, the rest, the *canaille* as it were, must take their chance? The rest are English as well as American; Australian, New Zealandish, and Canadian—any writers, in fact, who have no cheer leaders, or private reputation, or linguistic snob appeal. It may be unfortunate for them that they have not been embraced by the literary *ton*. But there is no animosity to American books as such. If they are unreadable, indeed, they have an excellent prospect of being extolled.

These words were largely true at the time. Some of them, although young men from the provinces have better chances today than their predecessors had in 1933, are still true. I think the star reviewers, who sought good where they found it, and such open-minded appraisers as Gerald Gould, Ralph Straus, and Howard Spring, who saw themselves as representing the larger public, did much to encourage unknown writers who had no Public School background; but the 'twenties and 'thirties did see much unconscious snobbery in the literary world. Only in the provincial press did older men, who perhaps were ignorant of the activities of London hostesses and the exclusions practised in the capital, continue to write as though John Smith from Halifax or Turnham Green was

potentially as important as any fashionable lad from Cambridge. I hope not to be misunderstood on this point. I therefore repeat words from my article: 'If a man has been educated
according to an established convention, if he has been taught
by the same masters, the same tutors, the same professors, he
will sympathize with work coloured by that convention and
by the set of ideas with which he is familiar. He praises whatever is acceptable to him.'

It may seem odd to very recent arrivals on the literary scene
that during the 'twenties and 'thirties, when we heard the now-
stilled clamour for contemporaneity, one of the neglected
writers of stature should have been Walter de la Mare; but this
was so. He was known, and greatly admired; but as he was an
original, not a deliberate innovator, there was little in his work
for fashion to seize upon. Moreover he was prolific; if he were
now to be busy I am afraid he would be labelled in select
quarters as 'commercial'. True, when a very old man he was
made, first of all, a Companion of Honour, and then—after
some private campaigning in which he had no part—a member
of the Order of Merit; but it is a convention in England that
when a writer is eighty he must be given either a Civil List
Pension because he is starving or a sort of semi-canonization
based upon longevity. We like octogenarians. They no longer
offend us. Though never mentioned, I believe, by Bloomsbury
or its attendant sprites, de la Mare was allowed to become a
saint. He was, in fact, a saint.

It was by length, rather than domestic familiarity, of acquaintance that I must measure my friendship with this beautiful
character. I probably first met him at the Cheshire Cheese
dinner where *Rhythm* was formally converted into *The Blue
Review*, and he was then writing a great deal for *The Saturday
Westminster*, edited by his friend Naomi Royde-Smith. It may,
however, have been as late as 1920, at a public dinner given by
the English Association. On that night, after fervently de-
nouncing every word of a speech I had made (I think I said, as
I still believe, that literary taste cannot be instilled by professors), John Bailey, contributor of leading articles to *The
Times Literary Supplement*, dragged de la Mare forward and

introduced us anew. The introduction, in any case, was needless: I felt that I had always known him; and this must have been the common experience.

Of course I never shared his daily life. No anxious consultations ever took place between us about the chances of love or illness. We worked together on the Royal Literary Fund committee, where we often sat side by side and for some reason were once sent out of the room almost hand in hand during an election; and whenever we met we spoke with unlimited relish of men, past events, old and new books, ideas, and fancies, while he urged me more than once to write authoritatively about old age. When I said that he, being rather more than ten years older than I, knew more about the subject than I did, he smilingly refused, on the ground that he was already too old for the task. As I am now in the same position, and the book written by John Cowper Powys was published twenty years ago, when its author was only seventy, the theme remains free for a younger hand.

Having seen de la Mare at any time during our long acquaintance, I went away enriched for many days by the exchange, to which I had contributed only a little merriment; but I understood more sensitively than before some of the innumerable delights of the contemplative life. Nothing was too small or vast for his comprehension. He would have been a friend for Sir Thomas Browne. He could equally well, on ground less hallowed, have been a friend for Max Beerbohm, as he would for poets as diverse as Henry Vaughan and A. E. Housman.

He once asked whether I had been given to eccentricity in dress as a young man, and admitted that he had taken extraordinary pleasure in wearing strange hats and coats of outrageous colours. It was hard to picture, for there was no sign of such extravagance when I knew him; but the amused memory proved how strong a power he had of entering into the humours as well as the dreams of youth. He would not have quarrelled with present-day fashions among the adolescents, which would have been received by him with the equanimity of wisdom. His sympathy, indeed, had no limits. I never knew him to belittle any of his contemporaries, although to the end his critical sense was so acute that he was unimpressible by fudge; and his modesty was such that he would invite and submit to comment from a number of men upon his own latest writing.

I think everybody who knew him felt a respect and affection even exceeding profound and long-continuing admiration of his genius. In my own case every meeting, although a year might have passed since we talked, was but the resumption of one previously left incomplete. 'I meant to ask you,' he would say on my arrival. Or 'I should like to know what you think about cobwebs.' Or 'Do you remember our talk among the ruins of Ancient Rome?' Always a question, or reminder, from which, as in all enjoyable conversation, the realms of earth and spirit would be drawn into harmony. He spent meditative days, and I expect that as he awaited a guest every previous understanding of and with that guest took its place in the pattern of his thought. At the encounter he was thus at once comprehendingly tranquil and radiant.

The perception is not only my own. It was the universal marvel. Other men knew him better than I: he had close friends; but just as he felt there was no such thing as death so he felt intelligence to be, not in the slang sense used to describe certain fictions, but in reality, a stream of consciousness. Some men, however kind, must be warmed gradually into ease. They are shy, well-intentioned strangers, feeling in the dark for landmarks recalling previous acquaintance. Not so de la Mare; with him there was no hesitation. 'I meant to ask you'; 'What do you think?'; 'Do you remember?' It was the sweet readiness of one questing mind to share every reflection, to seek every *rapport*, with another. This other was assumed to possess an identical appetite for the subtleties of knowledge.

Sitting at peace (I speak of the last years), without gesture, but ever humorous and philosophic, de la Mare serenely endured my own effervescence. If I tired him he gave no sign of weariness, but was amused to the last. He was interested in every manifestation of the human spirit; and he was as much stimulated by a child's answers as by the abstractions of a star-gazer. More stimulated, perhaps, because the child was nearer to his own poetic simplicity. No articulate creature was disdained. The inarticulate he supplied with words which they supposed to be their own, miraculously drawn from unsuspected inner wealth.

His prose style, so unknotted and unpretentious that dull readers, I believe, could yield to the enchantment without realizing its distinction, was more lovely than any other of our age. His verse, so apparently free from complexity that it could be skimmed by the uncomprehending as lucid commonplace, was as varied and as ingenious as its themes. It was dominated by de la Mare's own absorption in the simple, the unearthly, and the macabre. Imagination was its essence.

Another poet whose genius is being restored to us after a period of disregard is James Stephens. He belonged in early days to the life of Dublin, when plays by Yeats and Synge and Lady Gregory were being produced at the Abbey Theatre, A. E. was writing poetry, James Joyce and Oliver Gogarty drinking and arguing together, St John Ervine, who came from Belfast, writing his first plays and novels, and when a character from Peckham in one of Pett Ridge's novels remarked that 'anything about Ireland always makes me cry'. The aim of these writers was not to make people cry; it was to enrich their lives and, if they were English, to make them sit up. James Stephens's first book of poems, published in 1909, was called *Insurrections*.

In that book his motto was:

> What's the use
> Of my abuse?
> The world will run
> Around the sun
> As it has done
> Since time begun,
> When I have drifted to the deuce,
> And what's the use
> Of my abuse?

It was not a despairing philosophy. It was one of acceptance. And as the patient mind wove its further message it could state without impotent rage, in *The Red-Haired Man's Wife*, a fact which drove Lawrence to frenzy; the fact of 'otherness'.

> I am woman and glory and beauty, I mystery, terror and doubt.
> I am separate still,
> > I am I and not you:
> And my mind and my will
> > As in secret they grow,
> Still are secret, unreached and untouched and not subject to you.

In an age of exasperation at the senselessness of events and disaster to the Victorian belief in progress, such singing had no charm for youth. Therefore Stephens, whose interest in all things was detached, who looked on mankind with poetic scorn and consorted by preference with fairies, charmed but did not intellectually impress. He had no word for the rebellious or the distracted ('What's the use Of my abuse?'); he told stories because it amused him to play as imaginative children play; and being a magnificent talker he held his listeners entranced in the Irish manner with inexhaustible narrative. 'Once upon a time', 'There was a ship', 'Now you must know that a certain man . . .' The fairies were then not far away.

He was physically very small indeed, with an inappropriately large head, a rather long comedian's face and a mounting brow. At first one likened him to the Reynolds portrait of Oliver Goldsmith; but Reynolds made Goldsmith something of a Roman senator, whereas Stephens was evidently full of the slyest whim. Careless in dress, he often, to my recollection, appeared in a soft shirt without a tie, and conventional men looked a little askance, thinking him a droll but penniless fellow who might try to borrow a shilling or two. They were wrong. Stephens had the greatest pride, and was indifferent to conventional men. He carried his world about with him, and was lost to the hurly-burly.

In Dublin he had been employed at the Art Gallery; but when he afterwards came to London he had no occupation but that of author. Consequently he remained poor. He would leave his suburban home early in the morning to rove the streets, especially Charing Cross Road, which was the last human thoroughfare he was ever to see. As he roved his head was full of stories and memories which he would either write as verse or pour out as anecdote to his friends. In argument he could be, I understand, overwhelming, so quick and adroit was his management of words and ideas; but this overwhelmingness was outside my own experience. When we met, he did no more than talk his best.

He told extraordinary anecdotes, not malicious, but derisive, about other Irishmen such as Yeats, Joyce, and Gogarty, for whom he felt no respect, and about George Moore, who needed revision of the Connemara speech in *The Untilled Field* and would pay Stephens, but did not pay Stephens, vast sums for the help he received. The stories were always absorbing, usually amusing, and they stretched and interlaced for two, for three hours, or more, until the English habit of catching trains brought an end to the session. The teller did not tire. Nor did the hearer, even if, as sometimes happened, he had heard the story before.

Stephens had a curious and charming habit of bringing little presents for those he was to meet, one of these in my own case being a mysterious package which contained a brown-paper-covered copy of one of my own books. He had written in this not only a commendation of the book but an original poem. To me, who am neither Irish nor a Swinnertonian, the gift was embarrassing; but his delight in making it, and watching the packet's opening and the recipient's surprise, was so child-like and so endearing that he became in that moment a character from folklore.

One of his best friends in London was Norah Hoult, the very good Anglo-Irish novelist whose book of stories *Poor Women*, when it was first published, made a strong impression upon readers of taste, and whose later work, although little read by genteel reviewers, gets better and better. It was Norah Hoult who, although I already knew Stephens through casual encounters in larger company, brought us together for long talk-filled lunches. For her, Stephens represented unpractical genius at its zenith; and she did him many kindnesses. She even allowed him to exercise his gift for darting ridicule upon her strong religious beliefs, and although this ridicule may have wounded it never, I thought (as I joined in the teasing), went beyond the limits of tact. It did no more than release Stephens's tongue from any risk of disuse.

Norah Hoult knew, as I discovered later for myself, that Stephens rose as a talker to his greatest heights when happy; and this meant when a second bottle of wine had been broached. We always provided the second bottle; and if necessary, and if time had allowed, would have introduced a third or fourth. The second was enough to make him irresistible, and he was in no sense a toper. He talked from happiness in congenial company.

He was not a wit or a maker of *bons mot* in the manner of Wilde. Narrative was his strength, narrative adorned with fancy and irony; that curious bitter-flavoured laughter which makes Irish talk so much more astringent (as well as copious) than the English variety. W. J. Turner, the Australian poet, music critic, and one-time associate member of the Squire-archy, wrote in his miscellany *The Duchess of Popocatapetl* a passage contrasting the two. Before speaking of Yeats and Stephens, whom he knew well, Turner indulged in some heightened praise of English talkers, whom he described as the best in the world because they have most respect for the truth.

> The English mind [he said], at its profoundest, delights in *andante poco allegretto* in order to give time and space to the divagations, exceptions, qualifications, conditions, extenuations, diversions, digressions, and reservations in which the colossal, powerful, wide-reaching, deep-scouring, and subtle English mind delights. . . . Such a great talker as James Stephens often needed such an English guide, and was at his best when one was forthcoming to take him gently by the hand and lead him away from the flats on which he loved to

cut capers and perform somersaults for the audience whom he always, in his Irish hatred of the human race, despised.

Did he hate the human race? Not with the venom of Joyce; and if Turner was here making the mistake of supposing Swift to have been an Irishman because he was born in Dublin ('If a man is born in a stable, it doesn't mean that he's a horse') his generalization is undermined. The Irish are ruthlessly combative, and they have centuries of envy and hatred of the English to indulge; but unless they appropriate Swift to themselves only Joyce is the embodiment of hate for the human race. I think Stephens hated nobody, but that he was not sentimental. His faery fancies were as free from archness as the tales of Grimm. His acceptance of what is called 'otherness' embraced knowledge of the fact that he, too, was 'other'. Nor had he the highbrow's pride in being different from common people. He felt himself naturally a God, and was untroubled by his own physical smallness because he knew his speedy, resourceful brains would never fail.

I once saw Stephens talking to Augustus John, who in those days was a big and rather splendid figure. Neither was conscious of any contrast in physique; both were engrossed in their conversation. I was with a party at a distance, and do not know what they discussed; but this was an occasion when, if I had been Boswell, I should have stolen up with elongated ears to listen, for both were great men, and they were assuredly not asking each other to pass the salt.

The third of my poets is Siegfried Sassoon, who began by expressing in verse the enthusiasm and disillusion of his wartime generation, went on to become literary editor of a Labour journal edited by George Lansbury, tired of the paper's futility, and wrote in quiet prose of great distinction the story of his own life as a fox-hunting man, cricketer, and associate of others among the Georgian Poets. He was never one of the destructive wits who iconoclastically attacked traditional forms, never one of the intellectuals, but a simple lyric poet who had seen and hated war, and who wanted above all things to submit all his sensitiveness to the good tranquil things of life. He was simple; not a simpleton.

Having married, he retired to a very large house in the country and devoted himself to the composition and private publication of what he specifically called, in one instance, *Rhymed Ruminations*. It was his aim

> To find rewards of mind with inward ear
> Through silent hours of seeking;
> To put world sounds behind and hope to hear
> Instructed spirit speaking.

That was the quest. It led him into the woods and into the study; it drew him more and more apart, not from his true friends, whom he ever valued, nor from continued interest in the arts of music and design, but from clamour. He ceased to frequent even literary society, except for visits to Cambridge, where he renewed the delights of Fenner's, talked with contemporaries and cricketing undergraduates, took pride in the doings of his one son, and was able to relish the girl undergraduate's solemn admonition to Robert Graves that 'Poetry isn't meant to be enjoyed; it's meant to be analysed.'

Withdrawal from London led by degrees to inevitable but grotesque supersession in the eyes of fashion by more competitive spirits. Credit was given to others for the innovations of his verse. The life he chose to live, in which perhaps he hoped to carry over to younger poets an influence which he had already exercised in wartime upon Wilfred Owen, had a different consequence. It was that busy assessors of quality, who did not see his privately-printed volumes, knew nothing of the progress in thought which ultimately carried him into the Roman Church. They were aware only that he had written a biography of the now-disregarded George Meredith; and on his seventieth birthday they only mildly applauded his Collected Poems.

As one who always felt strong affection for Sassoon as a man, who appreciated the love of quietude which produced the beauty of his rhymed ruminations, but who had no sympathy with his final acceptance of clerical supervision, I travelled happily in his mental company for forty years and more. I know the constraints imposed upon him by the aggressiveness of intellectuals; I understand why he has wished to be more and more alone in the pursuit of truth; I think him under-rated now as a poet by those who prefer more positive concern with the times. I see in his fortune with the public the result of too little personal ambition and a modesty which has led him to avoid tragic, controversial, and tumultuous themes. This fortune is an accident of the age, which, because these things can be argued about and fought for, sets discord and experiment in the arts higher than reflective aloofness.

As a man, Sassoon has always been, I think, shy. His conversation, although spiced with brief and memorable literary comments (never sentimental comments, but pithy and colloquial, as when he said of an admired contemporary 'I always thought him a bit of a frump'), has been happiest in its moments of concern with cricket and cricketers. His letters, often crammed into two small pages of minute handwriting, have always been candid and communicative, so that they vividly picture scenes and problems in terms of the happiest humour. In person he has continued lean and athletic, playing his favourite game until well on in middle years and I suppose (but do not know) riding horses as he always did; and I think one would sense in his face and bearing familiarity with those endearing animals. His speech has always been abrupt, not staccato, but a little hesitant; his laughter often accompanied by impulsive movements of the arms which in a less reserved person could have been carried further, into delighted back-slapping.

No back-slapping has ever occurred. He has never been hail-fellow-well-met. But in greeting one he loves he has always gone forward very eagerly, with boyish zest. His great pride is in his Thorneycroft blood; and it is to his mother, who was a Thorneycroft, that his deepest affection, throughout life, has been given.

Original Sin

•

19 IN ONE of Talbot Baines Reed's school stories for boys (*The Willoughby Captains*, 1887) there is an inky and ungrammatical junior named Bosher who keeps a diary; and Bosher's grand philosophical discovery is: 'How vast is the world. I am small in the world.' Reed was evidently amused by the truism, and when his book was written it was a merely ridiculous observation. With the 1914–18 War, however, everybody saw that the little man, the man who in all countries was taken from his daily work to be slaughtered in uniform, could still not effectively control the bosses who turned him into cannon fodder.

These bosses in the past had been kings, nobles, and the Church. Now they were men very little larger than himself who had been elected to Parliaments intended to represent and protect whole populations. It was shown that Parliaments were composed, not of Solons, but of quite insignifioant mortals who cheered and waved order papers but in the long run, as Gilbert's sentry pointed out, 'voted just as their leaders tell 'em to'. We had again Bosher's discovery: 'How vast is the world. I am small in the world.'

Who, then, made the wars that nobody wanted? The financiers, said some; the armament manufacturers, said others; the old men (said the young), who are incompetent. Norman Angell had shown that wars did not pay, so the financiers seemed to be absolved. The old men, blaming the enemy's arrogant breed and disrespect for treaty, disclaimed responsibility. In England there was a Royal Commission to investigate the war-fomenting activities of arms manufacturers which included at least two journalists, J. A. Spender and Philip Gibbs, who—despite differences in outlook and education—were convinced pacificists and men of experience in the elucidation of facts. Its findings made no impression upon mankind. On the whole incompetence—drift, *laissez faire*, Liberalism—seemed to be the best answer. Unless, of course, it was the Devil, who to this day has his devotees.

We had been taught by the Victorians that Progress, meaning an increase of morality in human relations, but perhaps only commercial prosperity, was a great fact. The British Empire's humane rule extended from pole to pole, and was the subject of criticism only from envious nations which, starting late, had found the British already established everywhere. The Union Jack was the symbol of power and liberty. True, we had unemployment; but with successive extensions of the right to vote and the spread of popular education our people had attained a level of intelligence and independence never before known. It was a marquess who said: 'We are all Socialists now.' And when the twentieth century opened it was hailed as 'the century of the common man'.

The sense that common men had been killed and maimed and terrified for four and a half years, and that for all the trumpeting of war leaders about 'making the world safe for democracy' no new security was to be enjoyed, was widespread. The arrival of a new form of oligarchy in Russia which denounced kings, nobles, and the Church, and promised to assure through a classless society the virtues of perpetual peace, was endorsed in Britain, as the French Revolution had been endorsed more than a hundred years earlier, by many who agreed that a classless society would make wars impossible.

This view was particularly attractive to the young and ardent, who saw in the destruction of kings, nobles, and the Church a hope that they would cease to be small in the world. Returning soldiers, who found no jobs waiting for them, and who felt themselves to have been betrayed by politicians of all classes, remembered that their recent enemies had also been small men as little responsible as themselves for starting the

War. *Little Man, what now?*, a German novel which put this point, was widely read in England. Two slogans were common at the time. One was: 'The world owes me a living'; the other, taken from a Communist Manifesto: 'You have nothing to lose but your chains.' Both were impregnated with bitterness.

Owing chiefly to the self-discipline of the common man in Britain, but also owing to the fact that in this country there was no traditional enmity between the classes, revolution did not follow. It would come, said Sidney Webb, by 'the inevitability of gradualness'. Therefore Communist ideas did not seize the imagination of the people. They did inspire in the youngest among educated men and women a fever for social, political, and intellectual change.

This fever succeeded the assaults of Strachey upon the Victorians and the revolutionary efforts of those who sought innovation in the Arts and 'death to Humour'. It was accompanied by a quasi-scientific belief among older men that one must concentrate on the mass, not the individual, as a far more interesting study. This view, which I think originated in Germany, was enunciated to me by Joseph Hergesheimer, who as a consequence ceased to write novels. The individual and the Middle Class were both finished. H. M. Tomlinson did not agree; but in writing to me he summarized the phenomenon:

The old middle class [he said] which hammered out political and economic theory for all the world (and produced the revolutions in Europe and America); . . . the people of that class wrote the best we have on our shelves, translated the Scriptures into noble English, got rid of kings who did not understand where they were, did most of the inventing for the industrial and agricultural revolutions, changed common thought with its adventures in natural philosophy (Darwin, Clerk Maxwell, Faraday), gave us what music we have—in fact, gave us a name and a standing. That little lot is submerged. We are now an amorphous mob.

Others, besides Tomlinson, perceived dangers in the new cleavage. Even sponsors of a classless society realized that until all were free there was a need for leaders. The age of the common man was in conflict with an age demanding power for a new aristocracy based on education and command of ideas. Although politicians, in search of votes, flattered Tom, Dick, and Harry (together with the new and quite incalculable voters, Jane, Emily, and Dorcas), they knew, as other observers knew, that in society, the Arts, the factories, and every other human activity, chaos, which some called Liberalism and some Humanism, could not be allowed to continue. 'There must be authority.'

About a year after the publication of *The Willoughby Captains* a little boy was born in St Louis, in the State of Missouri, U.S.A. His name was Thomas Stearns Eliot, and he was the younger or youngest son of one Henry Ware Eliot, whose career and opinions are altogether beyond my knowledge. He was serious, became very studious, and my surmise, which I shall later explain, is that he may have been self-distrustful. At any rate, he quickly recognized that 'the world is so full of a number of things' as to need the discovery of some unifying principle to make it intelligible or even tolerable.

In his search for this principle he attended, first, Harvard University, then the Sorbonne, and at last Oxford University, at which places he learned to read widely in the Greek and Latin Classics and to make acquaintance with the graces and intricacies of French literature. In imagining his search I am reminded of some lines in FitzGerald's *Rubáiyát of Omar Khayyám*:

> Myself when young did eagerly frequent
> Doctor and Saint, and heard great Argument
>   About it and about; but evermore
> Came out by the same Door as in I went.

He was not satisfied. When he turned to English literature he found himself bored by the verbosity of our poets, repelled by the personalities of Milton and Shelley, and scornful of

Matthew Arnold, whose philosophy as expressed in *Culture and Anarchy* and its successors seemed to him inadequate. As for the Georgians, his contemporaries, he felt and expressed whole-hearted contempt. They were as bad as many said they were; and even worse than that. He turned in distaste from those who sought the material welfare of their species, such as Francis Bacon and Hobbes, Bentham, the Mills, Ricardo, T. H. Huxley, and H. G. Wells. The world they envisaged was one in which he could not breathe. Gilbert Murray's attempt to bring Euripedes into unclassical homes took many sentimental words to express the superlatively pregnant Greek; William Archer's wooden translations of Ibsen were an outrage upon a great Scandinavian who was poet as well as teacher. These material-ists and turgid songsters up and down the past two centuries represented unspeakable stupidity. They also represented a chaos of belief and performance. *Ecrasez l'infame!*

Eliot, and others, wanted English poetry to be as strict, as hard and simple, as French poetry. Though he never, as far as I am aware, extolled a line of Racine's (as Lytton Strachey did) as 'very, very lovely', he could spare from admiration of the transcendental beauty of Dante much esteem for Baudelaire and Verlaine, whose work contained something as different as possible from the endless sonorities of English romantic verse. The French had standards of language and prosody which satisfied his demand for poetic precision. Although nowadays he disclaims the classical scholarship for which he made a name by a long essay on Elizabethan translations of Seneca as well as the destructive assault on Murray's Euripides, it was the classic, as opposed to the romantic, which he really admired. He ex-plained his preference with the utmost severity in many critical pieces.

In recent years, Eliot has remarked upon the effect on others of his own early critical dogmatism. 'When we are young,' he said in a speech in Leeds, 'we are confident in our opinions, sure that we possess the whole truth; we are enthusiastic or indignant—and readers, even mature readers, are attracted to a writer who is quite sure of himself.' 'Even mature readers', one notes; but in reality it was to the young of the immediately post-1914–18 War period that Eliot made his greatest appeal. I recall a passage read long ago in one of Turgenev's novels, *Rudin*, from which I have omitted several disparaging sentences, because they do not apply to Eliot. My quotation does, I think, explain what I wish to say hereafter. Turgenev says (Mrs Garnett's translation, 1900, pp. 118–19):

Rudin . . . had a well-arranged intellect, and a prodigious memory, and what an effect that has on young people! They must have generalization, conclusions, incorrect if you like perhaps, but still conclusions! . . . Try to tell young people that you cannot give them the whole truth, and they will not listen to you. . . . He read philosophical books, and his brain was so constructed that he extracted at once from what he had read all the general principles, penetrated to the very root of the thing, and then made deductions from it in all directions—consecutive, brilliant, sound ideas, throwing up a wide horizon to the soul. Our set consisted then—it's only fair to say—of boys, and not well-informed boys. Philosophy, art, science, and even life itself were all mere words to us—ideas if you like, fascinating and magnificent ideas, but disconnected and isolated. The general connections of these ideas, the general principle of the universe we knew nothing of, and had no contact with, though we discussed it vaguely, and tried to form an idea of it for ourselves. As we listened to Rudin, we felt for the first time as if we had grasped it at last, this general connection, as if a veil had been lifted at last.

Besides writing these confident essays, which as I have suggested were often welcome condemnations of older writers, Eliot had another appeal to youth. His poetry was marked by lovely rhythms, and expressed as nothing else in current literature was doing the popular disillusion, disgust, and sense of frustration. All saw that political leaders, for one reason or another, but chiefly from lack of principle, could not maintain a clear line of conduct. Whereas Gladstone, Palmerston, and Disraeli could sit down and write reports to the Sovereign in longhand, modern statesmen had no time for thought or co-ordination. Everything must be improvised, as sandbags are hastily reared to battle against inundation. The sound of many voices on the air did but add to the impossibility of quiet.

It was not—it never is or should be—the business of youth to be patient. The world was visibly in chaos; human beings were seen, through the eyes of Freud's disciples, as sick from child-hood, their pleasures corrupt, their deceits and hypocrisies manifold; and while the little man suffered as a little man, he became, in number, a mob which nothing was being done to discipline. Eliot said later that it was never his aim to speak for the younger generation; his disgusts were his own. Neverthe-less his was the positive voice of criticism. As Malcolm Mugger-idge said in another connection: 'Popularity is achieved by making manifest the contemporary mind.'

In doing this Eliot received aid from unofficial acolytes. I remember reading of a delightful episode in which a convinced Eliotonian undergraduate discerned that an undergraduette whom he met that day for the first time was not of the Faith. He detained her with exposition for half an hour; at the end of which (assisted by charm and good looks) he had made a whole-hearted convert. The persuasiveness and determination of other enthusiasts spread far and wide. Once, after I had endured what I hope was my last operation for hernia, my nurse made a habit of introducing other nurses into the room, ostensibly to admire the straightness of my legs or the un-blemished beauty of my feet, but really to entertain a patient who was quite well enough to receive company all day long. One of the visiting nurses was a charming junior from over-seas, between whom and myself the following duologue occurred:

NURSE, in a tone of astonishment: 'I thought authors were all quiet, thoughtful people.'

MYSELF, fully informed by the Press: 'If you want to see a quiet, thoughtful author, you must find out which room in this establishment is occupied by Mr T. S. Eliot.'

NURSE, excitedly: 'Is he really here? How wonderful! But

how could I explain why I was there? Could I say you sleep with a copy of his poems under your pillow?'

MYSELF, in reproof: 'That wouldn't be true.'

NURSE, with cunning: 'I could bring my copy and put it there.'

MYSELF: 'But surely that would be very casuistical?'

NURSE, sadly: 'I suppose it would. Oh, but he's so wonderful! He says—you know—such wonderful things.'

MYSELF, ever willing to learn: 'Such as?'

NURSE: 'Oh, I don't know. In his poems, I know them almost by heart.'

MYSELF: 'Can you recite them?'

NURSE, a little disconcerted: 'No, I can't. But they're all . . . There's that splendid one about the breakfast-plates rattling.'

I had been speaking, it was clear, with an enthusiast. I made no effort to lessen her enthusiasm. I never do such things. I merely recorded the conversation on the tablets of memory, from which I now summon it in order to show that to a receptive mind the slightest hint carries significance unperceived by an ignoramus. I had read the poem which mentions rattling breakfast-plates, and had thought rather poorly of it; so I longed for enlightenment. Unfortunately at this point we were interrupted, and further literary discussion became impossible. I never saw this charming nurse again. On the following day I was sent home intact, and had to be satisfied with what my wife and daughter could do on the lower level of unashamed and unsentimental humanism.

Before going on to speak of Eliot's maturer philosophy, I remind the reader that after 1920 disgust and contempt were indications of the superior mind. Bergson had been weaving his spells in Paris before the War; Freud's *Interpretation of Dreams*, first translated in 1913, now reached the juniors; a new and rather confusing German theorist named Oswald Spengler, who complained in *The Decline of the West* that 'as yet there exists no theory-enlightened art of historical treatment', caught the mood of the hour. I cannot clearly recollect what *The Decline of the West* was all about, and as Spengler has dropped from attention I suspect that this is true of others; but he became for a short period what Americans call 'required reading'.

Concurrently with such potent influences was another, of great interest. Dr W. H. R. Rivers, a very learned ethnologist whom I used occasionally to see at the Reform Club before his death in 1922, believed that 'the ultimate aim of all studies of mankind, whether historical or scientific, is to reach explanation in terms of psychology, in terms of the ideas, beliefs, sentiments, and instinctive tendencies by which the conduct of man, both individual and collective, is determined'.

Rivers was a scientific inquirer of the most humane and humorous order, an adornment to a society 'worm-eaten with Liberalism', in Eliot's phrase, and much too disinterested in the pursuit of truth to be anything of a bigot or formalist. He would sit among less learned but quick-witted companions with a silent, smiling modesty endearing to all who saw the tanned face and rather wide mouth spread in noiseless laughter. His occasional brief remarks were never negligible—at least, to myself—and although we were never intimate I formed, as others did, deep respect for his character.

On one occasion it appeared that he had found both ridiculous and harmful a letter appearing that day in *The Times*. I think the letter advocated parental attempts to influence the child-mind during sleep; and he felt so strongly that I suggested a counter-letter to *The Times*. He replied with quiet boastfulness that he had never in his life written to the editor of a newspaper. At my remark that this abstention revealed an important psychological truth about himself, and a Freudian 'repressed wish', he laughed outright, not at all offended. I therefore claim him as a humanist.

He was more than humane, and the joke was less obvious than it may seem. As a lecturer at Cambridge and visitor to London he came into close contact with several of the Georgian Poets, and with great sympathy he encouraged them to discover the psychological sources of their own work. Since he was an ethnologist whose special subject was the civilization of primitive peoples, particularly the Melanesians, he did not claim to be a literary critic; but my belief is that he was the first to spread what afterwards was misinterpreted as the only possible approach to poetry—its analysis, not its enjoyment. I am sure that he first enjoyed whatever he read, and only when he had done this tried to assist the poets to understand themselves. It was a new approach; definitely a symptom of the age's tendency.

Another strong influence which at first affected only the few was that of a young man who had been killed in action at the age of thirty-four. His name was T. E. Hulme, and although he had published in his lifetime translations of Bergson's *Introduction to Metaphysics* and Sorel's *Reflections on Violence* he became known to the world as an individual only through a single volume of collected pieces, published in 1924, to which the title *Speculations* was given by its editor, Herbert Read.

This book contains some fine dogmatic statements on democracy, romanticism, and classicism. It is written very clearly, with many italicized words, and is the work of a most intelligent man, still immature, but already capable of thinking for himself. You could say of the book that it is often boyish, since Hulme, when he comes to a point of great moment, candidly and amusingly says, 'I must now shirk the difficulty of saying exactly what I mean.' He shirked it, not from cowardice, but from haste and the rush of thought, having swept impetuously into what all will recognize as the excited generalization heard in every youthful argument:

By the perverted rhetoric of Rationalism, your natural instincts are suppressed and you are converted into an agnostic. Just as in the case of the other instincts, Nature has her revenge. The instincts that find their right and proper outlet in religion must come out in some other way. You don't believe in a God, so you begin to believe that man is a god. You don't believe in Heaven, so you begin to believe in a heaven on earth. In other words, you get romanticism. The concepts that are right and proper in their own sphere are spread over, and so mess up, falsify and blur the clear outlines of human experience. It is like pouring a pot of treacle over the dinner table. Romanticism then, and this is the best definition I can give it, is spilt religion.

Hulme, following Sorel, had no use for pacifist democracy. He believed that a spiritual rot had attacked mankind at the end of the Middle Ages. Modern Liberalism, he said, was the 'sloppy dress' of the Renaissance; while romanticism ('which we may define as [the work of] all who do not believe in the Fall of Man') was a 'bastard phenomenon', originating in Rousseau. Only the Religious attitude was truly satisfying, because the Religious attitude conceives the state of Perfection. 'In the light of these absolute values,' says Hulme, who makes great play with the adjective 'absolute', and often prints it in italics, 'man himself is judged to be essentially limited and imperfect. He is endowed with Original Sin. . . . A man is essentially bad, he can only accomplish anything of value by discipline—ethical and political. Order is thus not merely negative, but creative and liberating. Institutions are necessary.'

I never met Hulme, and until *Speculations* appeared I had read no more than a few of the articles which he contributed to *The New Age* under Orage's editorship. Also, like Eliot, 'I am not arguing or reasoning or engaging in controversy with those whose views are radically opposed to mine.' Much as I admire his stimulating mind, I can now do no more than cite his opinions as having strongly impressed Eliot. The two men were temperamentally different, Hulme rejoicing in war, and Eliot, although he said 'pacifism can only continue as long as the majority of persons forming a society are not pacifists', being by instinct non-combatant. They united in insistence upon authority, upon the fact that Liberalism and Humanism represented 'sloppy dregs' or 'worm-eaten' thought, and that man is 'endowed with Original Sin'.

In Eliot's case, to judge by a reference in Leonard Woolf's *Sowing*, there was a sudden conversion from scepticism to what was not so much acceptance of Christ as a Saviour as vehement belief in the all-pervading rightness of the English Catholic Church. Like Master Bosher, he had always felt small in a vast world. Now he had found one single institution capable of supplying the authority which he and Middleton Murry had demanded.

For Bloomsbury, authority had properly resided in a crystallized Cambridge dialectic. For Murry it was something hitched to whatever star was then satisfying his vagabond loyalties, whether Lawrence, Hardy, Santayana, or what Eliot scornfully described as a 'highly respectable' version of Christianity. Eliot was not a member of the Cambridge set, and he cannot really at any time have accepted Murry's opportunism. What he wanted was some positive assurance with which to justify instinctive revulsions from materialism and the sort of highly coloured romanticism which eighteenth-century rational conformists called 'enthusiasm'. He detested the reach-me-down philosophy of men like Wells. Now he had a big brother —quite the biggest brother of all—to fight his battles for him.

He did not go as far back in condemnation of anti-classicism as Hulme had done. That would have affronted the memory of Dante; and Eliot had read more widely among the Elizabethans than Hulme, probably, ever had time to do. I doubt if he approved the legerdemain by which Hulme excepted Shakespeare from the denunciation of Romantic writers by calling him a dynamic Classic, or 'the classic of motion'. But he shared Hulme's hostility to slop under any name and to a glorious Guy Fawkes figure known to them both as Science.

Once more he was in tune with the times. The Russian Communists had knocked down Liberal ideas as readily as Grand Dukes. There was to be no more Humanism in their country; only dialectical materialism. In Italy a Left Wing leader followed the ancient Roman habit of marching on the capital at the head of his army, there to drive out bourgeois décadence. In Germany Hitler trained his brownshirts to exterminate a breed whose internationalism had corroded the pure gold of a master race. These three movements substituted dictatorship or oligarchy for flabby and expedient pseudo-democracy. Their leaders knew that an artist following his vision was as dangerous to authority as a counter-revolutionary army.

Hitler, it will be remembered, proclaimed all modern art as decadent, and ordered the removal of 16,000 paintings from the Munich Art Gallery. Krylenko, the Commissar for Justice in Russia, expressed what Malcolm Muggeridge described as 'a materialist interpretation of the Christian doctrine of Original Sin' when he said: 'In the specific nature of their functions there is no difference between the Soviet Court of Justice and the Ogpu. . . . Every Judge must keep himself well informed on questions of State policy, and remember that his judicial decisions in particular cases are intended to promote the prevailing policy of the ruling class and nothing else.'

This was authority with a vengeance! 'All,' added Mugger-idge, 'are miserable offenders who have erred and strayed from the Party line like lost sheep, and therefore deserve to be shot; but they may still hope to escape, if they are properly obedient and contrite, by virtue of their Government's infinite mercy.' The parody is unmistakable. Its application came very near home indeed.

Being a literary man, Eliot was neither Communist nor Fascist nor Nazi, although he said, 'I suspect that in our loathing of totalitarianism there is infused a good deal of admiration for its efficiency.' He saw that the three systems, whatever their professions, were fundamentally anti-Christian, as well as anti-Liberal. Their cruelties revolted him. But he was still pursuing, as he had done all his life, what he came to call Reality; and the confusion he saw in England made him admire what he mis-took for a firm control elsewhere of uneducated populations. ' "If we could only sweep this up," as the walrus and the car-penter said, "it would be grand." ' The notion possessed many other Anglo-Saxon writers.

Now a passing enthusiasm for Communist ideas affected many of the younger intellectuals, some of whom went to Spain to fight against General Franco and his abominable allies; and some of Eliot's remarks, taken by superficial critics as an endorsement of Fascism, were in truth directed against the more-glaring atheism of the Communist Faith. That Faith put into practical operation the ideas of Hobbes, of which he had already ('one of those extraordinary little upstarts whom the chaotic motion of the Renaissance tossed into an eminence which they hardly deserved and have never lost') declared his hatred. Fascists, whatever the brutality of their methods, did at least oppose Hobbes—and Communism. To that extent were they not commendable? How difficult it was to tread the path of truth; how difficult he found it to escape what was often malignant misrepresentation.

In this dilemma, the Church became more than ever a rock upon which sensitive minds, clinging to the notion of an *élite* as opposed to Casca's 'sweaty rabblement' or Dr Stockmann's 'compact Liberal majority', could rest. Eliot, like all converts, had become a zealot. To him, the Church was not a harbour against chaos; it was the consecrated symbol of authority. You could not have a true culture divorced from all-pervading Religion; and Religion divorced from the Church degenerated at once into slop. He had to lead his followers away from worm-eaten tolerance into a 'satisfying' (the word is Hulme's) calm. He had to live up to his bold declaration that he was 'classicist in literature, royalist in politics, and anglo-catholic in religion'. He did both these things.

He did them by leaping from reason to mystical dogma. 'A man,' Hulme had said, 'is essentially bad, he can only accomplish anything of value by discipline—ethical and political.' 'He is endowed with Original Sin.' Eliot's position, superficially akin to, but politically poles apart from, that of Krylenko, was formally stated in his book *After Strange Gods*:

> Literary criticism [he announced] should be completed by criticism from a definite and theological standpoint. In so far as in any age there is common agreement on ethical and theological matters, so far can literary criticism be substantive. In an age like our own, in which there is no common agreement, it is the more necessary for Christian readers to scrutinize their reading, especially of works of

imagination, with explicit ethical and theological standards. The 'greatness' of literature cannot be determined solely by literary standards; though we must remember that whether it is literature or not can be determined only by literary standards.

When Eliot began to write plays, this mystical dogma was the message he offered to those who read or saw performed what he had written: contrition, repentance, expiation. The characters in the modern plays belonged to a masked social order, in which artificiality and insincerity had altogether overlaid virtue, and a man had

> to keep on pretending to himself
> That he's a success—the man who in the morning
> Has to make up his face before he looks in the mirror.

Eliot wrote about this social order because all he knew about the multitude was that its members had 'damp souls' and 'unwholesome lungs'. It was an order in which the members, having in boyhood or girlhood assumed what Leonard Woolf calls 'a carapace' or self-protective outer shell, and having practised ever since the basenesses and corruptions of the smart set, were in decay. He arranged that a sense of sin should arise in these characters, either as a result of some emergency, or as a result of diagnosis on the part of a psychiatrist or some visitant with knowledge of their past lives. When this sense of sin struck, they could only part, or go away, or contemplate death. As Lord Claverton says, in *The Elder Statesman*:

> Perhaps I've never really enjoyed living. . . .
>   Some dissatisfaction
> With myself, I suspect, very deep within myself
> Has compelled me all my life to find justification.

Now the awkwardness caused to men and women by a sudden revelation of past misconduct has long been a theme for powerful and popular drama. Ibsen, Wilde, the early Shaw, Pinero, Henry Arthur Jones, and Maugham were all, in their ways, masters of the theme. Each dealt with it appropriately, Ibsen doing so better than his successors because his intense poetic imagination lifted the dramatis personae to tragic heights. The others saw theatrical possibilities, usually in adultery, and exploited them. The women in their plays had sexually immoral pasts; the men, unless blackmailed for some crime or treachery to fellow-criminals of older days, had to deal only with problems of forgiveness or self-sacrifice. Suicide offered a way out to some; in others a wise old man said, 'Go and sin no more'; in others again an odd effect was created by what may be called a counter-revelation. What had looked like tragedy became near-farce when tables were turned; and audiences went away to sin again with the utmost gaiety.

Eliot was much too serious to indulge even in comedy. Although some good sharp remarks are made in his plays they never drop for more than a moment from the melancholy plane of accusing morality. A nursing home in the country will bring understanding and remorse to the protagonists; some young people, not yet 'corrupted by secularism', will sweeten the atmosphere by their goodness (though one good girl for some reason goes bravely to a horrible death in the middle of *The Cocktail Party*); or an old man who once in youth ran over a corpse in the road and did not tell the police has his wickedness illuminated by two *revenants*. Having been teased by these *revenants*, Lord Claverton explains that although they seem to be active agents in his exposure

> They are merely ghosts:
> Spectres from my past. They've always been with me
> Though it was not till lately that I found the living persons
> Whose ghosts tormented me, to be only human beings.

Another character, in *The Family Reunion*, admits that 'there's a lot in my own past life that presses on my chest', and it must be said that to most readers Eliot's concern with un-quiet memory will appear to be obsessive. The feeling of guilt runs through his plays; guilt and the need for expiation. As *The Observer* said of *The Cocktail Party*: 'He has taken the ordinary West End drawing-room comedy convention— understatement, upper-class accents and all—and used it as a vehicle for utterly serious ideas.'

'Upper-class accents': there is a clue here to Eliot's popularity with the socialites who, as an old French dramatist said, 'bore themselves'. They needed a new sensation; he provided it. Such people, pursuing fashion, could not help wondering at times whether concern with what Hulme called the geometrical in art, with serial music, *Finnegan's Wake*, and the very latest disquisitions on novel technique provided by the Third Programme might not seem to an all-wise power as futile as the boys' collection of engine-numbers. They needed something less exacting than mathematics, economics, and relativity. Having had their wits sharpened at Public Schools and Universities, they were conscious of great superiority to the vulgar many and proletarians who clamour incessantly for more pay. Like Lord Claverton, they were not fugitives from justice, but fugitives from reality. It was delightful to be told that the Eliotonian metaphysic provided them with essential reality.

I have sometimes thought that the segregation of the educated young from their commoner fellows had disadvantages. It produces tremendously accomplished inexperience. As the twenty-three-year-old hero of *Crome Yellow* said: 'Books, Books. One reads so many, and one sees so few people and so little of the world. . . . In the world of ideas everything was clear; in life all was obscure, embroiled.' Such a person as myself, in active life from boyhood, misses ten years of possible mental training. He may read widely, as I have done; but he does it without professorial guidance. On the other hand his opinions escape the influence of fashion, and he mixes every day with all sorts of men and women, few of whom have been forced in early years, like their educated brothers, to assume masks. They are, for the most part, what they seem to be; and

their interests, though often represented as shockingly dominated by TV and the Pops, are still more often wider and deeper
than the intellectual has imagination enough to realize.

I know this by experience; and I could not be other than a
humanist, because there is no barrier between myself and those
who impulsively reveal to me their singular preoccupations
and urgent troubles. These preoccupations and troubles have
nothing to do with Original Sin; they call for no repentance or
expiation; they arise from extraordinary decency, and the wish
to do right. If Eliot had enjoyed my direct and varied experience of men and women, he would agree.

He does not agree. His disciples disparage the writings of
humanists because they are drawn from life and not from
theory. Eliot himself has always preferred to associate with
witty and bookish types, because he believes that in them the
best culture is to be found. His contacts with others have been
timid. One has only to notice in his works of laboured exposition the effort to be moderate and all-embracing, and to guard
against possible misrepresentation, to discover a didacticism
opposed to all free interchange of sympathy. There is no interchange of sympathy or points of view in the plays. Therefore I
do not find myself moved or edified by the abstract problems
of his characters. Except for *The Family Reunion*, in which old
beauties of rhythm return to enchant as before, and in which
the problem, however morbid, is direct and unfamiliar, I find
the plays thin and sentimental, and their language commonplace.

They contain no sharp, salutary pictures of human beings in
action, but only colourless discussions in which no opposition,
no self-defence, and no subtlety is allowed. Character-drawing
in depth, such as the novelist can luxuriate in, is difficult on the
stage, where simplification is essential, and no doubt Eliot has
been influenced by the flatness of morality plays with their
embodiments of Gluttony, Mendacity, and Avarice; but if one
thinks of Ibsen's *Ghosts*, or *The Wild Duck*, or, greatest of all,
Rosmersholm, the difference in quality is inescapable. Ibsen's
characters, also convicted of sin, had breath in their bodies and
minds in their heads. In Eliot's plays the strings are too tightly

held by the author, who cannot give his characters life and will, lest they dodge his prearranged moral.

I claim no importance for this objection, and I hope not to be regarded as hostile or offensive to Eliot, whose writings, whatever his veerings of direction, have unquestionably influenced young readers, and churchmen, very markedly for more than forty years. It is a proud record. He is a serious writer, and was a serious writer before he made his leap into theological dogmatism. I think that leap was a mistake. I regard the doctrine of Original Sin as a cruel hoax played centuries ago by bigots upon ignorant men, and now brought out of the cupboard as counterblast to a much more intelligent scepticism. The consequence of this revival has been to give half-baked socialites a pretext for metaphysical gymnastics and to encourage horrible spiritual pride—deadliest of sins. It is for the self-styled *élite*. It is invalid for the healthy-minded and non-carapaced generality, whether or not that generality regards Jesus Christ as the Son of God and a Saviour.

Best-sellers

•

20   I HAVE said that Eliot spoke for his age. That is true if you think of the age as made up of a comparatively small body of men and women generally described as persons of culture. These men and women, passing through the Universities of Oxford and Cambridge, published or read books on the errors of previous philosophers or the criteria of true judgment. They exposed as amateurish the attempts of those writers—such as Lamb, Hazlitt, and Coleridge —who had just discovered and wished to share with others the beauties of life or literature or painting. They wrote, sometimes well, sometimes pretentiously, in the weekly political journals; and they spoke, chiefly in the B.B.C.'s Third Programme, in accents which caused vulgarians to squeal with loathing.

These accents did not represent, as some believed, the acme of condescension. The microphone is extremely sensitive, and it thins the vowels of all but born broadcasters; while the loathed broadcasters themselves were often only trying to speak distinctly. When nervous, they exaggerated their mannerisms. Friends of mine have been horrified to hear in recordings of their own voices what one of them described as 'all the affectations I most detest'; and even I, according to the youngest and severest member of my family, 'sounded much more refined than you really are'. (A tape-recording made secretly while we were all talking at once over Christmas dinner vindicated me of public pretentiousness and gave the critic a shock about her own voice.) So thereafter, when, impatient of Olympian grandeur, we sometimes switched off I did not wholly condemn. I made certain reservations. As Dr Jung said in an interview, 'I'm not a bit taken in by intellectuals, you know. After all, I'm one myself.'

Intellectuals are read and heard by intellectuals or by snobs who hope to catch the right 'tone'. They do good work in giving new twists to the disagreements of other intellectuals, or explaining what they call 'tendencies' in literary history, or in pressing the claims to attention of their highly cultured friends. They have their place in the world. But they are not the whole world.

In this period other intellectuals besides Eliot and his supporters have existed, found admirers, and enjoyed varying fortunes. Dr F. R. Leavis, for example, has not written poetry or plays, but he has laid down the law as peremptorily as Eliot himself and done his utmost to destroy what he regards as worthless. This has made for his unpopularity with those whom he attacked. Having lately read some of his criticism for the first time, I find the manner—he describes it charitably as 'an indelicate bluntness'—rather too strident for my taste; but the matter admirable for its challenge to purely academic criticism and certain fashionable reputations. I shall therefore speak of him as an influence upon the latest age.

Despite prevailing contempt for their work, a few humbler men, playwrights, poets, and novelists, have dared to follow paths divergent from those favoured by intellectuals. Some of the humble ones (I have previously spoken of several) who once caught the spirit of flying time are now either lambasted, which is a compliment, or wholly ignored. They persist in doing what they can in the light of personal taste and personal experience. So do some newcomers, who at a first appearance receive startling praise, but, after success, become common butts. As Hazlitt and James Northcote agreed, 'the world will never admire twice; if an author was only equal to himself, he was always said to fall off'.

One reason for this is that a young writer puts his freshest thoughts into his first book. Twinkling genius is expressed for joy's sake upon every page. 'I wish you saw me,' said Sterne, who was always young, 'half starting out of my chair, with what confidence, as I grasp the elbow of it, I look up—catching the idea, even sometimes before it half way reaches me——' Subsequently it is impossible to 'warble wood-notes wild' with the same ecstasy, because careless rapture is gone. The writer has become self-conscious and self-distrustful. If he once succeeds, his innocence departs altogether.

He may still improve steadily in the practice of his craft; but that is a different thing. William Rothenstein says in *Men and Memories*: 'an artist learns, not through books or the opinions of others, but by hourly struggle with the difficulties of actual drawing and painting'. It takes exceptional energy and talent to produce a continuity of even mediocre books (mediocre, I mean, by comparison with the best); and too often this energy and talent grind to a standstill. I was told the other day that Francis Brett Young, long before his death, knew himself to be at the end of his never-prodigious inventive powers. He had once at least rewritten as a novel what he had already written as a short story; and this was a sure sign of exhaustion. I think his talent perceptibly declined after the flowering marked by *Portrait of Clare*.

In another instance, where success had bred doubt, a bitingly brilliant and much lamented youngster named Denton Welch, whose first novel, *Maiden Voyage*, I greatly admired, produced a half-length sequel, and then wrote to me—as a well-wisher not personally known to him—asking what he could possibly do next. He had used, he felt, all his authentic material. Unexpected death solved this problem. If he had lived Welch would have had to learn to write about people other than himself. The professional must always do so. The dreary business of contracts and making a living then kills all but the fecund or the persistent. Those men are wisest and most fortunate who can rest, as E. M. Forster has done, upon early triumphs and write little more.

It was otherwise in the past, when—setting aside Shakespeare and Ben Jonson in the theatre—such ferocious inventors as Balzac, Dumas, Dostoevsky, and Dickens, always in need of money, poured out novels in multitude and seemed inexhaustible; when Henry James and W. D. Howells produced book after quiet book and James, without bothering about his income, could enjoy the delight of consummate craftsmanship until the end of a long life. The contemporary novelist, unless to the regret of all he dies young, will always tend to outstay his welcome, with certain impatient reviewers, if not with the public.

Here is an instance, and an explanation. I once, while casually reading a foreign critical journal at my club, came across a severe column about a book of my own. It was rather insulting, I remember, although I forget the details. The reviewer, however, while in a full flight of denunciation, was visited by a strange thought. 'Of course,' he said, 'the book is better [or 'much better'] than many which I praise highly; but Mr Swinnerton shows no *promise*.' As I was seventy at the time, I at first thought this complaint very silly; but a moment's thought showed its justification. The writer's excellent habit was to encourage novelists whose books bore the bloom of youth. Just so does one smile with pleasure at the grace of an immature girl. I, having written many books, lacked endearing gaucheries. I sympathized with the reviewer.

A long list of books facing the title-page is always depressing. One has not read the books; their titles suggest industry, not inspiration, and recall James McWhirter, who painted Highland cattle every year until his one subject became a joke. Everything familiar stales. Beautiful as the Emperor Concerto is, the music critic listening to it for the fifty-second time in nine months will sigh for almost anything new, however discordant it may be to his ear. He can express an opinion of the new; of Beethoven nothing more is to be said. How much worse, then, is the position of a reviewer faced with the twentieth or thirty-fifth novel by a writer whose very name spelt dullness for others when he was in his cradle. 'Give us the new!' he cries.

There is another aspect to this preference for youth. It may be no more than a fad. I was once in company with three men of letters, one of whom announced firmly that the best novelist alive was a man who had written two books (he wrote no more). Our friends made no comment. I, having read both books, admitted that I thought them pretty good. The man was silent. Soon afterwards, having lapsed into melancholy, he left us. When he had gone, Compton Mackenzie (I think) said: 'You've made —— very unhappy. He's only enthusiastic about books that nobody else has ever heard of.'

This is a commoner idiosyncrasy than one might expect. It is at the root of much scorn for those popular novels that everybody seems to have read. The assumption, expressed crudely, is: 'I am so severe a critic that I care only for the best. The best cannot be appreciated by others. Any book admired by others, therefore, must be contemptible; and I cannot admire it.'

I was reminded of this incident when skimming a book by Mrs F. R. Leavis, which was published in 1932 under the title *Fiction and the Reading Public*. The book is extremely contemptuous of modern 'best-sellers', which it contrasts with the best-sellers of other days, and while sparing a moment to scorn 'the yawns and indolence and stiffness' of Sir Walter Scott, and 'run a critical eye over a novel or two' by Dickens, comes down most heavily on Gilbert Frankau, Philip Gibbs, Edgar Rice Burroughs, A. S. M. Hutchinson, and the 'preposterous' Ethel M. Dell. Two of these authors have 'minds of no greater calibre and sensibilities as crude and undeveloped as those of the lowest level of the reading public'. Arnold Bennett is disdained; Hugh Walpole, although tolerated, is treated little better. The best-seller of the 'twenties is something abhorrent to 'the ordinary cultivated person'. Only Virginia Woolf, E. M. Forster, D. H. Lawrence, and T. F. Powys are to be admired.

Now, what is a best-seller? I have a letter in my possession from a writer who, although a good writer, was often insulted by those who warmly praised much inferior but more intellectually pretentious work. He is dead, and my quotation from it can do him no harm. The letter says: 'I am classed with the best-sellers. For the private information of Swinnerton, who prefers to judge by facts, the half-year's sale, New York, of my "works" was as follows: 3 sold, 1 returned. Postal order: 1/2 (one shilling and tuppence). My oath.' I add my own guarantee that the letter is as I have now copied it.

So in this case the reputed best-seller was not, after all, a best-seller. Would that fact invalidate criticism based upon a false assumption? Mrs Leavis's book was written thirty years ago, when the writer had apparently just completed her schooling. There are good things in it, as well as examples of youthful high-flying prejudice; and as the author's opinions may have changed in thirty years I shall not discuss them. I shall only refer to her list of best-selling titles between the year 1578, when Lyly's *Euphues: the Anatomy of Wit* was a rage among the polite, and 1930, when *The Good Companions* and *Vile Bodies* are bracketed.

Mrs Leavis cannot have had access to comparative sales. She wrote from that ghastly accumulation of trivia known as 'research', which enabled her to quote very impressively James Lackington, who by the way was a remainder-bookseller, *The Annual Register*, and Frank Mumby's *Publishing and Bookselling*. To these authorities she added extracts from pronouncements by literary and advertising agents, the results of questions addressed to some librarians, and the distasteful scrutiny of bookstalls and 'greasy' twopenny libraries. Like Mrs Todgers, she 'dodged among the tender pieces' of the superior past; she was too inexperienced to be able to distinguish between novels which in their years of publication sold ten thousand, twenty thousand, fifty thousand, and a hundred thousand, these being figures known only to the respective publishers. From outside, like cats at night, all best-sellers look alike.

I do not condemn those who see them thus. Even I, long in the publishing trade, and in receipt of many curious publishing confidences, am still surprised to learn of extraordinary varia-tions in sale. A book that 'everybody' is reading may reach its limit at five or ten thousand copies. Twenty thousand is exceptional. One very much boosted modern success barely touched thirty thousand. But another, such as Henry Handel Richardson's *Maurice Guest*, persists through the years, Paul Gallico's *The Snow Goose* quietly snowballs to far higher figures;

and *Dracula*, by Bram Stoker, which was first published in 1897, is said never to be out of print. More spectacularly advertised books fall a long way short of their optimistically estimated and advertised figures, and are ready for pulping within three months.

Why? Inferiority cannot be the sole reason for inflated sales. Nor can illiteracy and bad taste in the reading public. *Mathematics for the Million* and *The Kon-Tiki Expedition*, both of which owed much to the confidence, business acumen, and pre-publication effort of their publisher, Sir Stanley Unwin, out-sold most of the novels of their years. Some books about village and country life—I am thinking of those by Adrian Bell and Reginald Arkell—beat the slushiest of tales; others, not markedly inferior, make no impression at all. One Leeds book-seller sold innumerable copies through the years of Constance Holme's *Crump Folk Going Home*; his colleagues elsewhere knew nothing of the harvest they were missing. Blazing reviews mean little; the names one sees most often in the national press and literary weeklies are little esteemed in Ayr or Newcastle or Marlborough; even radio commendations and television interviews have no effect. What sells books is talk; personal recommendation.

I once, in a Brighton hotel, heard a neighbour calling to a fellow-visitor at the other side of the room. 'I've just read such a *pretty* book,' she shouted. 'It's what I call a really *nice* book! It's called *A Girl of the Limberlost*.' Now I am sure that Mrs Leavis, like myself, would have been repelled by that unctuous advocacy; but the lady knew her friend, and knew that they shared a taste for pretty books. She was lighting a candle that would travel round the world. The same thing happens at highly superior dinner-tables in Chelsea, St John's Wood, Bloomsbury, and, dare I say? Cambridge. There *A Girl of the Limberlost* was never praised; but a few now-forgotten books had their glad day of celebration. Do not let us mention them now.

Mrs Leavis's list of best-sellers, although she regarded it as representative, was admittedly not exhaustive. It moved, in the period covered by my present excursion, from *Peter Jackson: Cigar Merchant*, by Gilbert Frankau, in 1919, and A. S. M. Hutchinson's *If Winter Comes*, in 1921, to *The Middle of the Road*, by Philip Gibbs (1923), *The Green Hat* and *Beau Geste* in 1924, *The Constant Nymph* and *Sorrell and Son* in 1925, Gentlemen Prefer Blondes in 1926, and *The Bridge of San Luis Rey* in 1928.

No reference is made, *à propos The Bridge of San Luis Rey*, to another tremendously successful novel about a similarly fortuitous assembly, Vicki Baum's *Grand Hotel* (1930). Nor does the list include *The Young Visiters*, which in 1919 sold over a hundred thousand copies in England, double that number in the United States, and has continued to sell ever since; nor Francis Brett Young's *Portrait of Clare* (1927), Remarque's *All Quiet on the Western Front* (1929), and Charles Morgan's *Portrait in a Mirror* (1929). All, if the list was to be representative of current popular literary fashion, should have been named.

Fourteen such titles indicate how different the publics are for different sorts of best-seller. It is useless to lump them together as balderdash, drawing the conclusion that popular taste has deteriorated since 1578, and to condemn Gilbert Frankau, Warwick Deeping, and H. M. Tomlinson as if they all wrote sentimental novelettes for the illiterate. Some Elizabethan novels, remembered only because they helped Shakespeare to a few not very good plots, were entirely colourless; in the seventeenth and eighteenth centuries novels were published almost by the cartload, only to sink unnoticed by the historians; in the nineteenth the proportion of rubbish was as high in the early- and mid-century as it is today. Any argument, therefore, from the past is deceptive. Nobody but George Saintsbury ever read all the novels there were and Saintsbury jibbed at a great many of them.

Frankau, Deeping, and Tomlinson are not comparable, either as writers or in popularity. Each wrote as he did because he was made like that. *Peter Jackson*, in fact, expressed the temperament and much of the actual life of its author; and when I, as a publishers' factotum, described the author's earlier book, *The Woman of the Horizon* (1917), in a blurb as relating 'the amorous adventures of a lively and warm-blooded young poet' Frankau was the first to object. He said: 'That paragraph, old man. It's vulgar! And if there's one thing I'm *not*, it's vulgar.'

I liked Frankau, and thought he had more talent than those who sneered at him. He was an amusing sophisticated boy, an incessant rattle who often, in conversation, achieved wit of a flashy but always unselfconscious order. He seriously regarded his work as literature, and when he bragged about it (amid much leg-pulling) he was (a) keeping up his courage, and (b) speaking in character.

> I write not egotistically [he once announced in print], but out of the depths of tremendous and soul-shattering experience, when I say that every book of my own which attains to best-sellerhood leaves me an utter wreck on its completion. For a week after I wrote 'Finis' to *Peter Jackson* I was too weary even to re-read the manuscript, and for a whole fortnight after the completion of *Aliette Brunton*, I was so nervous that I dared not put a horse at a fence.

This absurdity is not the declaration of a man writing for his public. It is packed with the sincerity of delusion; and its simple boyishness explains why Frankau's novels made so many friends among those who also had been born to love and shine, vicariously if not in fact. I was once talking to Frankau at a function when a young woman effusively addressed us. 'Oh, Mr Swinnerton,' she exclaimed; 'you're so *well-known*!' And, more genuinely, 'Oh, Mr Frankau, I did think *Peter Jackson* such a *dinky* book!' She was right: it was a dinky book. Who is Mrs Leavis to deny that?

Frankau's was one public; the public that craved for the company of smart cigar-smoking men who put their horses at fences with perfect aplomb, and who made love to women in the moonlight or in conservatories while music from distant bands flooded the atmosphere with facile emotion. There were such smart men and women—very distasteful to Mrs Leavis

and myself—and Frankau was their exponent. Naturally all
who shrank from gawds and tinsel and fleshpots, preferring the
still-life refinements of Virginia Woolf, thought wretchedly of
the author. They did not understand that he wrote from life,
and that a particular set of people responded with rapture to his
performance. It was larger than Mrs Woolf's set; but like Mrs
Woolf's set it had its limits.

Frankau also wrote in wartime fluent patriotic and onomato-
poetic jingles in the manner of Kipling, whom he called 'my
master'; but his best work, *One of Us: a Novel in Verse*, had
both verve and ingenuity enough to justify in its day comparison with another novel in verse, *Don Juan*. It was a gay
young man's imitation of that celebrated work, and in 1912
was a best-seller to the extent of six or seven thousand copies.

The ground of its sale was novelty. Frankau, although
shattered in 1915 by contact with savage warfare, was naturally
adventurous, resilient, facile in emotion (he was three times
married), fundamentally quick, and good-natured. I see no merit
in condemning him for enjoyment of the life he loved and the
echo of that life in fiction. It is not the kind of life I admire, nor
was his the kind of work I enjoy. I think that in spite of his
disclaimer both were vulgar. All the same, many worse and
more vicious writers than Frankau have been lauded by the
highbrows.

The public which swarmed in far greater numbers to *Sorrell
and Son* was entirely different from Frankau's. It had no interest
in smartness. It wanted something sober about middle-class
family relationships in which right was not all on one side.
Whereas Frankau, the son of 'Frank Danby' (also a best-selling
novelist with such books as *Pigs in Clover* (1903) and *The Heart
of a Child* (1908)), was an old Etonian who, being asked to leave
after a prank, joined his father's tobacco firm, precociously and
flamboyantly travelled the world, and laughed, drank, and
flirted during hot nights in Havana, Warwick Deeping was a
very quiet ex-Cantab and ex-doctor (R.A.M.C. in Gallipoli
and elsewhere during the 1914–18 War), who loved gardening

and took an intelligent if not scholarly interest in ancient British history.

Strangely enough, his first book was a mild companion-piece to Maurice Hewlett's *The Forest Lovers* called *Uther and Igraine*. It had none of the sensuous colouring of its model, and was little noticed. Deeping continued to write undistinguished novels until in 1925, with his thirty-fourth work, he produced that thing of shame, a best-seller. *Sorrell and Son* spread to sales never approached by Frankau's books. It was a very popular novel indeed, worthy of closer study than Mrs Leavis had time to give it by anybody wishing to explore best-selling attributes. It was subdued, patient, and to some natures poignant; it may possibly have reproduced a situation which recurs very often in middle-class families. A reader will notice that Deeping's style was colourless; so was Deeping himself. He was completely unpretentious, meagre in appearance, narrow-headed, a little legal, and without animation. Sincerity and competence were his two qualities. His handicap was industry.

Women in country homes, women in boarding-houses, women in London suburbs and provincial towns all knew that Deeping would tell them an undisturbing story in words which they could understand. They had no radio, no television; they did not want to read about the hunting set or smart amours (the passion for such things, they believed, had gone out with Ouida), nor about divorces, abnormalities, nor the problems of adolescence. Having read Archibald Marshall's demure miniatures in the Trollopian vein a few years before, they felt even more comfortable with an author as staid as themselves. For an hour or so after tea, in clean middle-class homes, over a bright coal fire in winter or in small gardens in the warm weather, they found themselves pleasantly amused. It was inconceivable that in liking these books they were likely to incur undergraduate scorn; they knew no undergraduates. They consulted no literary periodicals. They read Deeping as their mothers had read Edna Lyall and Annie S. Swan, Sabine Baring-Gould or the brothers Hocking; as their grandmothers had read Mrs Riddell, Mrs Hungerford, and Adeline Sergeant.

After *Sorrell and Son* Deeping's popularity declined. He

made no effort to exploit success; he avoided limelight; he several times returned in placid, uneventful tales to the historical backgrounds of earlier books. Just as R. D. Blackmore's best-seller *Lorna Doone* or William Black's *A Daughter of Heth* put all other novels by these authors in perpetual shade, so this one book, *Sorrell and Son*, which also sold a hundred thousand copies in the United States, where Frankau had no large public, is the only book of Deeping's to please a multitude.

Different again was the public, much wider and more fervid, for *If Winter Comes*. This book was favourite reading in 1921 and 1922, not only in country vicarages and suburban villas, but all over North America and in aristocratic homes in England. It aroused almost as much talk as *Robert Elsmere* had done in the eighteen-eighties, and its appeal was much more general than that of a once highly esteemed novel to which the ordinary cultivated person of the eighteen-eighties rallied in force.

A. S. M. Hutchinson had been editor of a London illustrated newspaper, *The Daily Graphic*. He had published three previous books, the titles of two of which hint at things to come (they were *The Happy Warrior* and *The Clean Heart*), before this extraordinary seller; and *If Winter Comes* contains the portrait of a colleague on *The Daily Graphic* who was described to me by James Bone as 'the most quixotic journalist I ever knew—and I have known many'. It was thus not a piece of sentimental imagining: it was, at its centre, as authentic as another allegedly sentimental invention by a journalist, Philip Gibbs's *The Street of Adventure*.

The portrait of a good man, who in real life unfortunately ended the quixotry of his career by suicide, was immediately praised as Christlike by, among others (I am told by Walter Allen, who has been studying best-sellers in order to write a whole book about them), Margot Asquith. It caused excitement among all simple-minded believers in the Ten Commandments. How different were those readers, or how different was their mood, from the unchastened publics which supped with worldlings in *Peter Jackson: Cigar Merchant* or *Gentlemen Prefer Blondes*!

In *The Bookseller*'s centenary issue, which brimmed with extracts from numbers issued between 1858 and 1958, one paragraph has especial point here. It is from the year 1922, and is as follows:

AGGRESSIVE ADVERTISING. The phenomenal success of Mr Hutchinson's *If Winter Comes* has been one of the notable features of the year's publishing. It is perhaps worth noting that when this book first appeared it made no particular mark and it was only when the publishers made special efforts to attract the attention of the reading public by vigorous and, indeed, aggressive advertising that it began to make way and, as everyone knows, speedily caught on and established itself as the best seller of the year.

Now advertising alone does not sell books. It can only do so when interest in those books has already been aroused. But much can be achieved by what may be called behind-the-scenes activity. A. S. M. Hutchinson himself, I believe, is as much in the dark about what happened as anybody else can be. Knowing nothing positive, I make a suggestion. Dr Robertson Nicoll was adviser to the publishers of this book, a religious man, a preacher, friend of David Lloyd George (then Prime Minister), and a most influential journalist and publicist. I think he probably read the book, praised it in his various columns in the Press, introduced it to the notice of those who formed, not an intellectual *élite*, but a considerable force. In this way he could have started an enthusiasm, as he did last century for Barrie and the Kailyard School. That the enthusiasm in Hutchinson's case, whatever the instigation, was general is certain.

A friend of mine, Harold Williams, who had been Russian correspondent to *The Daily Chronicle* until the Bolsheviks seized power (his wife was a Menshevik, or Liberal), became Foreign Editor of *The Times* under Northcliffe. One day he visited 'the Lord' (as Northcliffe was called), and found him with *If Winter Comes* in his hands. Northcliffe asked Williams whether he had read the book. On being told 'No', he exclaimed: 'Extraordinary. All about a man riding a bicycle down a hill.' As if aghast, he added: 'There's something I don't understand about *popular taste!*'

He determined to account for the success of the book (do not forget the hero's saintliness and his touching habit, probably based on fact, of calculating every day how far the momentum gathered by free-wheeling descent of a hill would carry him); and to this end he gave instructions that a decoy letter should be written to *The Times* praising it. I am told by Walter Allen that this letter, according to Lewis Hind, once editor of *The Academy* and a not impeccable witness, was at first to be written by Hind, but that somebody who is still anonymous was preferred. He wrote as 'a Critic'.

Every day for the following three weeks (I am still in Walter Allen's debt) correspondence appeared in the paper; and every day more and more people read and liked and hated and loved the book. Fury spread to the United States. It re-crossed the Atlantic, and became religious in quality and intensity. Hutchinson, who had meant only to celebrate his friend's exceptional character, found himself the most successful novelist of his generation, a best-seller *in excelsis*. Astonished, thankful, he remained what he had always been, a simple and modest believer in that humanitarianism which Marxists regard as a crime and that romanticism which T. E. Hulme scourged for confusing

> both human and divine things, by not clearly separating them. The main thing with which it can be reproached is that it blurs the clear outlines of human relations . . . by introducing in them the *Perfection* that properly belongs to the non-human.

Less warm-hearted, more akin to the appetite for smartness which accounted for Frankau's success, was the reaction to Michael Arlen's *The Green Hat*. Arlen—that was not his real name—was an Armenian who hungered for popularity as

Hutchinson had never done. He called upon me one unexpectedly hot day when the anthracite fire in my little office had for some reason been lighted, so that the room was like a Turkish bath, and his discomfort, heightened by nervousness, was obvious. I never found him, as a consequence, entirely at ease, and he did once go to the length of asking my editor if his new book could be reviewed by somebody else. This was not done. He was bright-eyed, thick-lipped, very high-strung, and eager to please. He liked fine clothes, good food, and good company; the cigar-laden atmosphere of American luxury hotels and the French Riviera, where he was much at home; and the company of Lady Russell and Somerset Maugham, who both gave him confidence and saw his real charm.

Hutchinson's simple belief in goodness was what convinced his admirers; Arlen's admirers felt naughty when they read *The Green Hat*. Hutchinson wrote his early books in a convoluted style which he later discarded; but the style represented an anxious attempt to escape triteness. Arlen aimed all the time at sophisticated Wildean wit. His smart society was much smarter and more pretentiously cosmopolitan than Frankau's. His books were not 'dinky'; they restlessly glittered in a manner which he relished as much as his readers. Alas, the readers were fickle as children at a Christmas party. They loved the sparkle of the tree, snatched the toys, and, thoughtless for their host, ran swiftly to another show. Having no different toys to offer, Arlen watched his denuded tree, which had so recently been covered with enticements, grow dry. The public had found more original and warrantable coruscations in the brilliant work of Evelyn Waugh, whose *Vile Bodies* Mrs Leavis linked, without comment and apparently without knowledge of a difference in public appeal, with *The Good Companions*.

Of these two reputations Evelyn Waugh's has been most in accord with the temper of the times, which has needed the comfort of fantasy and derisive wit. Incapable themselves of inventing and illuminating preposterous characters and turning every experience into material for exquisite laughter, many thousands of readers have been thankful for Waugh. He has had another advantage, this time with a more critical body, which has been able to focus his work within the formula and to speak of 'an Evelyn Waugh type' or 'novel'. Rightly or wrongly (I think wrongly) he has been, as they say in film and theatrical circles 'typed'. Had Waugh submitted to rule this would have been paralysing; but he has not done so. He has therefore kept his place, in spite of a perceptible inclination among reviewers to crab him as somebody who—like *Punch*—was better twenty years ago than he is today.

Crabbing has been more obvious in the case of J. B. Priestley; partly because Priestley has a less concentrated talent, partly because he has been outspoken in condemnation of others. Others do not like to be condemned; in the literary world they have a habit of punctually repaying injury. Being fecund, he has written many novels since *The Good Companions*, which was an overwhelming success, a number of highly original but not always agreeable plays, and much comment on the ways of politicians and social corruption. He, like the highbrows, is not pleased with the way the world is going; but he is no better pleased with the highbrows themselves; and although he deeply wishes to be liked he cannot control black moods which alienate those whom he would placate.

As a critic he has always written in the old generalizing manner which has been displaced by analysis and research. His novels, alternatingly genial and bitter, have been about men and women whose preoccupations are those of the majority. He has presented these ordinary men and women (and some extraordinary ones, too) in their own idiom; he has not condescended; he has seemed to be one with them. To the highbrow, who prides himself on being in a minority, this is an offence.

In any period [says F. R. Leavis, quoted by his wife] it is upon a very small minority that the discerning appreciation of art and literature depends; it is only a few who are capable of unprompted first-hand judgment. . . . The accepted valuations are a kind of paper currency based upon a very small proportion of gold. To the state of such a currency the possibilities of fine living at any time bear a close relation.

Priestley is not a perfectionist. He is interested in ideas, but in his plays and novels presents them, not academically, with the sense of Godlike wisdom, but obliquely, as a dramatic writer should do. *The Good Companions* was not only much longer than most modern novels (I do not think it was longer than *The Old Wives' Tale*); it had an ampler panoramic spread, and aimed at surpassing what Aldous Huxley called 'the innumerable and interminable anecdotes and romances and character-studies', although not by way of 'general theory, explanatory hypothesis, or co-ordinating philosophy'. A philosophy is there; but it is implicit. In other words, Priestley is not an intellectual, but a humanist.

Well, what does Priestley think? He wants a better world in the material sense; he is not bothered by the doctrine of Original Sin; he wishes men and women to be happy, thinking individuals, and not the victims of mass pressures. He comes from Bradford, and has persisted in the use of a Yorkshire accent. It is one of his defences. The bluntness with which he expresses his views is also a relic of Yorkshire breeding; but I think it is maintained as counter to the insincerities of the genteel. He is very sensitive to criticism; has the northern habit of 'knowing best' and telling you so; once tried, as Wells did before him, to inject a few liberal ideas into the veins of Labour leaders, only of course to fail from ignorance of political chicane; and although he still provides good copy for the popular press just misses in this uncertain world the literary standing which thirty-five years ago he seemed sure of attaining.

That he will enjoy this standing with readers in distant generations seems to me probable. But the histories of English literature then published will have to be written by men who can estimate intrinsic quality rather than rare refinement of technical device.

The last best-selling author I shall discuss is Louis Golding, whose *Magnolia Street* was published—and very effectively published—by Victor Gollancz in 1932. Golding was a Manchester boy, a small Jew, born and brought up in poor circumstances, who by industry and talent passed with credit into Manchester Grammar School and Oxford University. At Oxford he wrote poetry before venturing into the novel. His first book, *Forward from Babylon*, gave a truthful account of his early days and his early reading, and he went on to less personal themes until he elected to describe in coloured language his perambulations of Italy, Sicily, and Palestine.

In all this work he was taking himself very seriously as a writer of aesthetic quality. He wanted success, but he wanted the esteem of his fellow-writers even more; a curious dualism in his character which produced contradictory actions. I had not very enthusiastically reviewed his first novel for *The Manchester Guardian*, and had met him once or twice without being much impressed by a personality which I thought dominated by the wish to get on. I was then asked to give an extra opinion of a manuscript, already rather doubtfully condemned in the office of his publishers, who had done poorly with previous books; and I considered the book a failure because instead of attempting high tragedy it accumulated common details of Jewish life. I was not interested in the theme, and was bored by what I described as its horizontal ambitiousness.

Very sensibly, Golding took that book, which was *Magnolia Street*, to Victor Gollancz, who as a Jew saw possibilities in it which I had missed. Gollancz elaborately prepared a campaign for its publication, and brought off one of the great successes of his enterprising life. *Magnolia Street* made an absolutely genuine hit. It was the best-seller of its year, and it was praised everywhere as an illumination of Jewish character. I doubt if anything like this had happened since the days of Israel Zangwill.

During the year 1943 I was surprised to receive a letter from Golding which said, in effect: 'For the past quarter of a century you have been persecuting me. Do, for God's sake, leave me alone!' As I knew nothing of this persecution, and certainly felt no animus towards the writer—nor indeed towards any other writers, since my normal attitude is compassionate—I replied sympathetically. Golding responded. Our real acquaintance then began.

I found him convinced that Hugh Walpole had also treated him scurvily, and that there was a conspiracy among literary men to revile his work. He was still, for all his interest in modern art, modern poetry, and the glory of the ancient Jews, the little boy in Manchester who had been taunted by little Gentiles, and had tried to forget his shame in jeering at little Italian boys who were also of the band. He had never forgotten my review of *Forward from Babylon*, nor my lack of enthusiasm for *Magnolia Street*; but from that time he sent me all his books, some of which, for example *No News of Helen* and *To the Quayside*, appeared to me to contain far better work than I had given him credit for in the past. I came to like him, not with great respect, because I thought his sense of persecution absurd, and some of his ways of gaining attention rather low, but as somebody pathetic. When defensiveness had been shed he was an interesting and amusing companion, and this is what he wished to be in his books, only one of which (he never showed any concern over this) was a best-seller.

Best-sellers of more recent years have changed in character. Some, like Thomas Armstrong's *The Crowthers of Bankdam*, have followed the old formula of the chronicle, and have made steady friends in consequence. Others, such as *For Whom the Bell Tolls*, *Lolita*, and Graham Greene's *The Heart of the Matter*, have apparently reached heights of sophistication undreamed of by former generations; but as I have not read them and have not met their authors, I have nothing to say in the terms of this book. *Lady Chatterley's Lover* has been the best-seller of all.

It has occurred to me, in surveying the scene, that the enthusiasms of 'ordinary cultivated persons' tends to be for books specializing in perfection of *manner*. Subtlety, irony (Mrs Woolf's subtlety was superior, I read in Mrs Leavis, to Jane Austen's; but in one passage 'one is reluctantly obliged to conclude' that a description 'was not intended to be ironical'), and gentility are the criteria. As the Third Fellow said in *She Stoops to Conquer*, 'Damn anything that's low, I cannot bear it! . . . May this be my poison if my bear ever dances but to the very genteelest of tunes.'

If I am right, and pride in fine taste is due, not to wide sympathy and preference for the best, but to a mere restriction of outlook to the familiar, I think such pride must figure among the deadly sins. It is akin to the snobbery with which a fine lady of the past used to draw her skirts away from a beggar. A cultivated accent, agreeable enough to the ear, is really artificial; and if the user of that accent scorns the accents of provincials a distinction of class is being made where the difference is only one of locality. To feel that one is among one's equals when one is reading a member of the Cambridge *ton*, where imagined characters are sublimations of one's self, is to do exactly what the reader of a best-seller about the hunting-field, the concert party, or a man who rides a bicycle downhill does in another walk of life.

This, I think, is the secret of the best-seller, that each person who reads it feels himself or herself to be 'in' it. Not 'the swim', although that does influence a few; but the actual scene. As late nineteenth-century life became too prosaic after long peace and prosperity, swords returned to fiction. They figured in the most popular romances, from Stevenson to Anthony Hope's *The Prisoner of Zenda*, Stanley Weyman's tales of French history and their reproductions, Henry Seton Merriman's dramas of conduct. The alternative came, diluted, from France in another style in the realisms of George Moore and George Gissing, Arthur Morrison and Edwin Pugh; but in these books the reader relished contact with grime, and was not involved in the action. The books were admired; they were not best-sellers. The best-sellers were the romances, which told of days when chivalry was in favour and the heroes always won their battles.

Subsequently middle-class people found themselves por-trayed in Galsworthy; and from the north and elsewhere found themselves understood in Arnold Bennett; the not too self-examining little men smiled but experienced the pathos of little fellows like Kipps and Mr Polly, who had their love-stories, too; and everybody in the new century was taken by the fact that with *Tono-Bungay* and *The New Machiavelli* Wells brought politics and big business into their houses. All the later best-sellers (Bennett was never a comparable best-seller; and is only classed by highbrows with the breed because like Jung he was impervious to their pretensions) have given some one section of society the opportunity for self-identification. The old penny novelette, in which an educated girl was forced by poverty to take a situation as governess in a titled family, to end as a countess, was an answer to dreams of ease and happi-ness. It was an earthly Heaven, and cheap at the price. Nowa-days no dreams of wealth are beyond attainment; but young people are dissatisfied.

In the genteel class they seek magic from psychiatrists and drugs or the carrot-dramas which are offered as the latest thing in subtlety. In other circles the drugs have a cruder flavour. The trouble is really that there are too few enjoyments in the world. Drink, sin, and religion remain the only things that matter. The normal sophisticated best-seller offers the second; its counter-part tells what happens to sinners, and exhorts them, after indulgence, to repent. Drink, of course, is always with us. In any case the newspapers and Television do the novelist's job of dramatizing persons and events more vividly than the novelist can do it himself. While he etches with more or less precision, they present photographic close-ups in which nothing is withheld from the eye. No wonder the novel has become no more than 'the book of the picture'.

The Latest Fashions

●

21 BEFORE turning to the latest fashions in literature, I shall say a few words about myself and my friends. As a boy I saw authors for a number of years from the other side of the publishers' counter, at an angle from which they seemed small and often tiresome. I cannot rid myself of this early vision. Only the great ones have magnanimity; the rest, whatever their 'carapace', are self-distrustful and morbidly sensitive creatures who, if their work does not sell, cherish a gnawing grievance, and, if it does sell, are subjected to the contempt of those whom they regard as the envious few. If, as more often happens, the work only appears to sell, but is really not much needed by the Public, a sense of failure, being added to resentment of contempt, may corrode what was originally a healthy enough talent. Contempt has been altogether overdone in the period covered by *Figures in the Foreground*. It is a sign of littleness and incomprehension.

Personally, as I shall be reminded, I am worm-eaten with Liberalism. I know too much about the conditions of authorship and publishing to be either envious or, in the prig-word, intransigent. I have never been a best-selling novelist, and I have always been indifferent to contempt. I hope I have not been tiresome to my publishers. Though humane, I have no sentimentality. I think some of my work has been surprisingly good; and it has at times been highly praised. But I am so constituted that I should make an almost perfect captain for a sinking ship, shepherding everybody else, including the ship's cat, into the boats, but missing nobility by accepting the last place for myself. It is not that I am modest or unselfish; it is that I have hardly any consciousness of myself at all.

I have been told in print that one of my novels 'will never die', and that I shall be forgotten as soon as I am buried, which latter expectation is quite acceptable. I have been called 'puritan', 'conscientious mediocrity', 'good second-class' (by James Agate, who felt extremely brave in using the term to my face, and was forced to add: 'that's very good, you know'), 'brilliant', 'dazzling', 'the nicest of authors', 'the most under-rated novelist alive', and, by Joyce Cary, whom I had accused in a review of talking to himself (as proved to be his habit), 'a first-class critic'. One lady, a stranger, wrote some years ago to apologize for having at a first reading missed the quality of one novel which she had since realized to be profound. 'After all,' she said, 'one doesn't appreciate a Beethoven symphony on first hearing it.'

That lady had a pleasant humour; and she credited me with a similar habit of talking nonsense for the amusement of others. She was right to do so. I have not the rollicking invention of a Rabelais or Dickens; but humour, or at least good humour, has been my friend throughout life. It is a good quality. It tells its possessor that although, like Bosher, he is small in the world, his smallness is no smaller than that of most other men, and need not cause depression. I have not been depressed. Indeed, I have never understood what other men are so conceited about.

I also have that kind of imagination—humour is its handmaid —which allows a man to put himself in the place of persons entirely different from himself. This is why I write novels. Sympathy with the shortcomings, the failures, and the suffer-ings (but also the triumphs) of his fellows does, I think, enrich a man's mind more than book-knowledge, of which I have plenty. As the result of this sympathy I believe myself to have been a good reviewer of other writers' books.

I do not care for writers in bulk; but have warmly liked some of them as individuals. These have become my friends; others would have been my friends if I had wished to lead a social and literary life. I have not so wished. I am not, as Henry

James wanted to be, just literary, since my interests are multi-farious; I am not a recluse; but while I enjoy conversation, wine, and contact with other brisk wits I am always happy to be alone. Apart from human love, my notion of earthly happiness is a summer day with my wife and daughter at the Hove Cricket Ground.

One result of long life is that one's friends die or move to distant counties, or even to distant lands. Before marriage I had a studio or an apartment in London and saw many cordial acquaintances every day; since marriage I have lived in the country and seen both friends and acquaintances more rarely. Now the journalists who kept me primed with inside political information at the Reform Club are gone; with the exception of Webster Evans and Edmond Segrave all the editors I ever worked for are gone; of my old literary friends—Arnold Bennett, H. G. Wells, Horace Horsnell, Pauline Smith, Philip Gibbs, and many more—most are dead and of those who survive Compton Mackenzie is in Scotland, St John Ervine in Devon, and Siegfried Sassoon in the Roman Church; while even newer friends (though they are of twenty years' standing and more) such as William McFee, Norah Hoult and Richard Church, or the much younger Winston Graham, live a long way away; and my at one time weekly visits to London are spread more thinly. I still see Martin Secker and other publishing friends; I do not live in the past; but my nourishments are fewer.

For this reason many of the new authors are no more to me than names. I greatly admire some of them, and am hopeful that they are striking out broad new paths in place of the blind alleys of their seniors. But the sole point of this book is its attempt to give *personal* impressions of those who have been known to me, in the hope that some small detail may assist a future inquirer. I chat, as Northcote did to Hazlitt, without the gift of Hazlitt's genius in recording and inventing, of those who contributed to the atmosphere of a past age. Younger minds must take up the narrative. To them I quote William Plomer's lines:

Laugh if you like at this monstrous detritus
  Of middle-class life in the liberal past. . . .
Laugh while you can, for the time may come round
  When the rubbish *you* treasure will lie in this place.

I mentioned St John Ervine just now. His fine book on Shaw will not be forgotten: it presented a Shaw unfamiliar to the gossip-writers and apparently unfamiliar to Miss Patch. But it is long since a play of Ervine's has been seen on the West End stage, and the young are probably ignorant of the work he did for the Abbey Theatre and the great success, first in the United States and afterwards in England, of those realistic dramatic re-creations of life in humble homes—*John Ferguson* and *Jane Clegg*—which, quite unconsciously by the authors, are being rewritten today in settings of the moment. These plays had power and nature in them; they still have that power and nature. The last of Ervine's plays to be staged here went against the spirit of the period, being written, not in praise of youth, but in criticism of it, not in praise of Communism but, outspokenly, as was always Ervine's wont, with the Protestant-ism of Northern Ireland.

That was Ervine's way. He was ever the trailer of his coat, and the attacker of bunkum and what he called 'sloppy senti-mentality'. He was for years dramatic critic to *The Observer*, rivalling his editor in eloquence and swingeing phrases and sur-passing him in economy of space. Those who did not know him thought he was ferocious; those who did know him en-joyed the dry saltiness of his manner and his enjoyment of the superficial oddities of character. It was he who, when Hugh Walpole boyishly invited the guests at his house-warming party in York Terrace to demand anything they wanted but did not see on the dinner-table, said he would like some Brazil nuts. Alas, Brazil nuts could not be supplied; the boasted com-missariat was found wanting. In vain did the embarrassed Walpole pretend that almonds were Brazils; that made us laugh all the more. And our laughter was as innocent as Ervine's request had been. Walpole thought otherwise. He engaged for

some years in a one-sided feud with the cause of his discomfiture, until his equally boyish impulse towards reconciliation
triumphed. The feud ceased.

My own friendship with Ervine and his wife has never been
interrupted. Indeed, when Ervine was asked in the course of
a party game which of his contemporaries he would prefer as
companion on a desert island he hesitated between John Drinkwater and myself. Walpole, when (being rather derisive of
Drinkwater's entertainingness) I reported this, exclaimed: 'Oh,
Frank! John, every time! I could manage him. I should murder
you in a week!' I do not know what Ervine would have done.
Nothing short of murder would in those days have quenched
our mutual loquacity.

Another dramatist, now dead, and for too long buried under
the weight of highbrow disapproval, was A. A. Milne, who
had the lightest of touches—so light that he has been regarded
as a sentimental trifler and writer of verses and tales for
children. He combined with a gift for persiflage the sternness
of a Covenanter, which I think restricted the range of his
dramatic performance. Any writer of imaginative work who
cannot give the Devil his due, as Shaw's 'blooming gaseous
folly' enabled him to do very amply, becomes moral-bound.
He dare not let sinners have a flutter. This is as true of Milne as
of Eliot. When Milne wrote nonsense he was always felicitous.
When he wrote a thoughtful play, *Success*, which showed a
tendency that would please the Original Sin brigade, he was
wrongly assailed by dramatic critics for a boastfulness which
they read into his title. When he essayed a big and ingenious
theme in *The Truth about Blayds* he failed because his moral
sense would not allow the essential elasticity.

The play exposed a poet who had become a G.O.M., by
passing off as his own the works of a dead friend. In this case
the gaff was blown in the first act, when the old sinner died;
after which his family was carried willy-nilly into continuing
hypocrisy. Nobody could have doubted Milne's disapproval of
that hypocrisy. He arraigned it; all lightness was lost; the

audience was made uncomfortable. This was a miscalculation due to the author's puritanism. Barrie, attending the first performance, was asked his opinion of the play as he left the theatre; his laconic reply, which seemed to me a critical masterpiece, was: 'I should have kept the old man alive.' Barrie himself, of course, petered out as a dramatist; but one has only to reconsider *The Truth about Blayds* in the light of his remark to perceive what a chance was lost through too narrow a conception.

Barrie has been out of fashion and is returning. It is the lot of genius, and a sign of what in another country was called 'the thaw'. The time is past when a highbrow could refuse in contempt to pass him the salt at dinner. I am glad of that. Barrie had great defects; but his best plays were very good theatre, and they were original at heart instead of being only superficially 'different.' Milne, less of a genius, but highly talented, was, as far as I know, never refused salt. His success, however, did offend those who believed that 'life is real, and life is earnest'. This belief rose to its height when the Marxists determined to end all perversion of Russian child minds by suppressing fairy tales, and when intellectual snobbery and Lawrentian fury at everything bourgeois joined political bigotry in a grand attempt to clean out the pigsty of frivolity. Milne was guilty of nonsense, which became criminal; he was also guilty—this I think was a real crime—of sentimentality. But to my mind his defect, and I greatly liked him and appreciated his gossamer fun, lay in the restriction placed, as I have said, upon his invention and sympathy. Sinners do very often enjoy a good deal of liberty, which can be made diverting. One does not need to be wormeaten with Liberalism to allow this, in an imaginative work, to go unpunished until the final curtain.

That was an age ago. Since then the drama has taken several turns. Shaw had his months of deification by enthusiasts, and was then sentenced to oblivion by Eliot, who called him an adolescent. He is rising again. Maugham's dubious star stands higher than ever it did; I am told that his plays are as effective on Television as they almost always were on the stage. We have largely forgotten Frederick Lonsdale, of whose plays only one, *On Approval*, has successfully borne that translation; but the others may yet have their revivals as examples of stage-craft in the 'tens and 'twenties. Noel Coward, so talented, so wonderfully skilled in the theatre, but so much less than over-whelming in his serious experiment *Design for Living*, reached the peak of his facile and delectable wit in the merry comedy of *Blithe Spirit* and the first act of *Private Lives*. He has followed his gift into sentiment and panorama, amid the contempt of those who have no comparable gifts. He has committed the impropriety of entertaining ordinary people, and making them laugh. Also making them cry a little, which if one has a hard and intolerant heart is an unforgivable achievement. He re-mains, I gather, unmoved; and his comments on the theatre are delightedly passed by word of mouth from the source to regions remote from Central London.

Terence Rattigan, again, whose wit and skill have been devoted to traditional comedy, has had great success in the theatre, with the result that he has been accused of lacking both intellect and seriousness. He is—oh, what a damning word that is!—'commercial', which does not mean, as one might think, catchpenny, but only enjoyable.

At first the attacks on these and comparable writers came from the extreme Left Wing, who adopted from Communism the notion that literature must celebrate and forward the class struggle. Then the emphasis changed, and as counters to Marx we had illustrations of (1) the Catholic standpoint, (2) the curious fanciful dredging of the self-conscious associated with the name of Christopher Fry, and (3) the emphasis on consci-ence, incoherence, and terrible psychological uncertainty, all of which expressed the anxieties, fears, and, more superficially, indignations of extreme pessimism about human nature and the world's future. Like the conventional novel, traditional drama became unimportant. Critically speaking, Shaw, Barrie, Gals-worthy, Granville Barker, Milne, Coward, Rattigan, and the rest of their several generations were, for the time being, finished.

St John Ervine went along with them. I have never heard his opinion of the novelties. I feel sure it would be expressed, if we were able to meet, with all the old quasi-Shavian forcefulness. I should not say a word.

I should not say a word, because, for me, Ibsen and Chekhov are still kings of the modern theatre, with *Rosmersholm* and *The Cherry Orchard* their masterpieces. Perhaps in further attendances I have never wholly recaptured the absorbed delight of my first encounters with those plays; but the admiration remains, and I think them greater in the qualities I value than any that have been written since. Both are dramas of character, as Shakespeare's tragedies are dramas of character; both carry the richest implications of tragedy, and fill the imagination as, otherwise, only great tragic music does. Both superbly accomplish what I only try vainly to do in my own novels, which are excusably mistaken for unsuccessful assaults upon Hollywood.

I should also say not a word because although I think some of the very fashionable Continental dramatists are as empty of considerable ideas as Pinero or inferior Wilde, it seems to me that the theatre is the ideal place for experiment. This is true not only of production but of composition. I do not much fancy a National Theatre, lest it be nobbled by 'the little West End clique', to end in aridity; but if it is run in a way to give imaginative men and women (and not those who only wish to display their own ingenuity) a chance to test genuine artistic impulses it may do. Otherwise the danger is that it may be another Glyndebourne, where splendid work in reviving the lesser operas of Mozart and Rossini, having been supported by socialites, has reached the many only through supplementary effort on the part of the B.B.C.

Besides Continental masters, Samuel Beckett, and the young dramatists who deal in ghosts and vacuums, we have seen some bold attempts to put not very pleasant real life on the stage. Success has been only partial; and the vein cannot be indefinitely pursued. In both theatre and novel the echoes of mean streets and the impatience of frustrated young men and women (frustrated because they lack the genius to go their own way and use experience to fit into a very rich and elastic pattern) will subside. A similar echo was heard in the 'eighties and 'nineties of last century, and again in the 'tens of this one; and something more than echo, something more than protest, is needed for the living drama. I think that will come. There is plenty of talent and plenty of ambition. What is needed is dissatisfaction with discontent. We need deeper insights and more constructive ideas.

The old adolescent Shaw, chatterbox though he became, and endless though some of his last acts were, understood the theatre. He had ideas of his own, and humour to make his audiences absorb those ideas as they laughed. He made them laugh twice at every joke, which showed sound economy; and he did not hesitate to give the Devil some of the very best lines in every play. He knew that he was clever enough as a drama-tist to get away with slapstick and custard pie; but he could also rely upon his enormous debating capacity to secure victory for his own view. When he debated with G. K. Chesterton he always insisted upon a show of hands at the end of the debate, to decide the victory. The victory was always his own. I once saw him startled by Belloc's chairmanic bell, which rang to say that only five minutes were left of his speaking time. In those five minutes he brilliantly summarized all his arguments, and almost brought the audience to its feet. Verbosity may have been his weakness; but it arose from the overwhelming number and speed of his thoughts.

The dramatists of tomorrow should learn this lesson from Shaw, who never complained, and who was incapable, accord-ing to Henry Massingham, of being angry.

During the 'thirties, as I have said, Communist ideas so dominated the minds of the intelligent young that poems were filled with the philosophy of Marx, everything was seen in terms of politics and economics, and even old writers, Shakes-peare, Bunyan, and the other worm-eaten Liberals, were re-valued in terms of the class struggle. W. H. Auden, Cecil Day Lewis, Stephen Spender, and others found the times not very responsive to poetry in the Ercles vein; but could echo their machinery, condemn their social injustice, and express much of the Marxian doctrine in current idioms. For doing these things they received much laudation from their contemporaries. It was felt that in so far as original poetry was possible after the death of the Georgians and the unique and not to be equalled achievement of Eliot they spoke with the true voice of a generation which at last had seen political light.

I cannot say, because I do not know, what the poets who were then young now think. I believe they did, at the time, speak for their generation, because we know how powerfully the revolutionary idea affects ardent spirits. When Southey, Wordsworth, and Coleridge were young they were moved to espouse the cause of Liberty. Shelley, taught by William Godwin, was a political revolutionary until he was diverted from that path by a reading of Plato. Byron wished to participate in the Greek campaign for emancipation. The younger Georgian Poets at first believed themselves destined to fight against tyranny, and some of them did, in fact, give their lives for that Cause. Therefore those who were caught up by post-war theories of government were in the tradition of all previous romantics; that their political doctrines were anti-romantic did not seem to matter.

The emotion passed. Christian dogma succeeded. But Renan, according to Wilde, said he would sooner live under a military despotism than under the despotism of the Church, because the former merely limited the freedom of action, while the latter limited the freedom of the mind; and in spite of the great influence of T. S. Eliot in making the Church sole arbiter of taste, and in spite of the dictatorial manner of Eliot's *fidus Achates* John Hayward, there is at present a reaction against that authority. Younger and still dissatisfied men have likened it to the Inquisition.

Accordingly the political notions of the 'thirties succumbed to the doctrine of an all-powerful Church, and that doctrine, having served its turn, is making way for a new anarchism. This new anarchism, on the whole, is a racy affair. It still uneasily guys the good as well as the pompous; it is muscular and sexually boastful, anti-female and anti-genteel; but, at least,

influenced by such powerful American writers as John Steinbeck, it has vitality. If its representatives are allowed by economic conditions to mature without becoming merely rich
professionals, it may produce great things.

We have lived through a disturbing half-century. The new
criticism which I told Hugh Walpole I wanted to see has done
its good work in destroying slop and smugness. It has hardened
into something derogatorily known as The Establishment, and
seeks to maintain power for a conservatism which the new
critics of 1920 did not, I believe, intend. I wish I could distinguish (I have neither time nor, now, precision of mind to do so)
the degrees in which it has moved or been diverted by circumstances or other influences from original music and austerity to
the doctrine of Original Sin, and from Original Sin to the
present lamentable crystallization; but that it is losing power I
feel confident.

What is the alternative? Is it indicated by the apparent rise
to respect of Dr F. R. Leavis? Leavis, as a portent, belongs to
the 'thirties. He edited a review, *Scrutiny*, from 1932 until 1953,
and this review is now being ransacked for light and leading.
True, it is dead, like so many other periodicals which too
severely restrict their contents; but some of its pronouncements
in their day set on edge the teeth of literary editors and others,
and these pronouncements are all to be reprinted for the
world's delectation, which suggests that they will not lie down.

Leavis still feels that he has been a persecuted man, and is fond
of quoting himself and boasting of vehement battles with other
professors. He is too often occupied in contradicting what
other writers have said about literary subjects, instead of going
clearly ahead with his own critical opinions as if the others did
not matter in the least. He is for war on every subject. And yet
many of his critical opinions are in accord with what I believe
to be essential practice.

The critic's aim [he says] is, first to realize as sensitively and
completely as possible this or that which claims his attention;

and a certain valuing is implicit in the realizing. As he matures in experience of the new thing he asks, explicitly and implicitly: 'Where does this come? How does it stand in relation to . . . ? How relatively important does it seem?

This, in my opinion, is the proper approach to a literature which is not yet in chains. It is the approach of inquiry, and does not apply the arbitrary test of an irrelevant dogmatic system. Unfortunately Dr Leavis is not helped by a style in which sentences, already involved, are swelled and made uncouth by parenthesis and divagation. I can understand why he has been unpopular with his fellow-professors; for although, as he says in his essay on Swift, 'it is pleasant to believe that unusual capacity for egotistic animus means unusual distinction of intellect' his egotistic animus is sometimes too violently expressed to be convincing.

At his best, however, as for example when he is deciphering the letters of Gerald Manly Hopkins to Robert Bridges, and reconstructing the missing replies of Bridges, he shows genius, and is deeply interesting. On Lawrence he is not only superlatively enthusiastic but illuminating. If I think him less so on other themes it will be understood that I claim only to be a free-lance in a country which has not lost its freedom with the passing of *laissez faire*.

A free-lance. This situation has its disadvantages; but it also has great advantages. The disadvantages are that one misses a *claque* and the support of those who prefer a writer to follow a line acceptable to themselves. The advantages are that one can enjoy the sense of going one's own way, regardless of fashion and regardless of critical reputation. I have gone my own way; and if I have any reputation at all it is as a result of very reluctant work. No author, whatever his inner arrogance, can tell whether he has succeeded or not. All I claim is that as man and writer I have never been sycophantic or ungrateful for affection and respect.

I have been for nearly eighty years a lucky and a happy man.

In looking back over a life connected with books and periodicals, which began with a little journal for family reading composed at the age of ten years, progressed through a rather petted two years' experience as office-boy and a quarter of a century of useful labour in the publishing trade, to half a century of novel-writing and journalism, I see that I have taken a critical interest in other men and not in myself. The result is a detached view of English literature as a whole and especially of those who have contributed to that literature since the last decade of the nineteenth century.

I am not ashamed of having written over thirty novels in fifty-odd years, because although I see that librarians nowadays report with satisfaction an increase in 'serious' reading I share Jane Austen's view, expressed in 1795, that novelists are unduly despised. I also appreciate the opinion of Thomas Gray, who in 1742, after reading *Joseph Andrews*, wrote to his friend West:

> The incidents are ill laid and without invention; but the characters have a great deal of nature, which always pleases even in her lowest shapes. . . . However the exaltedness of some minds (or rather as I shrewdly suspect their insipidity and want of feeling or observation) may make them insensible to these light things (I mean, such as characterize and paint nature), yet surely they are as weighty and much more useful than your grave discourses upon the mind, the passions, and what not. Now as the paradisiacal pleasures of the Mahometans consist in playing upon the flute and lying with Houris, be mine to read eternal new romances of Marivaux and Crebillon.

My novels have all been paintings of character and nature; not of eccentrics, but of normal people as I see them. Some have been better than others; and in one of them, which was under-valued when it appeared (the book was called *A Month in Gordon Square*), I believed I had created a character almost worthy to be compared with Emma Woodhouse. I also think that in three others, *Thankless Child*, *Death of a Highbrow*, and *The Doctor's Wife Comes to Stay*, I have not wholly failed. The last-named, indeed, brought me the most perceptive comment I ever received from a reviewer. It was in *The Spectator*, and it drew attention to the fact that the hero's considerable sense of humour was quite different from my own. It was a compliment and testimony to a subtlety which has been often missed in hasty reading.

For the rest, I am content to be forgotten as soon as I am dead. The fate has befallen better writers than myself; and I doubt if any other octogenarian will meet his inevitable doom with greater equanimity.

Index

o

267

D